Shakespeare by Stages

For *Andrew* and *Diana*

Shakespeare by Stages

An Historical Introduction

Arthur F. Kinney

Blackwell
Publishing

350 Main Street, Malden, MA 02148-5018, USA
108 Cowley Road, Oxford OX4 1JF, UK
550 Swanston Street, Carlton South, Victoria 3053, Australia
Kurfürstendamm 57, 10707 Berlin, Germany

First published 2003
by Blackwell Publishers Ltd, a Blackwell Publishing company

Library of Congress Cataloging-in-Publication Data has been applied for.

ISBN 0-631-22468-8 (hbk); ISBN 0-631-22469-6 (pbk)

A catalogue record for this title is available from the British Library.

Set in 10/12.5pt Sabon
by Kolam Information Services Pvt. Ltd, Pondicherry.

Printed and bound in the United Kingdom by T. J. International, Padstow,
Cornwall

For further information on

Blackwell Publishing, visit our website:

http://www.blackwellpublishing.com

Contents

Figures

Picture research by Charlotte Morris.

Preface

"People in throngs, of all classes and callings, gathered to see Shake-speare's plays," Alfred Harbage writes:

> They came in wherries, on horseback, and on foot, from Cheapside and White Chapel, Westminster and Newington, Clerkenwell and Shoreditch, deserting for an interval their workbenches, their accounts, their studies, their sports, their suits at law, and their suits at court. They preferred the pleasures of the Globe to the pleasures of Brentford and Ware, and if they did not pass coldly by the ale-house doors, at least they reserved enough pennies to pay the gatherers.[1]

The boisterous excitement Harbage imagined more than a half-century ago sweeping across all parts of London is confirmed by contemporary reports and observations. Shakespeare's Globe was located outside the city walls in Southwark, but the location was a good one, drawing on the crowded suburbs, and just upriver from the houses of nobility and the palace of Westminster and downriver from the royal palaces of Hampton Court, Greenwich, and Richmond (where performances could earn a large set fee of £10). Travelling with a sketch book and taking notes on his trip from Utrecht to London, Johannes de Witt, famous now for his drawing of the Swan Theater, jotted down in 1596:

> There are four amphitheaters in London of notable beauty, which from their diverse signs bear diverse names. In each of them a different play is daily exhibited to the populace. The two more magnificent of these are situated to the southward beyond the Thames, and from the signs sus-

pended before them are called the Rose and Swan.... Of all the theaters, however, the largest and most magnificent is that one of which the sign is a swan, called in the vernacular the Swan Theater; for it accommodates in its seats three thousand persons, and is built of a mass of flint stones (of which there is a prodigious supply in Britain), and supported by wooden columns painted in such excellent imitation of marble that it is able to deceive even the most cunning.[2]

In 1626 Fynes Moryson reports further in his *Itinerary* that:

The City of London alone hath four or five companies of players with their peculiar theaters capable of many thousands, wherein they all play every day in the week but Sunday, with most strange concourse of people.... as there be, in my opinion, more plays in London than in all parts of the world I have seen, so do these players or comedians excel all others in the world.[3]

English actors were performing all over England and Scotland and on the Continent as well: in Germany, Holland, Belgium, Denmark, Poland, France. And the English playwrights supplied them with a great deal of material – between the 1580s and 1630s some 44 authors recorded more than 850 plays; in the *Epistle* to one of them, *The English Traveller* (1633), Thomas Heywood noted he himself "had a main finger" in at least 220 of them. By comparison, Thomas Dekker wrote 64 plays, at least 44 of them in whole or in part for the entrepreneurial Philip Henslowe between 1598 and 1602; Philip Massinger wrote all or parts of at least 55; Henry Chettle, 50; William Shakespeare and James Shirley, 38 each; and Thomas Middleton, 31. Yet in most cases – Shakespeare and Middleton seem to be exceptions – only a small percentage of those plays recorded actually survive today.

Even the plays by Shakespeare that we have may well not be wholly his. Although it is likely that he wrote most of them alone – *Pericles* and *Henry VIII* are likely exceptions – plays were in his time always a collaborative art, subject to revision by actors and audiences in performance and subject later to copyists, compositors, printers, and proofreaders when they were printed. Throughout this book we will look at the various forms and forces in such ongoing collaborative efforts. Such performative changes, and perhaps possible errors in printing – along with the fact that Shakespeare also earned his living as an actor and for much of his life as a sharer or part-owner of his acting company – might have explained the delay in the publication of his plays and, when they were on occasion printed, the absence of his name on the title-page. Plays were infrequently printed; and while it was for a long time thought that this was caused by the playing companies wishing to keep singular hold on their property, it now seems apparent that plays when they were published did not sell well in a market crowded with works of religious controversy, wondrous news, and household manuals. Shakespeare's name probably did not appear as an author's until 1598, more than a third of the way through his career, when Cuthbert Burby included it on the quarto of *Love's Labor's Lost* (it is hard to know when the second quarto of *Richard II* appeared). What happened more often was the advertisement of books on their title-pages *as scripts*: "as it hath lately been acted," "as it was played," even at times naming the location (Whitehall; before the Queen) – perhaps even more by naming the company, such as the Lord Admiral's Men or Lord Strange's Men. Perhaps another reason that authorship was almost never given until the late 1590s is that those in the theater knew how collaborative a playscript soon became: one of the central themes of this book.

In Shakespeare's age, when playwrights were hired by companies to write plays that suited the needs and composition of the acting company, the venues they played, and the audiences they played to, collaboration must always have been a primary concern. Knowing the conditions of playing and of playgoing, then, helps us to understand (or at least speculate with some firm basis) why Shakespeare wrote some of the plays in the ways he did and, beyond that, how they may have been acted. But he was also regulated by local and provincial governments who found the audiences inherently undesirable because they were drawn from the lowest levels of society as well as the highest, because they could be given to revelry but also riots, and because as crowds they attracted thieves – and plague. As early as February 25, 1592, for instance, Sir William Roe, lord mayor of London, wrote to the archbishop of Canterbury:

> Our most humble duties to Your Grace remembered. Whereas by the daily and disorderly exercise of a number of players and playing houses erected within this City, the youth thereof is greatly corrupted and their manners infected with many evil and ungodly qualities by reason of the wanton and prophane devises represented on the stages by the said players, the apprentices and servants withdrawn from their works, and all sorts in general from the daily resort unto sermons and other Christian exercises to the great hindrance of the trades and traders of this City and profanation of the good and godly religion established amongst us.[4]

The great historian of London, John Stow, omitted references to theaters altogether until, finally, the 1598 edition of his popular *Survey of*

London. He too takes the side of the lord mayor. Plays, he says, began with local customs and rituals, with amateurs, but:

> in process of time it became an Occupation; and many there were that followed it for a Livelihood. And which was worse it became the Occasion of much Sin and Evil. Playhouses thronged. And great Disorders and Inconvenience were found to ensue to the City thereby. It occasioned Frays and evil Practices of Incontinency. Great Inns were used for this Purpose, which had secret Chambers and Places, as well as open Stages and Galleries. Here maids, especially Orphans and good Citizens' Children under Age, were inveigled and allured to privy and unmeet Contracts.

Shakespeare must always have been aware of such sentiments: Falstaff's rioting and Christopher Sly's drunkenness show us that. Thus regulations, like the size and structure of the stage and the costumes and properties purchased by his playing company, became material conditions that inspired and restricted Shakespeare. They are also what this book is about.

Acknowledgments

Perhaps the most congenial and generous subset of Renaissance scholars, critics, and writers are theater historians, who cheerfully share their findings and ideas with one another. I am not the first – nor will I be the last – to benefit from their discoveries; the works I draw on will be found in the bibliography. I am grateful to all of them. Some of the information and interpretation in this brief book are drawn from sessions of English 891D, "Material Shakespeare," a graduate seminar held in the autumn of 2000 at the Renaissance Center of the University of Massachusetts in Amherst. There we were joined by visitors who submitted suggestions and in some cases subsequently read this book, saving me from many errors: John Andrews, Alan Dessen, Werner Habicht, Roslyn Knutson, Jerzy Límon, Scott McMillin, and Sheila Walsh. The book also reflects discussions and debates with members of the seminar: Walter Chmielewski, Edward Cottrill, Jennifer Crutcher, Joseph Earls, Kimberly Elliott, Melanie Faith, Nicole Kelly, Jeneen Lehocky, Christine Monahan, Rachel Salvidio, David Swain, Kathleen Thaw, Lisa Tiffany, and Claire Wilson; Jeneen Lehocky and Claire Wilson helped with the proofreading, and my editor at Blackwell, Fiona Sewell, was scrupulous as always. I am also indebted to the frequent wise counsel of S. P. Cerasano, Andrew Gurr, Grace Ioppolo, and Stanley Wells. Without their help this would have been a very different book. What I can claim are any remaining faults.

Newcastle, Australia
Amherst, Massachusetts, 2002

Every writer must govern his pen according to the capacity of the
stage he writes to, both in the actor and the auditor.
The Printer to the Reader, *The Two Merry*
Milkmaids, or The Best Words wear the Garland (1620)

1

Stages

All the world's a stage,
And all the men and women merely players.
They have their exits and their entrances,
And one man in his time plays many parts.
Jaques in *As You Like It*

The design of Shakespeare's Globe Theater that we may carry in our mind's eye – taken from early sketches or picture books or even the reconstructed Globe on the south bank of the Thames in greater London today – is essentially that of a round theater with three tiers of galleried seats on three sides. Along the fourth side a great stage juts out to cover nearly half the open yard raised nearly to the eye-level of standing spectators, whom the Elizabethans called "groundlings" or sometimes "standings." At the back of the stage is a wall separating it from the tiring room (or attiring room, where costumes and properties were kept) with two doors for entrances and exits, usually unlabelled but perhaps representative nonetheless – of England and France for *Henry V* or Montagues and Capulets for *Romeo and Juliet* or Orsino's and Olivia's separate households in *Twelfth Night*. Between the doors is a third door, or curtained space, to admit entrance to, or to conceal, large properties such as the table at the Boar's Head tavern in *1 Henry IV* or Desdemona's bed in *Othello*, to be revealed and wheeled out when called for. Above the rear of the stage is a balcony from which Christopher Sly may have witnessed the tale of Kate the curst and Petruchio and from where Pandarus may have pointed out the Trojan soldiers to Cressida, while over the stage is a roof decorated

1

with stars (known as the "heavens") above which was a primitive winch for slowly lowering the eagle of *Cymbeline* or Juno in *The Tempest*. Two large posts on stage support the roof; doubtless they held Orlando's love poetry in *As You Like It* and served as hiding places for eavesdroppers like the King of Navarre and Berowne in *Love's Labor's Lost*, Iago and Othello spying on Cassio and Bianca, or even Leontes keeping watch on Hermione and Polixenes on an otherwise bare stage. In the stage floor itself is a trapdoor large enough to accommodate two men that serves for further entrances and exits and supplies symbolic potential: there is a decided resonance in the fact that the Ghost of Hamlet's father appears and disappears from the same region where Ophelia will be buried, just as, with that discovery space between the doors at the back of the stage, there is resonance in comparing the bed and later the tomb of Romeo and Juliet or, in counterpoint in the same play, the liturgical materials designating Friar Laurence's cell in acts 2 and 3 and the merchandise of the Apothecary in act 5. In this last instance, in fact, both the Friar and the Apothecary will produce from their shelves a special potion in a vial to offer Juliet and Romeo respectively, the first to feign death, the second to guarantee it.

These features of Shakespeare's stage – largely void of sets and properties – are the conditions he had to work with. Staging was traditionally minimal. Country "stages" might be little more than an open space before a simple curtain, or a curtained room or booth, or a curtain with two doorways. Such open spaces might be in marketplaces on marketdays, or in open fields bordering villages, or even in the grounds of a manor house. There were also inside venues in the country where access to the play could be more easily controlled, where a charge could be levied for admission, and where there was protection from inclement weather. Such venues might be the upper room in an inn or guild hall, where the low ceilings and small space made for congested audiences. There were also larger spaces, as in the main room of the guild hall or a civic meeting-room such as a courtroom. Innyards, too, served as a natural place for a play, since the balconies of the inn could serve as galleries for playgoers and there was ample room in the innyard itself for the stage and for groundlings. There were also the great halls of manor houses and of Oxford and Cambridge colleges as well as the halls of the Inns of Court in London. These were especially welcoming, since at one end they had a balcony or musicians' gallery above and two doors beneath, and sometimes a raised dais as well. It has been argued, in fact, that public playhouses such as the Globe were not so much inspired by combining pageant wagons and bearbaiting arenas as they were by combining great halls and innyards.

The inns of London, in fact, set examples for the public performances of plays in inns at Norwich, York, and Bristol: the Bel Savage on Ludgate Hill below St Paul's Cathedral; the Bull in Gracechurch Street running north from London Bridge. Upper rooms were refurbished for plays at the Bell and the Cross Keys, also on Gracechurch (Gracious) Street. At the same time, open-air theaters were being built outside London's city walls, in the "Liberties" free of the jurisdiction of the lord mayor and council of aldermen of London. The first of these, the Red Lion, was built by the grocer John Brayne in 1567 in the eastern suburb of Stepney; in 1576 he built another playhouse (with his brother-in-law James Burbage) called the Theatre in Shoreditch, on the main north road out of London. Simultaneously, a public playhouse was erected in Newington Butts in Surrey, on the main road south out of London. Last came the Curtain, near to the Theatre but somewhat smaller, where in 1597–8 Shakespeare's company,

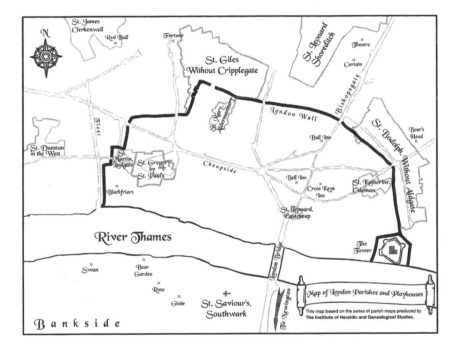

Figure 1 London theaters during Shakespeare's career.

From Rosyln Lander Knutson, *Playing Companies and Commerce in Shakespeare's Time* (Cambridge University Press, 2001). This map is based on one of London produced by the Institute of Heraldic and Genealogical Studies, from their series of genealogical aids, which includes *The Phillimore Atlas and Index of Parish Registers*; it is reproduced by kind permission of C. R. Humphrey-Smith and the Trustees of the Institute.

the Lord Chamberlain's Men, would stage performances of *Romeo and Juliet* and open *1 Henry IV*, *The Merry Wives of Windsor*, and *Much Ado About Nothing*. All of these public buildings, rounded or square, were based on the Roman amphitheater, with three galleries of spectators holding 1,500 or more people and a yard which could stand another 1,000. Unlike their Roman exemplars, however, the galleries were divided into sections, or bays, approximately 12 feet across at the front, 16 feet at the rear, and a little more than 10 feet deep.

London had inside playing places in Shakespeare's early years as well. Several schools, such as the famous Merchant Taylors School where the poet Edmund Spenser was educated, used their halls to stage plays and playreadings in Latin both to teach the language and to teach strategies of rhetoric, fundamental staples of the grammar-school curriculum. A small playhouse was built into one of the bays flanking the sanctuary of St Paul's for the choristers, Paul's Boys. In the 1580s there was also the "first Blackfriars," the hall of the former Blackfriars monastery, where two boys' companies merged under the writer John Lyly until the Privy Council closed them down in 1590.

Shakespeare, along with his fellow playwrights, thus inherited a long tradition of staging and its possibilities within which to compose his plays. Understanding how he explored, exploited, and capitalized on such factors as the physical space, the acting company's talents, the costumes and properties that were available, and the audiences whom he must please all helps us to understand something of the way he worked. It helps us understand more fully what he created, too, and helps us to begin to re-create the plays for ourselves.

Looking at the Evidence

Such an understanding of stages in Shakespeare's time rests in good measure on a handful of documents still extant. First of all, there is Arend von Buchell's copy of a drawing made by Johannes de Witt of the interior of the Swan Theater, discovered in 1880 in Amsterdam. The sketch shows a stage, two doors at the rear, two carved posts holding up the "heavens," and above that a hut, trumpeter, and flag (to denote a performance), all surrounded by three galleries of spectators. Some scholars have questioned the accuracy of this sketch because it shows two doors, not three, and no discovery space, and thus seems limiting: while a Swan play, Thomas Middleton's *A Chaste Maid in Cheapside*, clearly designates stage entrances *"at one Door... At the other Doore,"*

Figure 2 The Swan Theatre by Arnoldus Buchelius, after a drawing by Johannes de Wit, 1596.

University Library, Utrecht.

the same play has a scene of childbirth that would require a large bed onstage, and the drawing shows no means of getting it there.

A second document is the diary of Thomas Platter, which records for the year 1599 (in the modern translation of Clare Williams):

> daily at two in the afternoon, London has two, sometimes three plays running in different places, competing with each other, and those which play best obtain most spectators. The playhouses are so constructed that they play on a raised platform, so that everyone has a good view. There are different galleries and places, however, where the seating is better and more comfortable and therefore more expensive. For whoever cares to stand below only pays one English penny, but if he wishes to sit he enters by another door, and pays another penny, while if he desires to sit in the most comfortable seats which are cushioned, where he not only sees everything well, but can also be seen, then he pays yet another English penny at another door. And during the performance food and drink are carried round the audience, so that for what one cares to pay one may also have refreshment. The actors are most expensively and elaborately costumed; for it is the English usage for eminent lords or knights at their decease to bequeath and leave almost the best of their clothes to their serving men, which it is unseemly for the latter to wear, so that they offer them then for sale for a small sum to the actors.[1]

These annotations of a playgoer, a foreigner at that, complement two contracts that have also survived.

The first contract, a manuscript in the Edward Alleyn Papers at Dulwich College for the Fortune Theatre in Cripplegate, was drawn between Philip Henslowe, Alleyn, and Peter Street and signed on January 8, 1600. In part, it notes that:

> The frame of the said house to be set square ... with a good sewer and strong foundation of piles, brick, lime and sand both without and within to be wrought 1 feet of assize at the least above the ground. And the said frame to contain three storeys in height: the first or lower storey 11 foot ... in height, and the third or upper storey to contain 9 ... in height.... And which stage shall contain in length 43 feet of lawful azzize and in breadth to extend to the middle of the yard of the said house. The same stage to be paled in below with good strong and sufficient new oaken boards ... And the said stage ... [to have] convenient windows and lights glazed to the said tiring-house. And the said frame, stage and staircases to be covered with tile and to have a sufficient gutter of lead to carry and convey the water from the covering of the said stage to fall backwards. And also all the said frame and the staircases thereof to be sufficiently enclosed without with lath, lime and hair, and the gentlemen's rooms and twopenny rooms to be sealed with lath, lime and hair...

And the said house, and other things before mentioned, to be made and done to be in all other contrivitions [i.e. contrivances], conveyances, fashions, thing and things effected, finished, and done, according to the manner and fashion of the...house called the Globe, saving only that all the principal and main posts of the said frame and stage forward shall be square and wrought plaster-wise with carved proportions called satyrs to be placed and set on the top of every of the same posts.[2]

Unlike the competitive Globe, then, the Fortune was square, not round, and it had a roof of tile, not thatch. The distinctive sign was Dame Fortune, smiling on the theater until it burned to the ground in 1621 (when it was rebuilt in brick, finally to be dismantled in 1649). The initial cost was £520 to the builders, £1,320 to Henslowe and Alleyn (the rebuilt theater cost £1,000).

This contract can be fruitfully compared with another contract from Peter Street, this time for the Hope Theater, erected in 1613–14 on the site of a bearbaiting arena called the Bear-garden (to which Ben Jonson alludes in *Bartholomew Fair*, the play that opened the Hope). The builder was directed to:

not only take down or pull down all that game place or house where bears and bulls have been heretofore usually baited, and also one other house or stable wherein bulls and horses did usually stand, [which are] set, lying and being upon or near the bankside in the said parish of St Saviour in Southwark, commonly called or known by the name of the Beargarden: but shall also, at his or their own proper costs and charges, upon or before the said last day of November, newly erect, build, and set up one other game place or playhouse fit and convenient in all things, both for players to play in and for the game of bears and bulls to be baited in the same.[3]

Although the contract for the polygonal Hope Theater specified the Swan as the model rather than the Globe, its origins as a bearbaiting arena, where dogs baited a bear chained to a post until the bear was killed, is especially suggestive. It reminds us that drama, like bearbaiting, is based in an *agon*, a conflict or contest of wills. Petruchio and Kate in *The Taming of the Shrew*, Hamlet and Claudius, and Prospero and Caliban in *The Tempest* all wage a contest at the heart of their respective plays, but it is Macbeth who is most keenly aware of life as drama and contest. At first he is in conflict with himself: "why do I yield to that suggestion Whose horrid image doth unfix my hair And make my seated heart knock at my ribs" (1.3.133–5), then with his wife: "Prithee, peace. I dare do all that may become a man; Who dares do more is none"

(1.7.45–7), and at last, with assured death: "They have tied me to a stake. I cannot fly, But bear-like I must fight the course" (5.7.1–2).

But the Hope Theater was effectually a latecomer. Shakespeare's Globe had a different origin. When Burbage's lease ran out on the Theatre in Shoreditch in 1598, the players, under the direction of Peter Street, pulled it down between Christmas and January 20, 1599, and ferried the timbers across the Thames to Southwark to build their new playhouse neighboring the Rose and the Swan. Because the timber was already cut, the Globe was finished in six months: it was, in effect, a prefabricated building, with its beams morticed and tenoned and held at the joints by the customary dowel pegs, nails being expensive. John Orrell has hypothesized that the Globe was a polygon with twenty sides constituting a circumference of 330 feet and a diameter of nearly 100 feet.[4] Three galleries were fitted on a foundation wall of brick and rested on oak posts weighing two tons and rising vertically 32 feet to the top of the outer walls. The walls themselves were lath and plaster; the roof, thatch; and the yard had a one-in-ten decline toward the center, where a wooden pipe took water underground and northward out of the building. The yard itself was covered with a mixture of ash, clinker, and hazelnut shells which, trampled down, created a hard surface. The stage faced north so that players and the lords' seats above the stage were protected from sunlight, while the stage roof or "heavens" had a thatched ridge that directed rainwater away from the stage and out into the yard. The back of the stage could accommodate hangings: black drapery if the play was a tragedy; a woven tapestry of Venice, if that was the play's setting. A sign might be carried across the stage – "Athens," for example, for the opening of *A Midsummer Night's Dream* – as another means of establishing the setting on a bare stage and confirming the dialogue of the play. The playhouse sign is thought to have displayed Hercules carrying the globe, with the motto, taken from John of Salisbury, that all the world is a stage: "Totus mundus agit histrionem," echoed by Jaques in *As You Like It*.

Directions of plays written for the Globe bear out its fundamental, conventional features. There must have been two doors: *Pericles* mentions "*one door*" and "*the other.*" There must have been a curtained space at the rear of the stage; not only does Polonius need to hide behind "an arras" in the closet scene of *Hamlet*, but there is a "tent" referred to in *Richard III* and *Troilus and Cressida*, as well as in the crucial scene between Brutus and Cassius in act 4 of *Julius Caesar*. There must have been a playing-space above for the balcony scenes in *Romeo and Juliet*, for Richard II's appearance at Flint Castle, and for pulling Antony up to Cleopatra. And there must have been a trap, not only for the "old mole" in *Hamlet* but for a dungeon in which Malvolio is exorcised by Feste disguised as Sir Topas the curate in *Twelfth Night* and from which apparitions appear (and into which they later disappear) in *Macbeth*. From 1599 on, Shakespeare wrote most of his plays with the Globe Theater in mind.

He wrote plays, that is, for a building and a business in which he had invested. The cost of the first Globe was shared by eight men – Cuthbert and Richard Burbage, sons of James Burbage who had built the Theatre, who each owned 25 percent, and five actors – Augustine Phillips, Thomas Pope, John Heminges, William Kempe, and William Shakespeare – who

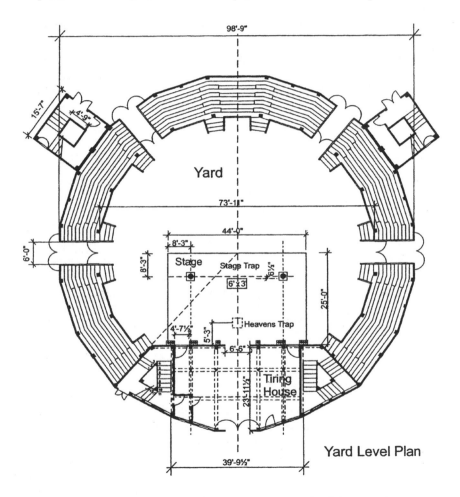

Figure 3 Jon Greenfield's plan for the reconstructed Globe, Southwark, © Pentagram Design Ltd.

each owned 10 percent. Assuming the financial arrangements were the same as those documented for the second Globe Theater which would replace it, these sharers had a lease on the property which included several buildings as well as the theater. They paid rent for the property and the cost of upkeep. In turn, they collected rent from the other properties and half the money collected for seats in the galleries and above the stage. The players themselves, responsible for producing the plays and paying their own wages, kept the other half of the money collected at the doors and all of the money paid by those who stood in the yard. Thus Shakespeare earned money as a shareholder and paid out money as an actor; he had good reason to write frequent and popular plays that would insure attendance.

Twenty-three professional theaters – 17 public playhouses and inns and 6 private playhouses – were built in and around London between 1567 and 1642, the largest number for any city in Europe. Shakespeare's company also played in a private theater known as Blackfriars. Richard Burbage bought the old Blackfriars monastery within the city walls and built the Blackfriars Theater in 1596, leasing it to a boys' company; in 1608, when Henry Evans let the lease drop, he divided it into seven equal shares owned by Richard Burbage, his brother Cuthbert, Heminges, Henry Condell, William Sly, Shakespeare, and Thomas Evans. This indoor theater converted a large medieval hall known as the parliament chamber, since three parliaments had once assembled there. It was at least two storeys in height, since the north end had two floors, and its ceiling may well have resembled the hammerbeam roof in Westminster Hall. This more intimate playing-space was used in the cold winter months. It had three wooden galleries in a horseshoe shape around the pit where playgoers sat on benches. The hall measured 66 feet by 46 feet. Serving as a model for two later London playhouses – the Cockpit or Phoenix built in Drury Lane in 1617 in what was then the separate city of Westminster, and Salisbury Court in the Whitefriars' former monastery within the city walls in 1627 – Blackfriars seated 600 spectators in the galleries, on benches in the pit, in boxes adjacent to the stage, and even on three-legged stools on the stage itself: at least 15 playgoers might come up on the stage to sit, stand, or recline against the walls. Candles provided light for Blackfriar performances and the five-act structure we impose on Shakespeare's plays probably orginated in the intervals when wicks were cut back and the candles newly lit. These material conditions – so different from those at the Globe – may have suggested to Shakespeare the possibilities for the intimacy of scenes that mark his late romances: *Cymbeline, The Winter's Tale, The Tempest.*

Five years later, in 1613, sparks from a cannon fired for a performance of *Henry VIII* set off the thatch of the Globe and it burned to the ground, to be replaced by a second Globe on the foundations of the former Globe built a short distance from the Rose. In the late 1980s, the Hanson Trust, digging on land by Southwark Bridge for a new office block, uncovered the foundations of the Rose Theater; the stage was found to be between 25 and 80 feet; subsequently, when the Rose was enlarged by pushing the back wall farther back, the stage was rebuilt at roughly the same dimensions. Somewhat later, under a legally protected eighteenth-century building, archaeologists also discovered a portion of the second Globe. As Andrew Gurr reported in the spring 1990 issue of *Shakespeare Quarterly*:

> What the initial dig seems to have turned up is the foundations of the stair turret on the east-northeast side and sections of the related foundations.
>
> These sections consist chiefly of a broad block of the chalk aggregate, or "clunch," forming the base of the outer wall, and attached brickwork. The chalk comprises part of two adjacent sides of a polygon. Attached to it are the brick foundations of the stair turret lobby, together with the foundation walls of a passageway running from the lobby into the yard. A layer of gravel found outside the stair lobby opening was probably laid as a pathway from Maiden Lane to the theatre. Also visible is one section of the brick foundations for the inner wall, positioned 10.5 feet center to center (3.2 meters) in from the outer lobby wall. A very rough calculation, based on the apparent angle in the outer wall and the angle shown by the bricks of the inner wall, suggests that the span of each section of the outer walls of the polygon was the standard builder's measure of one rod, or 16 feet 6 inches...
>
> The interior dimensions of each bay in the Globe's galleries would seem to be similar to the Rose's or slightly larger, although the overall size of the Globe was a third greater than its predecessor. An outside diameter of 105 feet for the Globe is markedly bigger than the Rose's 74 feet... The yards of the two theatres were evidently also designed to be similar. Around the inner wall at the Globe was found the same mixture of ash and hazelnut shells that appeared in the yard at the Rose, presumably laid to form a permeable layer and a soft footing for the standers in the yard.[5]

However similar the two Globe theaters were, they differed remarkably from the Banqueting House at Whitehall where Shakespeare's company, known as the King's Men from 1603, played before King James. This was a "long square" 332 feet in circumference with a 40-foot ceiling and tiered seating. The king himself was positioned centrally to the front so that he formed part of the view of every other playgoer. Fashioning plays after 1603, Shakespeare probably kept this in mind in scripting and

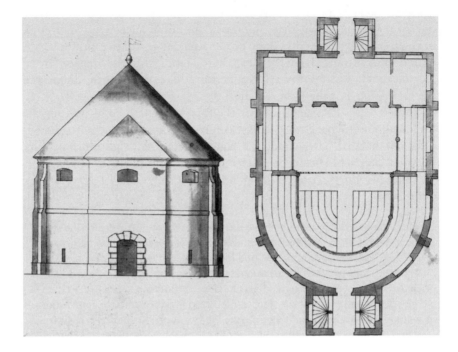

Figure 4 Inigo Jones's ground-plan for an indoor theater, *c.*1616. The width of the stage is thought to be 20 feet and the outside dimensions for the stage and flanking boxes 40 feet.

The Provost and Fellows of Worcester College, Oxford, photo courtesy Courtauld Institute, London.

blocking his works; after 1608, he would also have in mind the possible transfer of plays from the big outdoor Globe Theater to the smaller performance space at Blackfriars.

The Fluid Stage

What these various stages had in common, however, was their essential emptiness; they were bare platforms that were spatially neutral until the playwright himself defined them. Once defined, though, they remained flexible, open to constant redefinition, expanding or contracting as the movement of scenes required. Nor need distances on the stage remain consistently realistic. As Bernard Beckerman has noted:

12

Essentially the stage was a fluid area that could represent whatever the author wished without the necessity for him to indicate a change in stage location. The actors did not regard the stage as a place but as a platform from which to project a story, and therefore they were unconscious of the discrepancy between real and dramatic space. How far behind Malvolio were the "box tree" and his tormentors? How far from Brutus and Cassius are Caesar and Antony when Caesar sneers at Cassius' "lean and hungry look"? Is the eye meant to take in both parties at once? In performing these scenes, the Globe players probably concentrated on making the observation of Malvolio and the scornful characterization of Cassius dramatically effective. That this frequently necessitated the substitution of imaginary for real distance must have passed unobserved both by the players and the audience.[6]

The arbitrary assignment of space also permitted various changes of scene with correlated shifts in perspective. From act 2 to act 5, *Richard II* shifts from somewhere on the open Welsh coast to, more narrowly yet in the same space, Flint Castle and the base court, and finally to the close confinement of Richard's prison cell. Likewise, the playwright can collaborate with the spectator's participatory imagination in changing from the public market of Antonio's Rialto to Portia's private chamber in Belmont and then, widening again, from the Venetian courtroom to the meadow outside Portia's house; from Orsino's drawing room to the seacost of Illyria; and from Lear's royal palace to a barren heath in the midst of a storm to the white cliffs of Dover, and from random wandering to close imprisonment.

Muriel Bradbrook has also noted the capacity of the bare stage for an infinite variety:

There may be a battlefield with two tents side by side at an idealised distance (*Richard II*, 5.3). The pastoral "Scene individable" of *Love's Labour's Lost* shows the entrance to the king's palace and the princess's tent. There are "split" scenes like *Romeo and Juliet*, 4.5, and *Measure for Measure*, 3.1, where the place changes by the opening or shutting of the curtains on the inner stage [the discovery space], transporting the characters on the outer stage to the new locality. There are unlocalised scenes like *1 Henry IV*, 4.4 (which does not happen anywhere in particular), and a character is often delocalised for a soliloquy (e.g. Iago in *Othello*, 4.3, a "split" scene). The stage may represent a street leading to the senate house and the senate house itself (*Julius Caesar*, 3.1) or a long stretch of moorland (*Richard II*, 2.3 . . .).

There are in fact no "scenes" in the sense of separate units, and no locality except where it is indicated in the [lines]. The few localising stage directions, "Enter in the forest of Gaultree" (*2 Henry IV*, 4.1), or "Scaling ladders at Harfleur" (*Henry V*, 3.1), are supported by the text [although they may have been added by the printer]. When an important group of characters or when all the characters leave the stage there is a sense of pause.[7]

The open stage is conducive too to simultaneous spaces and actions so that with the Gadshill robbery attempt in *1 Henry IV*, the luckless travellers, Falstaff and his gang, and Prince Hal and Poins may all be onstage at once, though in separate groups; if so, the audience could see them react to one another, even though the robbery, at night, severely limits the vision of the characters themselves. Or scenes on one part of the stage may not be visible to those on another part, as Duke Senior's banquet in 2.5 and 2.7 of *As You Like It* is not seen by those in 2.6, and actors on one part of the stage may not be heard by others.

Scenes can alternate easily on an essentially bare stage and thus comment on each other. Shakespeare frequently structures his history plays by alternating public and private scenes, showing how they correlate, interrelate, and even cause one another, as Rumour helps interpret reports of Bardolph and Morton to Northumberland at the opening of *2 Henry IV*. Tragedies may work the same way – as in the alternation of the battlefield and the castle in *Macbeth* and the public and private scenes in *Othello*. *Romeo and Juliet* is broadly configured in this way: the four crowded public scenes – the initial brawl, the Capulet ball, the death of Mercutio and Tybalt, and the final visitations to the graveyard – where nearly the entire cast assembles and reassembles, contrast starkly with the political, social, and religious shortcomings that fracture the citizens of Verona. Played against these congregations, the more personal scenes – on the balcony, in the friar's cell, in the bedroom, before the apothecary – reflect the same dysfunctioning but at higher personal risk and cost. This manipulation of staging gives meaning and reinforces it. *Coriolanus* offers another example. From the crowded press of battle when Coriolanus storms the walls of Corioles and then, alone, enters the city, we are prepared for his solitary opposition to the Roman senate and, from that defeat, for his solitary meeting with Aufidius and then, in Aufidius' presence, with his mother outside the city walls. This time he is not alone, and his decision, far from the solitary victory at Corioles, results in his death and ritual mutilation.

Such configurations of characters – their blocking on a comparatively empty stage – is one way Shakespeare can not only suggest but visually reinforce the meaning of his spoken lines of dialogue and soliloquy. Scenes resonate in other scenes and help us understand them. Thus the gauntlets thrown down by Mowbray and Bolingbroke in act 1 of *Richard II*, relying on their trial by chivalric combat to determine the truth of their mutually cancelling accusations, is parodied by Aumerle and his enemies at the beginning of act 4, showing how respect for the rites of knighthood have been displaced by the power of realpolitik. The appearances of Benvolio as negotiator and peacemaker – with Old Capulet; with Tybalt – establish him as a moral norm who is, tragically, ineffective. Hearing of Antonio's contract and bond with Shylock in act 3, Portia forges her own contract and bond with Bassanio by giving him a ring and swearing him never to forsake it; she breaks both contracts disguised as the "learned doctor" Bellario in act 4. The appearance of the Ghost in *Hamlet* on the ramparts of Elsinor anticipates the other armed soldier who appears marching across the upper stage – Fortinbras – and may help to explain Hamlet's election of him as ruler of Denmark and forewarn us of his martial appearance at the end of the play. Act 1 of *Othello* builds from a dialogue through an argument among Brabantio, Iago, and Othello to a crowded public scene where, at a meeting of the Venetian senate, Brabantio puts Othello on trial. The pattern is repeated in act 5: from the fatal dialogue of Othello and Desdemona through the discovery of her death by Emilia, the play ends with a second crowded scene where once again – and for the last time – Othello is tried by Venetians. Prospero opens *The Tempest* by catechizing his daughter with his own confession; he will end the play by promising the same for Alonso and his train: "the story of my life, And the particular accidents gone by Since I came to this isle." Confessing his complicity in his exile to Miranda, he is able to confess his faults once more and so, cleansed, return to Milan, "where Every third thought shall be my grave."

Such freedom in setting forth scenes seems to have drawn broadly on medieval staging, in which a pageant wagon with a formal platform scene – called the *locus* – was in constant dialogue with the space on the ground before it, bordering on the audience and given to more informal and even intimate, shared speech – the *platea*. The *locus* provided conventional and even detached speeches, more or less aloof, while the *platea* allowed jesting, riddling, and punning, and this general practice may have lasted into the Elizabethan period. Thus as Robert Weimann points out, "Launce's audience address in *The Two Gentlemen of Verona* (2.3.1–32) constitutes a *platea*-like opening in response to what, in the preceding scene, is the localized action in Julia's house in Verona,"[8] both modes conventional. Speaking downstage in the *platea*, Philo tells Demetrius at the start of *Antony and Cleopatra*:

Nay, but this dotage of our General's
O'erflows the measure! Those his goodly eyes,
That o'er the files and musters of the war
Have glowed like plated Mars, now bend, now turn
The office and devotion of their view
Upon a tawny front.

(1.1.1–6)

His conspiratorial confidences are in sharp distinction from the opening lines of Antony and Cleopatra entering from the back of the stage onto the *locus*:

Antony   If it be love indeed, tell me how much.
Cleopatra There's beggary in the love that can be reckoned,

(1.1.14–15)

and their formal stichomythia. This clear distinction between an impersonal and even illusionistic *locus* removed from the playgoers – the palace of Westminster, the French court, the Athenian court, the Roman or Venetian senate – and the downstage area where soliloquies and direct asides characterize and even privilege clowns, servants, porters, and gravediggers, helps to distinguish both class and character. Thus the *locus* of Henry IV's court opens onto the *platea* of the Boar's Head Tavern and Gadshill; the little academe of the King of Navarre opens past the Princess of France to the shenanigans of Don Armado, Holofernes, and Costard; the court of France opens out into the Arden of Duke Senior's men, love poetry, and gendered disguise; and the strict governance of Angelo and the strict obedience of Isabella give way to the brothels and whoremongering of Mistress Overdone, Pompey, Lucio, and Bernardine in *Measure for Measure*.

In the smaller auditorium of the Blackfriars Theater, too, more formal actions upstage contrast with more intimate interpretations downstage. In 1.2 Leontes asks Hermione to persuade Polixenes to stay longer in Sicilia, and as she moves away from him, he says as an aside to the audience:

Too hot, too hot:
To mingle friendship farre is mingling bloods.
I have *tremor cordis* on me. My heart dances,
But not for joy, not joy. This entertainment
May a free face put on, derive a liberty
From heartiness, from bounty, fertile bosom,

> And well become the agent. 'T may, I grant.
> But to be paddling palms and pinching fingers,
> As in a looking-glass; and then to sigh, as 'twere
> The mort o'th deer – O, that is entertainment
> My bosom likes not, nor my brows.
>
> (1.2.110–21)

His speech directs both the action and gestures of all three actors. In 2.3 his dialogues sequentially with a servant, Paulina, and Antigonus are in deliberate contrast in their intimacy to the formal court scene which follows on the *locus* in 3.1. At the end of the play – in 5.3 – they seem to converge, to pull the play to conclusion. His strained personal request of Paulina now – "O Paulina, We honour you with trouble. But we came To see the statue of our queen" (5.3.8–10) – leads to the upstage appearance, at the *locus*, of Hermione, but at Paulina's command she comes downstage in a gesture of reunion and, perhaps, of reconciliation:

> 'Tis time. Descend. Be stone no more. Approach.
> Strike all that look upon with marvel. Come.
> I'll fill your grave up. Stir. Nay, come away.
> Bequeath to death your numbness, for from him
> Dear life redeems you.
>
> (5.3.99–103)

Once again, Shakespeare blocks his own scene in the writing of it. But he also provides – in descent; in redemption – the very themes of the work, in the language and in the staging. They too are united.

Staging Time

Fluidity on the Shakespearean stage is not only a matter of space – where the boundaries between the conventions of *locus* and *platea* can blur in spaces of liminality, as when Navarre and his men meet the princess and her women in *Love's Labor's Lost* or Cressida moves from the forces of Troy to those of the Greeks. There is also a fluidity of time. Many – perhaps most – of the events in Shakespeare's plays take place in what we might call real or normal time: Titus' arrival with Tamora as prisoner in *Titus Andronicus*; Valentine's farewell to Proteus in *Two Gentlemen of Verona*; the queen's colloquy with the gardeners in *Richard II*; Mercutio's fight with Tybalt; Bassanio's choice of a casket; Brabantio's arousal from bed; Lear's division of the kingdom. But, indistinguishably at other

17

moments, Shakespeare deploys his story and his drama through what John C. Meagher has called expanded, condensed, multiple, or displaced time. The opening of Hamlet is one of his examples of expanded time:

> The first scene of *Hamlet* is not particularly long, but it begins with the bell having struck twelve, and ends with morning having arrived. The ghost has twice appeared before "just at this dead hour," says Marcellus, who has previously specified that the last time was on the stroke of one. About forty lines have been spoken between what is apparently just after midnight and what is evidently one o'clock. The ghost vanishes at the cock-crow (Capulet has heard the second cock at three, in *Romeo and Juliet* 4.5), and in about twenty-three lines the morn walks over the eastern hill in russet mantle.[9]

Elsewhere, in *A Midsummer Night's Dream*, Theseus complains to Hippolyta at the start of the play that their wedding is still four days away, yet one night in the woods and the nuptials are celebrated.

Condensed time for Meagher is employed in the second scene of *Romeo and Juliet* following the normal time of 1.1:

> In *Romeo and Juliet* 1.2 Capulet announces to Paris that his "old accustomed feast" takes place tonight, invites Paris as "One more, most welcome," and then hands his servant the list of invitees, giving him the mission to bid them come.... but it is hardly realistic to have one of the most substantial citizens of Verona send out his invitations right on the brink of the occasion, just after informing his daughter's noble suitor that he had not been put on the guest list....
>
> The foreshortening of the feast's beginning is fairly extreme; but the part of the celebrations that we see is hardly less condensed. The routine for masquers was to perform their costumed dance, then take ladies from the assembled company to dance with them. After that, they may depart or stay through the "revels," the general ball. It is not likely that Shakespeare allowed enough time for more than a token masque-dance and a token "commoning" of the masquers with the lady guests....
>
> When Capulet, genial host that he is, pleads with the masquers to stay for the customary buffet after the dancing, we are to understand that the general dancing is almost over, which is a further condensation; but when he realizes that they are determined to part, and thanks them for their masquing contribution, Shakespeare speeds up the temporal condensation about as far as it can be pushed. Naturalistically, we would now expect Capulet to return to his invited guests and lead them to the banquet – but Shakespeare, having already accomplished almost everything that is dramatically necessary, has Capulet break up the party and head for his sleep, in a single line! ("More Torches here: come on, then, let's to bed.")

In these instances, dramatic time does much more than provide a story line; it also provides an emphasis on the theme of runaway time as well as a perspective for playgoers.

The most commonly acknowledged multiple time in Shakespeare's works is the double time in *Othello*: the play opens with the recent marriage of Othello and Desdemona, although Iago argues without evidence that Desdemona has been an adulteress for some time. During the voyage to Cyprus, when Iago is on the ship with Desdemona and Othello follows in another vessel, Iago can apparently find no cause for such charges. Yet he makes such an accusation shortly after their arrival, and Othello becomes suspicious.

But there are many other instances. Meagher notes the peculiar juxtapositions of time in *Richard II*:

> Shakespeare has Richard send Bolingbroke into exile in 1.3, arranges for Richard to receive Aumerle's up-to-date report of Bolingbroke's journey partway to the coast in 1.4, and concludes that scene with the news of John of Gaunt's illness, whereupon Richard scrambles to get to his uncle's bedside as quickly as possible. The next scene opens with moribund John, includes Richard's arrival and John's death and Richard's confiscation of the inheritance of Bolingbroke (in more or less normal time) – and concludes with the dangerous and secret news that Bolingbroke is about to land in Yorkshire with powerful support (to regain that inheritance).

King Lear is another case in point:

> 5.2 contains less than a dozen lines, but it also contains the decisive battle between the predominantly French forces of Lear and Cordelia and the British troops led by Albany, Goneril, Regan, and Edmund. It begins with the parade of Cordelia and Lear, with their army, over the stage, after which Edgar enters with Gloucester, places him in a secure place that is apparently visible to the audience, and exits. We then get one stage direction: "Alarum and retreat within," followed by Edgar's reentry with the news that Lear's side has lost.

The reported battle has moved swiftly, yet simultaneously the playgoers remain watching Gloucester in real time. Such startling juxtaposition must mean to call our attention to the common theme of survival, pitting the passive Gloucester against the active troops conducted by both France and Britain, yet the passive Gloucester and the active Lear and Cordelia will meet the same fate. Multiple time, then, reinforces other more direct lines in the play about whether justicers are above, the significance of the late eclipses of the sun and moon, even the excellent foppery of the world. The first scene of *1 Henry IV* splits both time and focus to rejoin them: the scene opens with Henry IV organizing a crusade to the Holy Land, relieved at what appears to be the end of civil war, only to learn that Hotspur is withholding prisoners. As Hotspur betrays Henry's rule, so Henry will betray his own religious intentions. Such Shakespearean manipulations of time directly affect the playgoers' interpretations.

Utilizing the Stage

Slippages in place and time on the Shakespearean stage thus underscore certain ideas and relationships, often defining through analogy. The two doors at the rear of the stage, for instance, are put to service:

> *Enter the King of Fairies, at one door, with his train; and the Queen, at another, with hers.* (A Midsummer Night's Dream, 2.1.59)

> *Alarum. Enter a Son that hath killed his Father, at one door; and a Father that hath killed his Son at another door.* (3 Henry VI, 2.5.54)

> *Enter at one door Pericles talking with Cleon, all the train with them. Enter at another door a gentleman with a letter to Pericles. Pericles shows the letter to Cleon. Pericles gives the messenger a reward, and knights him. Exeunt Pericles at one door and Cleon at another.* (Pericles, scene 5)

> *Alarum, as in battle. Enter Martius, and Aufidius at several doors.* (Coriolanus, 1.9)

By assigning doorways, and thus entrances and exits, to different forces, Shakespeare can move swiftly to identify newcomers and their probable relationships to playgoers. Thus he might utilize one door for Ephesus and another for Syracuse, or London and the North, York and Lancaster, England and France, Egypt and Rome, Venice and Belmont, the Greek camp and the Trojan camp, or even for families, as with the feuding Montagues and Capulets. In the histories and tragedies, such groups may never be reconciled, but in the comedies, the reverse is likelier: just as the King of Navarre and the Princess of France meet, so do the Antipholi and Dromios, the Athenian aristocracy and their mechanicals, the merchants of both Antonio's mart and Portia's household, giving to spectators the special joy of fulfilled expectations. One editor of *The Comedy of Errors*, T. S. Dorsch, has suggested that the play makes use of the two doors and the discovery space as the Phoenix, the Porpentine, and the Priory; at Gray's Inn, where the play was presented in 1594, two outer doors behind these three, he remarks, could remain open as Syracuse and Ephesus.[10] But the Globe could also be called upon: with the two doors representing Ephesus and Syracuse, their common arrival at the discovery space where they discover the prioress leads to the reunion of everyone.

Despite the drawing of the Swan by Johannes de Witt that shows only two doors, there may have been three, if we count a central discovery space, at the Globe. It was used by Shakespeare (as well as other playwrights) to conceal those asleep (*Lear*, 3.6) and to reveal dead bodies (*Timon of Athens*, 5.3; *Pericles*, 1.1). But it was also used as a playing-space: as Timon's cave (*Timon of Athens*, 5.1.29) and the cave used by Belarius, Guiderius, Arviragus, and Imogen (*Cymbeline*, 4.2.0); as Friar Laurence's cell and the cell of Prospero; as Tom o'Bedlam's hovel. Closed, it could provide a back wall that could serve King John as the gates of Angiers, Henry V as the gates of Harfleur, and Martius as the gates of Corioles; as an arras hanging, it could conceal Polonius, Falstaff (in *The Merry Wives of Windsor*), and Miranda and Ferdinand playing chess; opened, the arras could disclose Juliet (she "*falls upon her bed within the curtains*," 4.3) or Portia's three caskets ("Go, draw aside the curtains, and discover The several caskets to this noble prince," 2.7). It could reveal large properties – thrones, beds, tombs. And it could allow a triumphant change of mood and pace: it is likely that, at the close of *As You Like It*, both the restored Rosalind and Hymen emerged from the discovery space, just as, years earlier, the Lady Abbess Emilia miraculously steps forth from the priory at the end of *The Comedy of Errors*.

Above the discovery space, the balcony is a crucial playing area in *Romeo and Juliet* and for Cleopatra as she has Antony, dying, hoisted to her presence. But Bardolf must be there, too; he tells Falstaff "there's a woman below" (*Merry Wives of Windsor*, 3.5). The balcony plays a role in the siege of Orleans: "*Enter on the walls La Pucelle, Dauphin, Reignier, Alencon, and Soldiers*" while, below, Joan cries out, "Advance our waving colours on the walls" (*1 Henry VI*, 1.6–2.1). It is the place from which young Arthur jumps to his death: "The wall is high, and yet will I leap down" (*King John*, 4.3). "*Enter above*" and "*Aloft*" are not uncommon directions for players at the Globe. Richard II appears above Northumberland at Flint Castle: "may it please you to come down? Down, down I come, like glist'ring Phaethon." Even the funeral orations for Julius Caesar may come from the balcony: "The noble Brutus is ascended" (3.2.11), and later Antony is asked to "go up" (3.2.65).

Armies "passing over," however, may come in one door, cross the stage, and exit through the other, given their numbers. There was also a window there, important to the plot of *Much Ado About Nothing* when Claudio thinks Margaret to be Hero (3.3). Explicit extant directions make these uses of the balcony certain. But it might well have been used for much more: Christopher Sly, for instance, watching the tale of Kate the curst and Petruchio unfolding beneath him and silently making his own analogy. Fortinbras twice passing over the scenes in Denmark reminds us that he is at the edges of Claudius's kingdom; but it is also possible that Egeon keeps reappearing, searching for ransom required for his life by the Duke of Ephesus.

The trap in the middle of the stage, in the *platea*, serves the gravediggers in *Hamlet* as they dig in unsacred ground and find Yorick's skull (5.1), but it must also be the earth in which Timon digs – "Earth, yield me roots" (*Timon of Athens*, 4.3.23) – and the sea from which Pericles's fishermen pull the "rusty armor" (*Pericles*, 2.1.) It is the pit in *Titus Andronicus* into which Bassianus' body is thrown and where Quintus and Martius fall, smearing themselves in his blood and thus appearing guilty of his death (2.3). It is also, most commonly, infernal. Joan de Pucell's familiar spirits are "culled Out of the powerful regions under earth" (*1 Henry VI*, 5.3.10–11); it is where the spirit rising for Mother Jordan the witch is commanded by Bolingbroke to "Descend to darkness and the burning lake!" (*1 Henry VI*, 1.4.39). This may be why the trap seems so fitting a place for Malvolio and why Feste thinks of exorcism as the way of bringing him back onstage. But ghosts may issue from the trap, too: in *Richard III* at Bosworth Field (5.5); in *Julius Caesar* before the battle of Philippi (4.2); in *Macbeth* when Banquo appears bloodied at the coronation banquet (3.4). Hamlet's father seems doomed to remain in the trap as one who "*cries under the stage*" (1.5). There is also the odd stage direction in *Antony and Cleopatra*: "*Music of haut boys under the stage*" (4.3.11). But it is used most frequently by the weird sisters in *Macbeth*, who enter and exit by it; later, they may use the trap to summon "*A show of eight kings, last with a glass in his hand* [mirroring Macbeth]; *and BANQUO* (4.1).

On either side of the trap were the twin pillars holding up the canopy or "heavens." They may or may not have served as trees for Orlando's love poetry for his Rosalind, but they surely were used in the scenes of eavesdropping. Behind the pillars Claudius and Polonius could spy on their scripted scene with Ophelia and Hamlet and comment on it; here the Duke and Provost withdraw to listen to Claudio and Isabella (*Hamlet*, 3.1; *Measure for Measure*, 3.1). Sir Toby Belch, Sir Andrew

Aguecheek, Maria, and Fabian gather behind one or both posts to observe Malvolio in his yellow stockings and crossed garters (3.4). Rosalind overhears and oversees Silvius displaying his lovesickness to Corin and to Phebe herself (*As You Like It*, 2.4; 3.5). Hamlet and Horatio observe the funeral procession to the trap under cover (*Hamlet*, 5.1): "couch...awhile, and mark" (216). Surely this was a handy staging device, but it must also have been a crowd-pleaser, for Shakespeare delights in a whole series of eavesdroppings in *Love's Labor's Lost*. Although stage directions were not necessarily authorial, but added, perhaps, by printers, they are still suggestive of staging. Thus Berowne steps behind a pillar (*"stands aside"*) to overhear the King of Navarre (4.3.19); the King *"steps aside"* to overhear Longaville (39) and he in turn *"steps aside"* to listen to Dumaine (73) before Berowne begins a series of discoveries (147). And Shakespeare multiplies the eavesdropping as well in the double scenes of *Much Ado About Nothing* in which Don Pedro, Leonato, and Claudio gull Benedick (2.3) and Hero, Margaret, and Ursula gull Beatrice (3.1). As for the canopy displaying the heavens, only this makes sense of Hamlet's directions to Rosenkrantz and Guildenstern to view "this most excellent Canopy the air; look you, this brave o're-hanging firmament, this majestical roof fretted with golden fire" (2.2.290–2).

Shakespeare's players used these physical features of the stage to establish relationships with one another – meeting, hiding, spying, departing – as their entrances and exits alone marked the play's scenes and, most often, indicated a change of locale. Often the players on the *locus* entered with formal speeches – as Richard II and Lear do – but occasionally, as with Roderigo and Iago, they may walk all the way to the *platea* before beginning a hushed conversation (*Othello*, 1.1.1–6), just as the commoners do in *Julius Caesar* (1.1) or Gloucester and Kent, in hushed tones, at the start of *King Lear* do. Frequently there is a delay between a direction for an entrance and the character's first lines (as with Borachio in *Much Ado* [1.3], Juliet in *Measure for Measure* [2.3], or Edmund in *Lear* [1.1]); while it was once thought that hasty compositors mis-set the type in quarto and folio, it is likelier that entering from the rear of the stage and moving toward the *platea* could take as many as fifteen steps and perhaps four to six lines. This gives Romeo time to contemplate Juliet before they first meet (1.5.39ff) and Beatrice time to prepare a suitable quip for Benedick (*Much Ado*, 1.1.95–6). Orlando and Old Adam discuss Oliver before and during his initial appearance (*As You Like It*, 1.1.1–24). The Ghost drifts on in his first appearance in *Hamlet* even as Marcellus and Bernardo talk about him (1.1.19–49).

J. L. Styan contends Shakespeare uses the device of the slow entrance to establish character as well as relationship, situation as well as personality, and cites *All's Well That Ends Well* (1.3). Here, he says:

> the Countess of Rousillon invites the audience to observe the condition of Helena's unhappy love as the latter passes at a distance on another part of the stage, even the balcony, unaware that she is being watched. Following her entrance there is a long delay before she speaks, and as the audience scrutinizes Helena's slow approach, the older woman explains with compassion how it is with the young. Her moving lines begin,

> > Even so it was with me when I was young;
> > If ever we are nature's, these are ours; this thorn
> > Doth to our rose of youth rightly belong;
> > Our blood to us, this to our blood is born. (123–6)

> It is not yet time for moral verdicts, but the wisdom of the Countess receives special weight by her stillness on the stage set against Helena's exposure as she moves wistfully downstage.[11]

Shakespeare condenses this narrative of entrances in *Troilus and Cressida* when Pandarus gives thumbnail sketches of the Trojan warriors (1.2.163–273). Conversely, Bernard Beckerman writes:

> The longest delay in an entrance, sixteen lines, occurs in *Coriolanus* (V.iii.19ff), when Coriolanus describes the delegation of Volumnia, Virgilia, young Marcius, and Valeria approaching him. By no means could it require a speech of that length for the actors to reach him, no matter from what part of the stage they may have entered or where he may have been standing. During his speech they become the visible expression of the inner struggle that he is about to undergo. If they move, they must move very slowly; if they stand still, they compose a picture. It is highly unlikely that the Globe company tried to "naturalize" this entrance by giving the entrants business or movement which would divert the attention of the audience from the effect their entrance was having upon Coriolanus.[12]

Entrances were not merely narrative, were not used merely to establish character, but were also situational – we think of the vilification of Kate and the praise awarded Bianca (1.1.50ff) or Portia's understanding and counsel to Bassanio (3.2).

Minor characters such as servants often exit rapidly, but this is not usually true of more major characters, as Antony and Cleopatra continually attest. In *As You Like It*, Rosalind has considerable difficulty in leaving Orlando after the wrestling match and imagines herself called back (1.2). But this seems to be delayed because, Andrew Gurr and Mariko Ichikawa report, three lines for an exit seems the norm. They cite as evidence Whitmore in *2 Henry VI*, the First Murderer in *Richard III*, Catesby in *Richard III*, and Bardolf in *2 Henry IV*. In the instances of major characters – Titus, Mistress Ford, Othello, Lear – they cite four lines as the norm.[13] But as with the long entrance of Helena in *All's Well*, Gurr and Ichikawa see extended or delayed exits as especially telling:

> Towards the end of *King Lear*, 3.7, the blinded Gloucester exits, led by a servant. As the F1 stage direction for their exit indicates, the servant unbinds Gloucester and begins to lead him away immediately after Regan's command: "Go thrust him out at gates, and let him smell His way to Dover" (3.7.91–2). Clearly Gloucester is still making his stumbling exit when Cornwall repeats his wife's order two lines later: "Turne out that eyelesse Villaine" (3.7.94). These harsh words would not only reinforce our sense of Cornwall's cruelty but intensify the painfulness of Gloucester's departure.

At times, exits and entrances are deliberately coordinated, as in *Richard II* with the exit of Richard in 3.2 overlapping the entrance from the other door of Bolingbroke in 3.3. The increasing despair of Richard and the efficient entrance of Bolingbroke underscore the slow defeat of one and the rapid rise of the other, and increase the intensity of such a juxtaposition.

Macbeth textually blocks scene after scene to reinforce meaning. In 1.3, for instance, the hero described in 1.2 meets the three sisters of 1.1, and the confrontation is incendiary. In 1.7, Macbeth's separation from the king and from the welcoming dinner, during which he thinks of regicide, is a prelude to 3.1 when Banquo is alone onstage, likewise concerned with regicide; in 3.2, Macbeth's exit by one door followed immediately by Lady Macbeth's at another visually demonstrates their separation, for always before they have been conspiring; by the end of the scene, he will keep her out of his plans to have Banquo murdered. Her isolation, which begins here, can be heightened visually in 5.1 when the doctor and gentlewoman remain in the *locus* and she wanders, carrying her taper, wiping her hands, down in the *platea*, around the edge of the stage.

But for Alan Dessen, entrances and exits can also be problematic. One of the most frequently contested entrances is Romeo's appearance to Friar Laurence in 2.3. As Dessen conjectures:

> To have Romeo enter just in time to deliver his first line in the scene ("Good morrow, father") may be a tidier solution (so some editors *have*

repositioned the entry from line 22 to line 30), but various possibilities emerge if Romeo is onstage for lines 23–30. For example, a Romeo who hears the friar talking about the presence of both poison and medicine within the same flower may be more likely to think of such poison (and the apothecary) in 5.1. Moreover, a playgoer who sees Romeo appear and meanwhile listens to the friar may be more likely to make a connection between "this weak flower" (in line 23, juxtaposed with Romeo's appearance) and Romeo, so that the friar's subsequent analysis, that builds to a postulation of "grace and rude will" (28) encamped in all of us, is not understood solely in highly abstract terms but is linked to the key chooser in the tragedy.[14]

As for exits, Dessen writes that:

> One recurring problem is found when a scene ends with a speech that seemingly should not be heard by some of the figures included in the final *exeunt*. For example, should Sir Oliver Martext's speech that ends *As You Like It*, 3.3, be understood as an *aside* (with Jaques, Touchstone, and Audrey still onstage) or as a comic speech addressed to the audience after a group *exeunt* (as in many modern editions)? Similarly, at the end of *Macbeth*, 5.3, should the Doctor's couplet be an *aside* with Macbeth still onstage or a speech directed at the playgoer after Macbeth has gone?

Then there is:

> the practical problem of what to do with a corpse. In some instances, the early texts do provide specific signals for the disposition of bodies (e.g., with Hotspur, Polonius, Hamlet, and Enobarbus), but the usual situation is silence. The richest example arises from the choice of how or when to dispose of the onstage corpse of Sir Walter Blunt in *1 Henry IV*.... If Falstaff closes the visor on (Blount's) helmet, what the playgoer would see is a corpse "semblably furnished like the king himself" (5.3.21) and therefore indistinguishable from Henry IV (who soon appears to fight with Douglas). How then will that playgoer view the moments that follow, especially Prince Hal's epitaphs over Hotspur and Falstaff, if such an "image" of a counterfeit king remains onstage? What would be the effect upon Falstaff's disquisition on Hotspur's body in which he uses the term *counterfeit* nine times? Since the Quarto provides neither evidence for Blunt's continued presence nor a signal for his removal, the editor or critic cannot be certain of the body's presence or absence, so what could be a highly visible and meaningful "image" is very much in doubt.

When that person (or body) appears and when that person (or body) exits can thus shift meanings and so can the consequent configurations.

26

Blocking, as Shakespeare demonstrates, therefore makes use of the physical stage: of the doors, the balcony, the posts, and the traps as well as the back of the stage for scenes of ritual and the front of the stage for more intimate soliloquies and asides. It is as if he pictured the play in his mind as well as heard it – thinking of himself as a spectator every bit as much as he thought himself an auditor.

Sound and Sight

Sound reinforces visual blocking. The plaster over lath which was used to construct the walls of the Globe, Bruce R. Smith writes, reflected back 86 percent of the sound waves that struck it, producing "standing waves" or "stationary patterns of vibration formed by many reflected sound waves, coming from many different surfaces, all superimposed on one another." He continues:

> Vibrations in wood may be short in duration, but wood catches the harmonic complexities of ambient sound. In effect, the stage of the Globe acted as a gigantic sounding board: made of reverberative material, it translated vibrations in the air above into standing waves in the air underneath, producing a harmonically rich amplification of the voices of actors positioned on top.[15]

Given the wooden canopy over the stage as well as the stage itself, the most powerful place to stand for projecting the voice would be under the canopy, not at the edge of the stage (where intimate, conspiratorial lines were delivered). There normal conversations, Smith says, would have a volume of 60dB as contrasted to shouts which might have 75dB, so that even when Orsino tells Viola that "thy small pipe Is as the maiden's organ, shrill and sound, And all is semblative a woman's part" (1.4.31–3), she too would have little trouble being heard given the excellent acoustics provided by the size, shape, and material of the Globe Theater.

In *A Midsummer Night's Dream*, Bottom reminds us that songs and dances are often means by which Shakespeare directs character and blocks action with the use of sound. Bottom's attempt to sing about woodland birds shows the limitations of his artistic abilities (3.1.120–3). The song Portia has sung to Bassanio not only directs him to the proper casket by supplying lines that rhyme with *lead* but announces her willingness to marry him (3.2.63–5). Benedick's superficial cynicism in *Much Ado About Nothing* –

I do much wonder that one man, seeing how much another man is a fool when he dedicates his behaviours to love, will, after he hath laughed at such shallow follies in others, become the argument of his own scorn by falling in love, and such a man is Claudio (2.3.8–12) –

is exposed when he too can recognize a "divine air" or song (2.3.58). The lyric to Feste's "O mistress mine," a melancholy song just right for Orsino, is sung to Sir Andrew Aguecheek and seems out of place (2.3.35–48); concluding with the line that "Youth's a stuff will not endure," Feste underscores the darker side of *Twelfth Night* and prepares us for the darker ending of his final song in the epilogue ("For the rain it raineth every day"). Desdemona's recognition of her own potential death is revealed in her willow song (4.3). Pandarus' song to Helen of Troy echoes the act and sounds of orgasm (3.1) while Ariel, despite the treatment he receives at the hands of Prospero, shows his own compassion for others when he comforts Ferdinand with "Full fathom five thy father lies" (1.2.399).

Dancing, too, carries significance, as Beatrice reminds Hero:

Hear me, Hero: wooing, wedding, and repenting is as a Scotch jig, a measure [pavan], and a cinque-pace: the first suit is hot and hasty like a Scotch jig, and full as fantastical; the wedding mannerly-modest as a measure, full of state and ancientry; and then comes repentance and, with his bad legs, falls into the cinque-pace faster and faster, till he sink into his grave. (2.1.66–73)

The witches' dances in *Macbeth*, the masqued Capulet ball (1.3), the country dance of *The Winter's Tale* (4.4), and the dance of the reapers in *The Tempest* (4.1) all set the tones of their respective plays. Conversely, the general ineptitude of the idealistic lovers of the court of Navarre is revealed when they try their hands at a dance of Muscovites (5.2), while Timon's worsening health of mind and body is signalled by a dance of "*Amazons, with lutes in their hands*" (1.2).[16]

Song and dance in Shakespeare usually occur in daytime scenes. But it was always daylight during afternoon performances at the Globe. R. B. Graves, in determining the angle and degree of sunlight on performances, has shown how the audience could accept night-time scenes in daylight. Indeed, such lighting is crucial if the playgoers are to witness some scenes set in the dark, as Macbeth's nocturnal arguments with his wife and his night-time conversation with the hired murderers (1.7; 3.4) and the observations on Lady Macbeth's sleepwalking (5.1) replete with accusations ("The Thane of Fife had a wife. Where is she now?" 5.1.36–7).

Daylight is necessary to comprehend the fight between Cassio and Roderigo (*Othello*, 5.1) and the Gadshill robbery in *1 Henry IV* (2.2). Given Shakespeare's utilization of daylight, he draws upon the material conditions of his playhouse to invigorate the imagination of his playgoers. In such a conventional agreement between player and playgoer, we can better understand why Shakespeare risks laughter in having Gloucester merely fall to the stage when he thinks he jumps off the cliff at Dover, for it works in parallel or analogical fashion: in the darkness of his blindness, Gloucester like Macbeth will imagine things are what they are not.

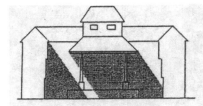

a. NE stage: 2 P.M. in summer

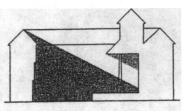

b. NE stage: 3 P.M. in spring or autumn

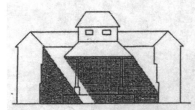

c. NW stage: 2 P.M. in summer

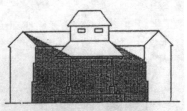

d. NW stage: 3 P.M. in spring or autumn

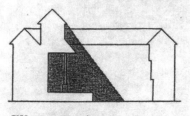

e. SW stage: 2 P.M. in summer

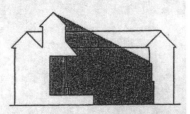

f. SW stage: 3 P.M. in spring or autumn

Figure 5   Conjectural diagrams of sunlight and shadow at the Swan Theater; the Globe Theater had a southwest stage (here e and f).

From R. B. Graves, *Lighting the Shakespearean Stage, 1567–1642* © 1999 by the Board of Trustees, Southern Illinois University, reprinted by permission of the publisher.

Conclusion

Shakespeare's stagecraft often relies on the unwritten contract with the playgoers' collaborative imagination, too. He relies on it when important actions occur offstage and are merely reported: Ophelia's report of a distressed Hamlet appearing to her ungartered; Gertrude's description of Ophelia's death; Mistress Quickly's announcement of the death of Falstaff; Enobarbus' description of Cleopatra on her barge; the report to Brutus of Portia's death. Other events we are made to imagine may remain deliberately ambiguous: whether Julius Caesar denied the crown; when (if ever) Othello's marriage to Desdemona is consummated; who murdered Thomas of Woodstock; the actual assassination of Duncan; the ordered conversion of Shylock. Some critical questions in the plays that have come down to us may have been clearly answered in performances at the Globe: does Christopher Sly learn anything from the actions of Petruchio? How does Iago finally leave the stage, sworn to silence? When does Lear actually die, and does he die still hoping (or thinking) his daughter lives? Fundamental lines, too, would have been resolved of ambiguity in their delivery. When Bolingbroke, returning to England, asks "How far is it, my lord, to Berkeley now?" (*Richard II*, 2.3.1), is he bewildered, anxious, or hungry for power? When Prince Hal, in his first thoughts shared with playgoers through soliloquy, says, "I know you all" (*1 Henry IV*, 1.2.173), is he joyful, smug, cynical, ambitious, or reflective? When Cordelia weeps at the beginning of 5.3, does she weep because her father is defeated and sent to prison or because her suggested reconciliation of their family has been deliberately ignored?

One of Shakespeare's signatures is to leave the fundamental narratives of his dramas untold, so that playgoers, like the players in the play, must piece together the sequence and interpretation of events. The abbess promises a full account of what happened to her at the end of *The Comedy of Errors*, but we do not know what she will tell or how she will tell it. Yet it has import in characterizing her decision to give up the veil and return to the secular life of a merchant's wife. Orsino promises to tell more about himself, too, at the close of *Twelfth Night*; Hermione yet may talk to Leontes, but only after the final lines of *The Winter's Tale*. And what will Horatio tell of Hamlet; Malcolm of Macbeth; Duke Vincentio to Isabella – will she accept him in the end? Such open questions are deliberate, for they keep the playgoers' imaginations active and engaged. The same happens with us. Even knowing the material conditions of Shakespeare's stage, its possibilities and its limitations, his plays still invite us to take part, too.

And one way accessible to all of us is to visualize the stage and the action on it. Although any play renders striking possibilities, *Romeo and Juliet* is one play that says as much through its staging as through its language. The entrances, for instance: when the play proper opens, Samson and Gregory come onstage from the Montague doorway, identifying their allegiance; meeting Abraham and another serving man from the opposite doorway – the Capulets' – establishes the opposition of families that will be the play's foundation. The subsequent procession of entrances moves up the chain of authority, from the servants, to the parents, to the prince himself. If Prince Escalus enters with his impressive train from the central discovery space, he sets himself in the position of reconciler – but if so, he dismisses that possibility when he asks to see the Capulets and the Montagues separately, precluding thorough negotiations. Meantime, the *platea* remains, at the forefront, equally available to both families and their allies, as the doorways at the rear of the stage do not.

Seen visually, the first meeting of Romeo and Juliet occurs on the main stage at the Capulet ball, where it is important that everyone, even if dancing, is disguised from the others by a mask. It is what allows greater mobility on the stage for each of the actors. When Romeo and Juliet drift away from the crowd to have their first intimate meeting, they move downstage nearer the audience, who can then share in the intimacy. But the next time we see them, they have ascended to a bedroom and the balcony outside it – an ascent too quick in the midst of a feud and anticipatory of the play's ending when they will fall again, this time to a supine position atop a shared tomb in the Veronese graveyard.

Moreover, if we think of the discovery space as the only space that can hold large properties, then it will be used for the scenes of Juliet's bedroom and the tomb itself; in both instances, she will lay down combining thoughts of love, betrayal, and death: it is a *liebstod*, the love of death anticipating the death of love. But that inner space at the back of the stage can also house smaller interiors, such as Friar Laurence's cell and the Apothecary's shop, aligning these two characters visually. Both of them take upon themselves the powers of life and death (or the appearance of death) and both, against their better judgment, conspire in the forbidden plans of the two young lovers.

At the play's conclusion, the candlelight employed during the night ball in 1.5 will be used only once more, in the graveyard of 5.3. What Juliet fears in 1.5 – "My grave is like to be my wedding bed" (1.5.132) – is turned into certain, deadly prophecy. It is a self-warning, and self-knowledge that she refuses to heed, just as Romeo will ignore the initial advice of the friar. For all of the comments about "a pair of star-crossed lovers" (Prologue 6) which contents the chorus, the play works hard – in staging as well as in poetry – to show how the characters – Romeo, Juliet, Old Capulet and his wife, the nurse, the friar – work their wills and through errors in human judgment give us a story unsurpassed in woe. And if Prince Escalus comes to this realization independent of the chorus, but in the same place onstage as he appeared in 1.1, surrounded by most of the same crowd of people, his stubborn refusal to witness the feuding Montagues and Capulets arguing over the better memorial suggests that, in many ways, the play has made no progress in the state of warring factions in Verona.

The lines of the play suggest such readings, of course, but the staging of them makes them indelible. In "reading" Shakespeare this way, we become collaborators with the playwright, too, just as his actors were. It is to those players that we now turn.

2

Players

Whatever is commendable in the grave orator is most exquisitely perfect in him [the excellent actor]: for by a full and significant action of body he charms our attention: sit in a full theater and you will think you see so many lines drawn from the circumference of so many ears, while the *actor* is the *center*. He doth not strive to make nature monstrous, she is often seen in the same scene with him, but neither on stilts nor crutches: and for his voice, 'tis not lower than the prompter, nor louder than the foil and target. By his action he fortifies moral precepts with example. . . . He adds grace to the poet's labors: for what in the poet is but ditty, in him is both ditty and music.

Sir Thomas Overbury, "An Excellent Actor,"
New and Choice Characters (1615)

Too often we think the exceptional period of achievement of the English theater results from such brilliant playwrights as William Shakespeare, Ben Jonson, and Christopher Marlowe. But a case can be made that the extraordinary accomplishment of English theater in the days of Elizabeth I and James I – throughout Shakespeare's lifetime – is equally due to the talents and skills of the best of the London players. The most noteworthy companies of players were the Lord Admiral's Men (under the patronage of Lord Howard until they became Prince Henry's Men in 1604); the Earl of Worcester's Men (until they became Queen Anne's Men in 1604); and Shakespeare's company, known from 1594 as the Lord Chamberlain's company (after their patron, Henry Carey, the first Lord Hunsdon and lord chamberlain to Queen Elizabeth) and then, from 1603, as the King's

33

Men, under the patent of authorization issued by James I. Such companies of professional players operated under licenses awarded by their patrons, received their protection, and wore their livery: in theory, then, they were servants to their sponsor and expected to add to his (or, rarely, her) dignity and magnificence through their service to him in household entertainments and adding to his reputation for beneficence through their public performances, while in fact they operated on a daily basis more like a guild. A large number of players and their managers came from guilds, in fact, such as the joiner James Burbage, the draper Francis Langley, the grocer John Brayne, the dyer Philip Henslowe, the haberdasher Oliver Woodliffe, as well as Robert Armin, goldsmith; John Heminges, grocer; Ben Jonson, bricklayer; John and Lawrence Dutton, weavers; Martin Slater, ironmonger; Richard Tarlton, vintner; and James Tunstall, sadler. Like freemen in guilds, they might have boy actors training as apprentices – as John Heminges had as apprentices Alexander Cooke and John Rice, and Richard Burbage had young Nicholas Tooley and Richard Robinson. And like guilds, as E. K. Chambers noted long ago, their association was fundamentally economic:

> The basis of [their] organization was the banding together of players into associations or partnerships, the members of which acted together, held common stock of garments [properties] and playbooks, incurred joint expenditures, and daily or at other convenient periods divided up (as sharers) the profits of their enterprise.[1]

Existing largely independently of their patrons, then, the shareholders of the Lord Chamberlain's–King's Men hired journeymen to play adult roles for fixed wages and took on boys as apprentices to individual players to act the roles of women and children, to be trained in their profession, and to insure the company's future.

We know the names of the 26 principal actors of Shakespeare's plays because they are listed in the First Folio of his works. S. P. Cerasano has noted that:

> when read by column, the order of names suggests roughly four "generations" of players, just over half of whom were still living when the folio was published in 1623.
>
> The first nine players in the inventory (William Shakespeare, Richard Burbage, John Heminges, Augustine Phillips, William Kempe, Thomas Pope, Henry Condell, William Sly) are those who comprised the company in August 1597, plus George Bryan who seems to have left late in the previous year. With the exception of Sly, Bryan, and Condell, all seem to have

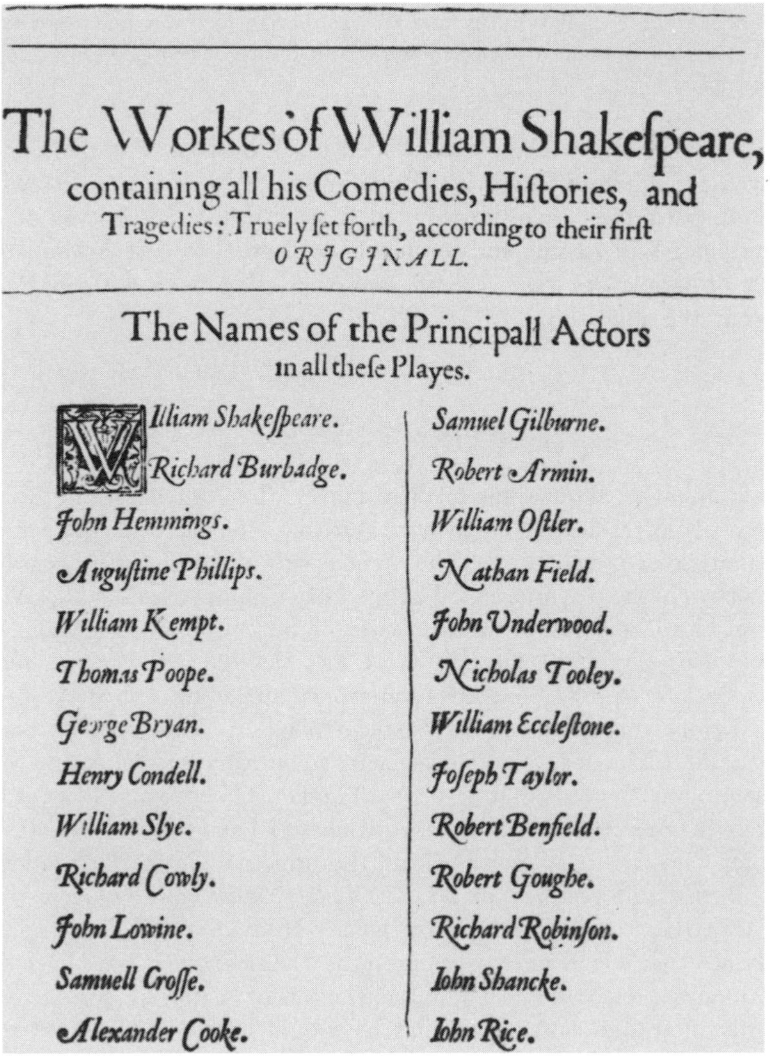

The Workes of William Shakespeare,

containing all his Comedies, Histories, and
Tragedies: Truely set forth, according to their first
ORIGINALL.

The Names of the Principall Actors
in all these Playes.

William Shakespeare.	*Samuel Gilburne.*
Richard Burbadge.	*Robert Armin.*
John Hemmings.	*William Ostler.*
Augustine Phillips.	*Nathan Field.*
William Kempt.	*John Underwood.*
Thomas Poope.	*Nicholas Tooley.*
George Bryan.	*William Ecclestone.*
Henry Condell.	*Joseph Taylor.*
William Slye.	*Robert Benfield.*
Richard Cowly.	*Robert Goughe.*
John Lowine.	*Richard Robinson.*
Samuell Crosse.	*John Shancke.*
Alexander Cooke.	*John Rice.*

Figure 6   Title-page of *Comedies, Histories and Tragedies*, 1623, sig. B2.
British Library.

held shares; so the compilers of the 1623 list placed the nonsharers last on
the list. This is the "generation" that built the first Globe playhouse in 1599.

The second generation (Richard Cowley, John Lowin, Samuel Cross,
Alexander Cooke, Samuel Gilburne, and Robert Armin) are those who
saw the company develop into the King's Men in 1603, when it assumed

royal patronage. Five additional players (William Ostler, Nathan Field, John Underwood, Nicholas Tooley, and William Ecclestone) were employed by 1611, some of them replacing others who had died or dropped out of the company.[2]

Each of the players might have a specialty – Burbage was the leading player, for whom Shakespeare wrote many of his major roles, while writing parts for clowns that suited the quite different talents of the entertainer Will Kempe and the more intellectual Robert Armin – but most of the players were versatile and could play many different parts, often in the same play.

King and Clowns

We know more about some of these players than others. We know, for instance, a great deal about Richard Burbage. The son of the player and theater owner James Burbage, he owned with his brother Cuthbert half the shares of the playhouse used by the Lord Chamberlain's–King's Men. He may have begun acting as early as 1584 (he was born in 1568); he was surely acting by 1590. He must have met Shakespeare then or shortly after, because in 1594 Elizabeth I summoned him along with Shakespeare and Kempe to perform at Greenwich Palace at Christmas. Burbage's remaining career was with Shakespeare's company and we know from contemporary records that he played Hamlet, Othello, and Lear; it has also been conjectured that he played Richard III and Romeo. In 1605 Sir Walter Cope wrote to Robert Cecil, the principal secretary to James I, that Burbage proposed to play *Love's Labor's Lost* before Queen Anne; on May 31, 1610, he was hired by the city of London to deliver a speech to Prince Henry in a water pageant on the Thames (it may have been that of Amphion). He was much admired; the earl of Pembroke, for one, said shortly after Burbage's death that he would not attend a court play because "I being tender-hearted could not endure to see [it] so soon after the loss of my old acquaintance Burbage." Burbage was also a businessman, inheriting from his father both the Theatre and the second Blackfriars. He was also a well-known painter. The earl of Rutland paid Burbage for "painting and making" an heraldic device in 1613 and, in 1616, for painting his shield. There is still extant "a woman's head on a board done by Mr. Burbage, the actor" at Dulwich College, London, and it is believed that a contemporary painting of him is a self-portrait. He seems to have been popular among his fellow players according to the sentiments in the wills of several of them including Shakespeare, Augustine Phillips, and Nicholas Tooley, his apprentice. After his death, Burbage seems to have been succeeded by Joseph Taylor.

The first extant reference to the clown Will Kempe is as "my lord of Leicester's jesting player" in a letter written by Sir Philip Sidney in 1586. Although little is known of his early years, he was presumably one of Leicester's players and may also have been his messenger between the Low Countries and London. The next possible reference to him, "Wilhelm Kempe, instrumentist," is on the payroll of Elsinore Castle in Denmark. By 1590 he was back in London, inheriting the place of Richard Tarlton, the leading clown; he became a shareholder until his retirement in 1599. He must have played Peter in *Romeo and Juliet*, because the second quarto of 1590 has as a stage direction in 4.5 "Enter Will Kemp" instead of Peter. But this is a small part and he doubtless doubled in others. He was probably also Balthasar, since the stage direction for 5.3.21 reads "Enter Romeo and *Peter*," and this cannot be correct, since Peter is a servant to the Capulets while Balthasar serves the Montagues. Kempe must also have had a part in the crowded scene of the Capulet ball; he was known for his dancing, and Shakespeare may have indicated this when he writes "A hall, a hall, give room! And foot it, girls! More light, you knaves, and turn the tables up" (1.5.26–7), because in his later poem *The Scourge of Villainy* (1598), John Marston writes, perhaps in parody, "A hall, a hall! Room for the spheres, the orbs celestial Will dance Kempe's jig." Kempe was a large man even if light on his feet and he likely played other parts similar to Peter's: the unnamed clown in *Titus Andronicus*; Launce in *Two Gentlemen of Verona*; Launcelot Gobbo in *The Merchant of Venice*. Kempe's name is put beside the part of Dogberry in the manuscript of *Much Ado About Nothing*; he may also have played Bottom and Falstaff in both parts of *Henry IV*. The quarto of *2 Henry IV* has the nonsensical direction "Enter Will" at 2.4.18, a little in advance of Falstaff's entrance ("Lo, here comes Sir John," 27), but there is even greater weight for this possibility in the play's epilogue: "If my tongue cannot entreat you to acquit me, will you command me to use my legs? And yet that were but light payment, to dance out of your debt" (15–17), since the only crime is Falstaff's – he has just been banished by the king – and Kempe's job after a play was to perform a jig:

One word more. If you be not too much cloyed with fat meat, our humble author will continue the story, with Sir John in it, and make you merry with fair Katherine of France; where, for anything I know, Falstaff shall die of a

sweat. . . . My tongue is weary; when my legs are too, I will bid you good
night, and so kneel down before you – but, indeed, to pray for the Queen.
(22–30)

This was in 1598, when Kempe may already have been making plans to
leave the company (he was gone by 1599), and it helps to explain why the
Falstaff of *The Merry Wives of Windsor* – aging, inept, bumbling, un-
creative – is so different in character and why there is no appearance by
Falstaff in *Henry V*. Upon his departure from the company, Kempe
danced from London to Norwich on a bet (and wrote about it in *Kempe's
Nine Days' Wonder* in 1600), receiving from the mayor of Norwich an
annuity of 40 shillings. He performed in Italy and Germany, then
returned to England to join Worcester's Men in 1603. He was known
not only as a clown but for his dancing; he ended Shakespeare's plays
with jigs (sketches with song and dance that were often obscene)
and "merriments" (improvised witty repartees). In 1609 Thomas
Dekker mentions that Kempe is dead, but he may have died as early as
1603.

Figure 7 Will Kempe dancing, from title-page of Kempe's *Nine Days' Wonder*.
He is accompanied by a man with a pipe and tabor associated with Kempe's
predecessor Richard Tarlton.

Robert Armin, the son of a Norfolk tailor, and a goldsmith's apprentice, succeeded Kempe as the company's clown. Unlike Kempe, Armin was small with a twisted physique, but he took on more substantial and more serious roles – Touchstone, Feste, Lavache – and became known not for his dancing, but for his singing, particularly the bittersweet songs Shakespeare wrote for him in *Twelfth Night*. He probably played Touchstone, whose criticism of William in *As You Like It* 5.1 is clearly a critique of Kempe. Armin has also frequently been thought to have played Lear's Fool (and thus perhaps have doubled as Lear's "poor fool" Cordelia, 5.3.304), but Cordelia was probably played by a boy, and it has therefore also been conjectured that Armin's talents might have been equally suitable for the role of Edgar, particularly as Tom o' Bedlam. Thus he may also have been Trinculo, the most serious and perceptive of the clowns in *The Tempest*.[3]

Other Company Members

The first extant reference to Augustine Phillips is in 1590, when he is listed as Sardanapalus in the plot of a play now known as *The Second Part of the Play of the Seven Deadly Sins*. As a member of Lord Strange's company, he was given permission to leave London during the plague of 1593, along

Figure 8 Robert Armin from title-page of *History of Two Maids of Moorclack*, 1609. He is in his traditional long coat.

with Kempe, Thomas Pope, John Heminges and George Bryan, and Edward Alleyn, who was a member of the Lord Admiral's Men. Phillips was back and resident in Horseshoe Court in the liberty of the Clink and the Southwark parish of St Saviour's in 1593; two of his daughters were baptized there in 1594 and 1597. He may have been a dancer, because he secured the rights in 1595 to publish his *Jig of the Slippers* from the Stationers' Company. His stillborn child was buried on September 27, 1597, and on October 5 his wife was churched in the parish of St Botolph's without Aldgate where he must then have been living; he moved back to Southwark and to Paris Garden in 1598 and returned to St Saviour's parish in 1601. He must have managed business affairs for the Lord Chamberlain's Men, because he was approached by members of the Essex conspiracy in 1601 to perform Shakespeare's *Richard II* on the eve of their rebellion and march against the Queen early in 1601. He acted as a moneylender in 1604, loaning "the sum of £105 of lawful money of England" to John Baumfeld; but he was making his own will in 1605 and died shortly thereafter. His will, which acknowledges he now had an estate outside London at Mortlake, left money to his wife, his family, his servants, and his preacher; there is also, typically, an:

> Item: I give and bequeath unto and amongst the hired men of the company which I am of, which shall be at the time of my decease, the sum of £5 . . . to be equally distributed amongst them. Item: I give and bequeath unto my fellow William Shakespeare a 30s piece in gold; to my fellow Henry Condell one other 30s piece in gold; to my servant Christopher Beeston 30s in gold; to my fellow Lawrence Fletcher 20s in gold; to my fellow Alexander Cooke 20s in gold; to my fellow Nicholas Tooley 20s in gold.

He appointed his wife Anne his executrix, but if she should remarry she would forsake that right and her inheritance from him, and his fellow players would succeed her, each receiving "for their pains herein to be taken, a bowl of silver of the value of £5 apiece."

We know far less about other members of Shakespeare's playing company. Like Kempe, Thomas Pope was in Danish service in the mid-1580s, assuming a later appointment at the court of the elector of Saxony in Dresden. He must also have been a business manager of the Lord Chamberlain's Men, because he served with Heminges as joint payee for court performances between November 1597 and October 1599. John Heminges and Henry Condell may have been the company's historians and, in effect, librarians, because in time they would collect the best of the playscripts and publish them as Shakespeare's *Works* in 1623. The royal patent establishing the King's Men in 1603 named Shakespeare,

Burbage, Phillips, Heminges, and five new members to the company –
Lawrence Fletcher, Condell, William Sly, Armin, and Richard Cowley.
Fletcher, the only Scotsman in the group, may not have been with the
company for long; he had a reputation in Edinburgh as a leading English
actor and he may have come down with the new king in 1603. Unlike the
others, there is no indication he ever performed at the Globe.

Cerasano has pointed out that various members of the Lord Chamberlain's–King's Men were not only professionally associated but shared
personal friendships and marital ties. There were also ties across company lines:

> Richard Robinson married Richard Burbage's widow, Winifred, after her
> husband died in 1619. John Heminges's daughter Thomasine married William Ostler (and Heminges had formerly married the widow of another
> actor, William Knell, a former Queen's Man who died in 1588). Robert
> Goughe married Augustine Phillips's sister in 1603, and another of Phillips's sisters is probably the Margery who married William Borne, a lead
> actor with the Lord Admiral's Men.

But Cerasano conjectures that the company existed as a kind of
"extended family":

> This is supported by the numerous mentions of players and their families in
> probate documents, particularly wills. To cite only a few, Augustine Phillipps bequeathed to "my late apprentice," Samuel Gilburne, "the some of
> ffortye shillinges, and my mouse Colloured velvit hose, and a white Taffety
> doublet, A blacke Taffety sute, my purple Cloke, sword, and dagger, And
> my base viall." Another apprentice received "the some of ffortye shillinges
> and a Cittern a Bandore [plucked string instruments] and a Lute." ... Shakespeare remembered Heminges, Burbage, and Condell in his last will and
> testament, and Robinson and Tooley stood witness to Burbage's will, which
> was written out by the scrivener of the King's Men, Ralph Crane. Nicholas
> Tooley, who had once been Burbage's apprentice, left various sums of
> money to friends, including members of Burbage's family, Condell's wife
> and daughter, and fellow player Joseph Taylor. Tooley forgave debts owed
> by two other King's Men, John Underwood and William Ecclestone, and
> left a further £10 to Cuthbert Burbage's wife in whose house Tooley died.

Cerasano also notes they generally lived near the theaters and near each
other: Shakespeare took rooms in the parish of St Saviour's, Southwark,
near Alexander Cooke, Robert Goughe, John Lowin, Augustine Phillips, William Sly, and Joseph Taylor; in St Mary, Aldermanbury (northeast of St Paul's Cathedral, near Blackfriars), Heminges and Condell lived

and, later, William Ostler, who married into the Heminges family and named his son Beaumont, after the playwright; while northeast of the London city walls, in Shoreditch, home of the Theatre and Curtain, Richard and Cuthbert Burbage lived, close neighbors on Halliwell Street, along with Richard Cowley, who named his two sons Cuthbert and Richard after the Burbages.[4]

Company Organization

Shakespeare's playing company was organized like the other companies: it was overseen by the sharers who invested in the company – at perhaps £70 per share – who divided their proceeds accordingly after expenses. One of them usually served the company as its business manager. According to Gerald Eades Bentley, this task entailed:

> authorizing the purchase of new costumes and costume materials; paying for new plays by freelance dramatists; getting scripts approved by the Master of the Revels, paying him for licenses for the theater and for occasional privileges, like playing during parts of Lent; paying the company's regular contributions to the poor of the parish, assessing fines against sharers or hired men for infringement of company regulations; calling rehearsals; collecting fees for court and private performances; supervising the preparation and distribution of playbills; and perhaps for paying the hired men.[5]

John Heminges's function as the manager of the Lord Chamberlain's–King's Men is documented from 1596 to 1630, since he was always the recipient of payments for court performances, even when he was joined by another sharer – twice by Thomas Pope, and once each by George Bryan, Richard Cowley, and Augustine Phillips. Around 50 such payments to Heminges are extant, amounting to well over £3,000. He was also the company representative in other matters: when in 1615 eight players from the four London companies were called before the Privy Council on charges of playing during Lent, he answered for the King's Men along with Richard Burbage. He dealt too with the office of the Master of the Revels, with whom he had a good relationship. On August 19, 1623, for instance, Sir Henry Herbert noted his allowance "For the King's players. An old play called *Winter's Tale*, formerly allowed of by Sir George Bucke and likewise by me on Mr. Heminges his word that there was nothing profane added or reformed, though the allowed book was missing; and therefore I returned it without a fee, this 19 of August 1623."[6] Clearly, he was a trusted servant of the crown.

The sharers augmented their company with hired men, sometimes a good many of them. They served as actors, musicians, prompters or bookkeepers, stagekeepers, tiremen or wardrobe keepers, and sometimes gatherers, who were responsible for collecting admission in their leather bags at the doors. Often these hired men were used on the stage for crowd scenes, such as the masked ball in *Romeo and Juliet* or the Roman citizens and soldiers in *Coriolanus,* or for small parts such as messengers and servants. Shakespeare wrote his musicians – probably a consort of six men or so – into such plays as *Romeo and Juliet* and *Othello.* The company bookkeeper did not prompt players in their lines during performances – the wall at the rear of the platform was far too thick and the actors on the platform far too distant from anyone behind the doors, although Tiffany Stern has recently suggested he stood behind the arras at the rear of the stage.[7] The bookkeeper was also in charge of putting necessary stage directions into the scripts, hiring copyists and scribes to make one or more fair (readable) copies from the author's foul (handwritten) papers, and making revisions required by the Master of the Revels or suggested in rehearsal or performance. Some plays that have come down to us show several staging directions, often in layers that suggest revision during or after performances. Working out the parts, the bookkeeper might also assign the minor parts which Shakespeare and other playwrights had not written for any particular player in the company. In addition, the bookkeeper acted as a kind of stage manager, seeing that properties were collected and ready, alerting musicians, supervising sounds offstage, and cuing players, usually with the aid of a Plot, or listing of entrances hanging near the doorways behind the stage. The tiremen were in charge of costumes, buying cloth or clothing, making costumes, and occasionally helping the players dress or quickly change costumes, often by throwing on or taking off robes and cloaks if they were to play different parts or a role at different times or places. Gatherers alone could be men or women, but only the men were ever asked to perform silent parts on stage. Since this job required the least amount of time, gatherers may in addition have served as stagekeepers, or janitors. They might also be asked to do other minor tasks, such as post bills announcing performances. These are the men Shakespeare has in mind when he writes in *Romeo and Juliet* "*Enter three or four Citizens with clubs*" (1.1), "*Enter Romeo, Mercutio, Benvolio, with five or six other Maskers, Torch-bearers*" (1.4), or "*Enter Father Capulet, Mother, Nurse, and Serving men, two or three*" (4.2); or in *Hamlet* Q2 "*Enter old Polonius, with his man or two*" (21); or in *Titus Andronicus* "*After them, Titus Andronicus, and then Tamara the Queen of Goths, and her two*

43

Sons Chiron and Demetrius, with Aaron the Moor, and others, as many as can be" (1.1).

While they were playing in London, the Lord Chamberlain's–King's Men usually had twelve men and four boys as the basic company of players. There was no legally sanctioned players' guild, although many adult players belonged to another guild. The boys were individually apprenticed, from perhaps the age of 10 or 12, to individual players who, acting as a combination of teacher and father, trained a future generation of actors. There was no set curriculum as there was no set period of apprenticeship (the boys' voices began changing often at the age of 16 or 17), but they were likely instructed in formal rhetoric, declamation (like that delivered in soliloquies), physical bearing and movement, and conventional expressions and gestures. The player John Rice, listed among the principal players in the Folio, began as an apprentice (or "boy") to John Heminges when he performed before James I at a Merchant Taylors dinner held for the king. Although there is no documentary evidence pertaining to a boy apprentice for the King's Men, a suit in the King's Bench for 1609 records the relationship between Martin Slater and the shareholders of the Whitefriars theater:

> Item, it is likewise…agreed…by and between the said parties that whereas by the general consent of all the whole company, all the children are bound to the said Martin Slater for the term of three years. He the said Martin Slater doth by these presents bind himself to the residue of the company in the sum of forty pounds sterling that he shall not wrong or injure the residue of the said company in the parting with or putting away any one or more of the young men or lads to any person or persons, or otherwise without the special consent and full agreement of the residue of his fellow sharers, except the term of his or their apprenticeship be fully expired.[8]

In return, the boys were given food, lodging, clothing, training, and experience. We know some of them, at least, in Shakespeare's company were recruited from the Chapel Royal and some others, perhaps, from other boys' companies: Nicholas Tooley apprenticed to Richard Burbage, James Sands and Samuel Gilborne to Augustine Phillips, Alexander Cooke and John Rice to John Heminges, Nicholas Burt and Thomas Pollard to John Shank, and Charles Hart to Richard Robinson. Ben Jonson especially honored boys apprenticed to him: he taught Nathan Field how to read Horace and Martial in Latin and perhaps playwriting; he referred to another boy player, Salmon Pavy, as "the stage's jewel" in an epitaph for him on his death in 1602 at the age of 13.

Repertory, Other Companies, and Revivals

All of Shakespeare's plays – as all of the works performed by the Lord Chamberlain's–King's Men and the other London companies – were performed in repertory. As Roslyn Knutson reports, plays were generally performed in three standard seasons: the fall season from August to October, the winter season from All Hallows to Lent, and the spring season from Eastertide to summer.[9] The most important time was the twelve days of Christmas (December 26–January 6), when plays were also performed at court; no plays were permitted during the holy season of Lent. During these seasons, though, unless there was a declared danger from plague or rioting, performances were held nearly every day. But the same play was never performed two consecutive days; rather it was repeated several days later, or a week or a month, or several months later; at any given time, the company would have between 12 and 24 plays in performance. Sequels or serial plays (like Shakespeare's first and second tetralogies, or parts of them – *1, 2,* and *3 Henry VI* and *Richard III*; *Richard II, 1* and *2 Henry IV*, and *Henry V*) were, conversely, usually performed on consecutive days.

The theatrical manager Philip Henslowe's *Diary* – actually an account book with all the financial transactions – records all the performances of his companies, but there is no comparable record for the Lord Chamberlain's–King's Men. The only record we now have is of a ten-day period in June 1594 when the newly formed Lord Chamberlain's Men briefly merged with the Admiral's Men, overseen by Henslowe at the playhouse in Newington Butts. Knutson has transcribed this series showing receipts in shillings for performances of plays:[10]

3 of June 1594	Rd [Received] at heaster & asheweros		viijs
4 of June 1594	Rd at the Jewe of malta		xs
5 of June 1594	Rd at andronicous	[*Titus Andronicus*]	xijs
6 of June 1594	Rd at cvtlacke		xjs
8 of June 1594	ne [new] Rd at bellendon		xvijs
9 of June 1594	Rd at hamlet	[not Shakespeare's]	viijs
10 of June 1594	Rd at heaster		vs
11 of June 1594	Rd at the tamynge of A shrowe	[*Shrew*]	ixs
12 of June 1594	Rd at andronicous		vijs
13 of June 1594	Rd at the Jewe		iiijs

Company	Season	Possible performances	Actual performances	Plays	New plays	Weeks in which new plays opened
1. Strange's Men	19 Feb. 1592–22 Jun. 1592	123	105	23	5	2, 8, 10, 14, 16
2. Strange's Men	29 Dec. 1592–1 Feb. 1593	35	29	12	2	2, 5
3. Sussex's Men	27 Dec. 1593–6 Feb. 1594	42	30	12	1	5
4. Sussex's & Queen's Men	1 Apr. 1594–8 Apr. 1594	8	8	5	0	
5. Admiral's Men	14 May 1594–16 May 1594	3	3	3	0	
6. Admiral's Men	17 Jun. 1594–26 Jun. 1595	328	273	36	20	2, 4, 5, 7, 9, 11, 14, 15, 19, 21, 22, 25, 26, 35, 36, 38, 42, 44, 46, 48
7. Admiral's Men	25 Aug. 1595–27 Feb. 1596	187	151	30	10	1, 2, 4, 6, 8, 10, 14, 20, 23, 26
8. Admiral's Men	12 Apr. 1596–28 Jul. 1596	107	84	25	7	3, 4, 6, 9, 11, 12, 15
9. Admiral's Men	27 Oct. 1596–12 Feb. 1597	109	75	18	8	6, 7, 8, 10, 11, 12, 14, 16
10. Admiral's Men	3 Mar. 1597–16 Jul. 1597	136	109	21	6	4, 9, 11, 13, 14, 18
11. Admiral's Men	11 Oct. 1597–5 Nov. 1597	26	9	6	1	1

Philip Henslowe's receipt for playing seasons of the Lord Admiral's Men at the Rose Theater until 1597 when his record-keeping ends, showing the number of possible and actual performances, the number of new plays and those already in the repertory, and the intervals between openings of new plays.

From Carol Chillington Rutter, ed., *Documents of the Rose Playhouse* (rev. edn) (Manchester and New York: Manchester University Press, 1999), p. 23.

Except for occasional performances at court or at London's Inns of Court, the law schools known for their revels, no other record survives.

In lieu of this, Knutson has drawn on title-pages of quartos, court records, and allusions to performances in private correspondence to piece together the probable new plays which Shakespeare contributed to the repertory of his company. Sometime after June 1594, the Lord Chamberlain's Men toured in the provinces and then played the winter at the Cross Keys Inn in London before moving north of the city walls to the Theatre in Shoreditch. They played at the Theatre until 1597, when they moved to the nearby Curtain Theater before, in 1599, moving to their newly constructed Globe Theater in Southwark, south of the city and across the Thames, approximately, from St Paul's Cathedral. When Shakespeare joined the company, he likely brought with him the plays he had already written, two of them recorded in the ten days with the Lord Admiral's Men: *Titus Andronicus*, *The Taming of the Shrew*, *1 Henry VI*, *The First Part of the Contention of the Two Famous Houses of York and Lancaster* (*2 Henry VI*), *The True Tragedy of Richard Duke of York* (*3 Henry VI*), *Richard III*, and *The Two Gentlemen of Verona*. During the years at Shoreditch he presumably added *The Comedy of Errors*, *Love's Labor's Lost*, and *Romeo and Juliet* (1594–5); *Love's Labor's Won* (now lost), *Richard II*, and *A Midsummer Night's Dream* (1595–6); *The Merchant of Venice*, *1 Henry IV*, and *King John* (1596–7), *2 Henry IV*, and *The Merry Wives of Windsor* (1597–8); and *Much Ado About Nothing* and *Henry V* (1598–9). Knutson suggests that these plays probably ran alongside other plays held by the company – *The Merry Devil of Edmonton*, *Mucedorus*, and *Fair Em*, and, possibly, *A Knack to Know a Knave*, *Edward II*, *Arden of Faversham*, *Edward III*, and *The Tartarian Cripple*. The repertory of the Admiral's Men might also have suggested certain plays to Shakespeare: as have other scholars before her, she sees echoes of *The Jew of Malta* by Christopher Marlowe (performed in 1594 and 1596) in *Romeo and Juliet* (1594–5) and *Merchant of Venice* (1596).

In 1599 alternative performances grew more frequent as more playing companies were formed. The Lord Chamberlain's Men dismantled the Theatre to erect the Globe in Southwark. The Boar's Head playhouse was enlarged; the playhouse at Paul's opened with a new company of Paul's Boys. The following year, the Admiral's Men also built themselves a new playhouse – the Fortune – and the Blackfriars reopened with a boys' company. Shakespeare's company, keeping to its large and diverse collection of plays, continued, adding his new plays to its growing repertory: *As You Like It* and *Julius Caesar* in their opening season; *Hamlet* (1600–1); *Twelfth Night* (1601–2); and *Troilus and Cressida* and *All's Well That*

Ends Well (1602–3); alongside probable revivals of *Richard III* (printed in 1597, 1598, and 1602), possibly the *Henry VI* trilogy connected to it, and *Romeo and Juliet* (printed in an enlarged and revised version in 1599). These new plays, too, might not have been entirely random. The *Ur-Hamlet*, an earlier, anonymous play now often attributed to Thomas Kyd but lost, may have given Shakespeare a plot, but performances of Paul's Boys, who opened the new playhouse at Paul's with a two-part play of revenge by John Marston, *Antonio and Mellida* and *Antonio's Revenge*, and *The Spanish Tragedy* revived by the Admiral's Men in a text revised for them by Ben Jonson, may have given him impetus. The Admiral's Men also presented their own set of plays on the Wars of the Roses, *2 Henry Richmond* (implying part I), while Worcester's Men made an initial payment for *Shore's Wife* and Derby's Men played *Edward IV* in two parts. On June 22, 1603, the Admiral's Men paid Jonson for a play entitled *Richard Crookback* and commissioned a two-part play on *Sir John Oldcastle*, reminding their audience that its hero was not a fat knight as in Shakespeare's *1 Henry IV* but a respectable, historic Lollard. Such competition may have been in part friendly – Shakespeare had worked with Ben Jonson and acted in his plays, and his earlier echoes of the work of Christopher Marlowe may suggest elegiac respect or even his own acting as a boy in the company Marlowe wrote for – and it is possible that, in tandem, the various companies were sharing audiences and creating joint audiences for their various repertories. (It is also possible, of course, that this intense period of history plays was especially timely during the transition between the reigns of Elizabeth I and James VI and I.)

In 1603 Shakespeare's company received a new name, the King's Men, and new letters patent providing them the right:

> to show and exercise publicly to their best commodity, when the infection of the plague shall decrease, as well within their now usual house called the Globe within our County of Surrey, as also within any Town Halls or Moot-halls or other convenient places within the liberties and freedom of any other City, university, town, or borough whatsoever within our said realms and dominions.[11]

The acknowledged plague lasted nearly a year, and the London playhouses did not reopen until April 9, 1604. But then, while the company playing at the Fortune began a series of plays about the heroes of Foxe's *Book of Martyrs* and the Queen's Men at the Red Bull developed a repertory of plays filled with battles, epic travels, and romance, Shakespeare

Year or year extent	Month or season	Kind of closure
1563–4	30 Sept.–Jan.	
1569	31 May–30 Sept.	
1572	?	
1574–5	15 Nov.–Easter	
1577	1 Aug.–31 Oct.	
1578	10 Nov.–23 Dec.	
1580	17 Apr.–31 Oct.	
1581	10 July–18 Nov.	
1582	summer–autumn	
1583	summer–26 Nov.	
1584	?summer	
1586	11 May	precautionary restraint
1587	7 May	precautionary restraint
1592	23 June–29 Dec.	
1593	1 Feb.–26 Dec.	
1594	3 Feb.–1 Apr.	
1596	22 July–27 Oct.	
1603	19 Mar.–29 Apr., 1–12 May	[Mar.–Apr.; June–][a]
1604	12 May–9 Apr.	[–Apr., June–Sept.]
1605	5 Oct–15 Dec.	[Mar.; Oct.–Dec.]
1606	? July–? Nov.	[Mar.–Apr.; July–Dec.]
1607	? July–? Nov.	[Jan.–Mar.; May–Dec.]
1608	? July–	[Jan.–Mar.; Aug.–]
1609	–? Dec.	
1610		[–Jan.; Mar.; July–Nov.]
1611		[Feb.–Mar.]
1612		[Mar.–Apr.; Nov.–Dec.]
1613		[Feb.–Mar.; July–Dec.]
1625	12 May–24 Nov.	
1630	8 July–28 Nov.	
1636	12 May–	
1637	–2 Oct.	
1640	23 July–29 Oct.	
1641	15 July–9 Dec.	

[a]Lists in square brackets give alternative estimates for the years 1603–13.

The dates of playhouse closings because of epidemics of plague, 1563–1642. From Andrew Gurr, *The Shakespearian Playing Companies* (Oxford: Oxford University Press, 1996), pp. 91–2.

wrote similar plays for the King's Men – *Othello*, *Measure for Measure*, *King Lear*, *Macbeth*, *Antony and Cleopatra*, *Pericles*, *Coriolanus*, and *Timon of Athens* – and brought back, for a new king who had presumably not seen them, *The Merry Wives of Windsor*, *The Comedy of Errors*, *Love's Labor's Lost*, *Henry V*, and *The Merchant of Venice*, and, quite likely, *As You Like It* and *Richard II* as well. The King's Men added to this list several other plays that were more or less similar: *Sejanus* and *Volpone* by Ben Jonson; *The Malcontent* by John Marston; *The Revenger's Tragedy* (possibly by Cyril Tourneur); *The Devil's Charter* by Barnabe Barnes; and *The Miseries of an Enforced Marriage* by George Wilkins; as well as *The Fair Maid of Bristow*, *The London Prodigal*, and *The Yorkshire Tragedy*, all of them resonating in Shakespeare's plays with situations, scenes, characters, and story lines. There was also the anonymous *Gowrie*, perhaps an early version of *Macbeth*. Meantime, the Admiral's Men were performing their own plays about the Scots: *Robert II, King of Scots* in September 1599 and *Malcolm, King of Scots* in April 1602, and, alongside Shakespeare's *Julius Caesar* and Jonson's *Sejanus*, the Admiral's Men staged Jonson's *Cataline* (1598–9).

Another major epidemic of plague shut the playhouses again for a year beginning in August 1608. When the theaters reopened, the King's Men took up winter performances at Blackfriars, presenting, among other works, Shakespeare's late romances. The astrologer and physician Simon Forman reports going to the Globe to see, in April and May of 1611, *The Winter's Tale* (new), *Richard the 2* and *Macbeth* (in revival), and *Cymbeline* (first performed in 1609–10). The Revels Office for 1611–12 and the Revels Account for the Christmas season of 1611–12 record performances of *The Tempest* on November 1, *The Winter's Tale* on November 5, and Beaumont's and Fletcher's somewhat similar tragicomedy *A King and No King* in revival on December 26. In 1612–13, the new plays included *Cardenio* (sometimes assigned to Shakespeare) and, with John Fletcher, *Henry VIII* and *The Two Noble Kinsmen*. But there were a number of revivals as well: Beaumont's and Fletcher's *Philaster*, *Much Ado About Nothing*, *The Maid's Tragedy*, *The Merry Devil of Edmonton*, *Sir John Falstaff* (perhaps *The Merry Wives of Windsor*), *Othello*, *Caesar's Tragedy* (perhaps *Julius Caesar*), *The Alchemist*, and *The Hotspurr* (perhaps *I Henry IV*). Yet just what playgoers saw is always open to question. Reporting on *Macbeth*, Forman recalled not the story of a king with great imagination or the fall of a tyrant, but "3 women feiries or Nimphes," Macbeth's bloody hands, the "prodigies" of nature on the night of Duncan's assassination, Banquo's ghost, and Lady Macbeth's sleepwalking – the most sensational bits.[12] Both in the quality of Shakespeare's writing and in the quality of playing by the King's Men, they remained the premiere company in a highly active theatrical period in London; and when they also went to play at Blackfriars, they were frequented by the highest aristocracy. Even royalty, which never attended public playhouses, went to Blackfriars.

Just how long performances of these plays took is still a matter of some debate. Ben Jonson says flatly in the prologue to *The Alchemist* that the play will take "two short hours." Fletcher and Shakespeare claim *The Two Noble Kinsmen* is just "two hours travel," and Thomas Middleton also claims "two poor hours" for *Hengist*, a King's Men play. But Jonson confesses that his longer play, *Bartholomew Fair*, which opened the new Hope Theater in Southwark, takes more time in performance: "*Spectators*, and *Hearers*" must "have a little patience" and "agree to remain in the places their money or friends have put them in . . . for the space of two hours and a half, and somewhat more." It has been argued that texts of plays of normal length – about 2,500 lines – now take us three hours or longer to say aloud and that what we have are "maximal texts" which were shortened even then in production. (*Bartholomew Fair* and *Hamlet* run to 4,000 lines.) Conversely, faster delivery (which may well have been the case in the aurally conditioned culture of Shakespeare's time), along with the overlapping of entrances and exits, no pauses for change of scenery, and no intermissions (refreshments were sold throughout the play by pedlars in the yard), might shorten the plays to two hours or so. In our own time, the Shenandoah Shakespeare Company, based in Staunton, Virginia, has kept most plays to just two hours by utilizing small casts who double and triple parts with clothes put on from trunks onstage and who talk rapidly. That plays could last until dark at the public playhouses in the autumn is probably behind Lord Hunsdon's request to the lord mayor of London on October 8, 1594, when his Lord Chamberlain's Men were playing briefly at the Cross Keys Inn in Gracious (Gracechurch) Street, that:

> I pray you the rather to do for that they have undertaken to me that where heretofore they began not their plays till towards four o'clock, they will now begin at two and have done between four and five, and will not use any drums and trumpets at all for the calling of people together, and shall be contributories to the poor of the parish.

The time seems sensible: for all social classes the main meal, dinner, was served between ten o'clock and noon and if the play ended at four or a little after, the playgoers could be home before dark. This seems to have become the norm: Thomas Platter records that he saw *Julius Caesar* at the Globe on September 21, 1599, "after lunch, about two o'clock," and goes on to report that this is the conventional time for performances in the public playhouses. But from 1608 onwards, when the King's Men transferred playing to the indoor Blackfriars where so much changed – the size of the playhouse, the absence of stage pillars, a stage one-third the size of the Globe and that reduced by playgoers seated or standing on the platform – the matter of starting time might be less crucial. And it surely became inappropriate when the players went on tour in the provinces, playing in some towns and villages to playgoers who had completed a full day of work.

Touring

Players such as the Lord Chamberlain's–King's Men greatly increased their audiences and the stature and popularity of their art by touring; they also created a stronger influence on the nobility and gentry by playing at their country houses. J. A. B. Somerset has determined that companies on tour had "3,119 successful visits out of a total of 3,279 records [now extant], giving an actual success rate of 95.12 per cent" in Shakespeare's lifetime.[13] Touring could also mean performances at town halls, guild halls, market squares, or inns. Sally-Beth MacLean proposed and Andrew Gurr maintains that in Shakespeare's time the roads "were quite heavily used, and generally of a reasonable all-weather standard," that "No part of the country was more than two weeks' travel from the seat of government," and there were "inns with accommodation and food for travellers along every highway."[14] Playing companies such as the Lord Chamberlain's–King's Men travelled both by choice and by necessity, but either way it was in their best interests to maximize performances, especially where they had found good audiences previously; it led to profits and enhanced reputations, a means of self-advertising both in the towns where they played and to those playgoers if later they came to London. The players' success in drawing crowds could disrupt city life, however, eliciting the disapproval of local civic authorities, and provoking a contest of wills between players with the proper licenses to travel and play and local authorities who had the power to prevent their doing so. The most obvious route, according to Peter Greenfield, was to follow the Roman road (Watling Street) northwest out of London through Abingdon and Oxford to Coventry or, moving farther west, through Bath, Bristol, and Gloucester. Another route took the players to Exeter and Plymouth, although the

North Downs deterred them from Guildford and Farnham even though both possibilities were along the old Pigrims' Way from Canterbury to Winchester. Choosing Oxford over Gloucester meant struggling up the steep Cotswold Edge, but players often followed the rivers, such as the Thames and the Severn, instead. They also travelled by water along the Dorset and Devon coasts.[15] They walked on tour alongside covered wagons carrying costumes, properties, and playscripts, covering perhaps 25 miles a day; we learn from *Richard III* that from Tamworth to Bosworth Field was "one day's march" (5.3.13). But they went at what Gurr calls "surprisingly high speed": the Queen's Men travelled over 150 miles from Ipswich on December 17, 1588, to Dover by Christmas; Queen Anne's Men went from York on September 23, 1607, to Dunwich, Suffolk, by early October.[16] Canterbury seems (like Coventry) to have been especially hospitable. Expenses for such tours have been estimated at 10 s to 14 s a day.[17]

Beginning in 1559, travelling players could not perform in many towns until they had been licensed directly, or seen in performance by the whole corporation. The "standard procedure," according to Gurr, is recorded by R. Willis in *Mt. Tabor, Or Private Exercises of a Pentinent Sinner* (1639):

> In the City of Gloucester the manner is (as I think it is in other like corporations) that when Players of Enterludes come to town, they first attend the Lord Mayor to inform him what nobleman's servants they are, and so to get license for their public playing, and if the Mayor like the Actors, or would show respect to their Lord and Master [i.e. their patron whose livery they wore], he appoints them to play their first play before himself and the Aldermen and common Council of the City; and that is called the Mayor's play, where every one that will comes in without money, the Mayor giving the players a reward as he thinks fit to show respect unto them.

Likewise the York rolls for 1582 stated that "players of Interludes now come, and coming from henceforth to this city shall play but twice in the common hall of this city, viz. once before the Lord Major and aldermen &c. and th'other before the commons."[18]

Other town records explain such cautious limitations. In the Mayor's Court Books for Norwich on June 10, 1590, an entry reads:

> This day John Mufford, one of the Lord Beauchamp's players, being forbidden by Mr Mayor to play within the liberties of this city, and in respect thereof gave them among them 20 s, and yet notwithstanding they did set up bills to provoke men to come to their play, and did play in Christ Church; therefore the said John Mufford is committed to prison.

In Leicester Town Hall after performances by Queen Anne's players in January 1605, repairs had to be made to broken glass windows and chairs. Norwich encountered similar difficulties. The Assembly Proceedings for March 21, 1614, note that "Whereas Joseph Moore and other stage-players, servants to the Lady Elizabeth, came lately to this city and here attempted to play without leave from Mr. Mayor, at which their said plays were many outrages and disorders committed, as fightings, whereby some were wounded, and throwing about, and publishing of seditious libels, much tending to the disturbance and breach of His Majesty's peace."[19] The town records of Chester for October 20, 1615, displays even more anger at:

> the common bruit [rioting] and scandal which this city hath of late incurred and sustained by admitting of stage players to act their obscene and unlawful plays or tragedies in the common hall of this city thereby converting the same being appointed and ordained for the judicial hearing and determining of criminal offences, and for the solemn meetings and concourse of this house into a stage for players and a receptacle for idle persons.

As a consequence, "no stage players upon any pretense or color whatsoever shall be admitted or licensed to set up any stage . . . within this city or the liberties thereof in the night time or after vi of the clock in the evening,"[20] even when given noble patronage. Such scenes can be placed alongside the play-within-a-play in the Boar's Head Tavern in *1 Henry IV* (1.2), Falstaff's behavior in *2 Henry IV* (5.1), Sir Toby Belch's uncontrolled revelry in *Twelfth Night*, and moments throughout *The Merry Wives of Windsor*.

Still, the players had little choice but to go on the road when the plague struck London. But plague could visit the country as well as London. Even the Chamberlains' Accounts for the City of Canterbury for 1608–9 deny performances by Lord Chandos' players and Lord Berkeley's players.[21] Like Leicester in 1594–5 to Lord Morley's players and Southampton in October 1592 to the earl of Worcester's players, provincial towns refused to allow players to perform, although they paid them a gratuity out of deference to their patron. Shakespeare and his playgoers were well aware of the uncertainties, the suddenness, and the devastation that plague could cause; Friar John faces the plague in *Romeo and Juliet*:

> Going to find a barefoot brother out,
> One of our order, to associate me
> Here in this city visiting the sick,
> And finding him, the searchers of the town,

Suspecting that we both were in a house
Where the infectious pestilence did reign,
Seal'd up the doors, and would not let us forth,
So that my speed to Mantua was stay'd.

(5.2.5–12)

What may seem to us to be an easy plot device, then, would to Shakespeare's playgoers underline not only the potential horrors but the very
fragility of life for the Montagues and Capulets, Romeo and Juliet.

When London playing companies went on the road, they probably
travelled with a reduced repertory to save space, keeping their possessions
– their parts and their properties – in covered wagons to protect them from
both rain and sun. They may have reduced the number in their company,
too; present thought is divided on whether they went at full strength to
keep all of the company employed or reduced their numbers to something
like seven or eight men and one or two boys; in any event, they were also
accompanied by support staff. Shakespeare may have thought of such
possibilities as he was drafting and, in his mind, casting his plays: only
three parts in *Macbeth*, for instance, cannot be doubled in the Folio text:
Macbeth, Macduff, and Ross; and the play can be performed with a cast of
six or seven. And the Lord Chamberlain's–King's Men did travel: to
Shrewsbury, Ipswich, Oxford, Bath, Faversham, Maidstone, and Marlborough, among other places, and some of them – Oxford and Barnstable
in Devon – seem to have been regular stops; like most companies, Shakespeare's playing company probably had its regular routes. But during the
plague, the King's Men might also have sought refuge in the homes of their
fellows. Records show that the Lord Chamberlain's–King's Men toured in
1597; by August 27 they had played in Rye (and perhaps Faversham on
route), they were in Dover by September 3 and Bristol by the week of
September 11. They doubtless included Bath and Marlborough, too,
although stopping at the small village of Marlborough, Peter Davison
argues, probably meant they also found more lucrative audiences at the
neighboring great houses of Sir Edward Seymour, earl of Hertford, at
Tottenham House in the Savernake, and of the Pembrokes at Wilton
House.[22] In 1604 Augustine Phillips bought his manor house in Mortlake
not far from Richmond Palace; one item that is recorded paid to the
company is the cost of their travelling in 1603–4 from Mortlake to
perform at Wilton during a siege of the plague in London. Later, in
1625, Henry Condell would also buy a house in the country, in nearby
Fulham. Just as easily, during the plague, the players may also have taken a
holiday or returned to their homes, as Shakespeare doubtless went, on

some of these occasions, to Stratford. The only other time they knew they would not be playing, after all, was during the season of Lent.

The Art of Counterfeiting

Much of the year, though, in public playhouses, at court, or on the road, the Lord Chamberlain's–King's Men *were* playing. "In the sixteenth century the term 'acting' was originally used to describe the 'action' of the orator, his art of gesture. What the common stages offered was 'playing,'" Andrew Gurr writes; "What the players were presenting on stage by the beginning of the century was distinctive enough to require a whole new term to describe it."[23] Playing was a matter of re-enactment, not embodiment; as Thomas Heywood put it in 1612, the player should "qualify everything according to the nature of the person personated."[24] The key concept was imitation, not duplication; as Cerasano has it, Shakespeare and his fellow players "did not attempt to *become* a character, but to *represent* a character, to convey emotion in such a way that the spectator could relate to a character's joy or grief." Thus playing "was about inspiring the audience."[25] The chief means for such a representation was known as counterfeiting. This understanding was derived from Aristotelian *mimesis*, advocated by Sir Philip Sidney in 1590 in his *Defence of Poesie* and promulgated again in 1593 by Henry Peacham in his *Garden of Eloquence*: "Mimesis is an imitation of speech whereby the orator counterfeiteth not only what one said, but also his utterance, pronunciation and gesture, imitating everything as it was, which is always well performed, and naturally represented in an apt and skillful actor." Even I. G., in his *Refutation* of Heywood in 1615, recalls a "jesting-Player" who "so truly counterfeiteth everything, that it seemed to be the very persons whom he acted."[26] These players are "the abstracts and brief chronicles of the time," as Hamlet reminds Polonius (2.2.503–4), personators imitating the past to counterfeit it in their imitations of yet another story, "Aeneas' tale to Dido" (2.2.426–7) in "an excellent play, well digested in the scenes, set down with as much modesty as cunning" (2.2.420–2). His subsequent advice to the players, as he interpolates their play and their cunning with his own, is a set of directions for counterfeiting that is somewhere between stock convention and what we know as realism, between overacting and an echoing reproduction:

> Speak the speech, I pray you, as I pronounced it to you – trippingly on the
> tongue; but if you mouth it, as many of your players do, I had as lief the

town-crier had spoke my lines. Nor do not saw the air too much with your hand, thus, but use all gently; for in the very torrent, tempest, and as I may say the whirlwind of your passion, you must acquire and beget a temperance that may give it smoothness. O, it offends me to the soul to hear a robustious, periwig-pated fellow tear a passion to tatters, to very rags, to split the ears of the groundlings, who for the most part are capable of nothing but inexplicable dumb shows and noise. I would have such a fellow whipped for o'erdoing Termagant. It out-Herods Herod. Pray you avoid it. (3.2.1–13)

Rather, he instructs "*two or three of the Players*" (3.2.0):

Suit the action to the word, the word to the action, with this special observance: that you o'erstep not the modesty of nature. For anything overdone is from the purpose of playing, whose end, both at the first and now, was and is to hold as twere the mirror up to nature, to show virtue her own feature, scorn her own image, and the very age and body of the time his form and pressure.... Go make you ready. (3.2.16–23; 40).

As mirrors of nature, they are reflectors of it.

Shakespeare and his fellow players seem to have delighted in such counterfeiting, and his own plays are redolent with opportunities. Hamlet's own play, "*The Mousetrap*," "the image of a murder done in Vienna" (3.2.217–18), begins with a dumb show counterfeiting the action to come (3.2.123) followed by Prologue (3.2.133ff) before a fuller imitation is performed, the play-within-a-play in *Hamlet*. Borachio stages a dumb show with Don John in *Much Ado About Nothing* when he asks Don John to bring Don Pedro and Claudio "to see this the very night before the intended wedding, for in the mean time I will so fashion the matter that Hero shall be absent, and there shall appear such seeming truth of Hero's disloyalty that jealousy shall be called assurance, and all the preparation overthrown" (2.2.36–41). Iago scripts a similar dumb show with Bianca, who he tells Othello is really his wife Desdemona as she approaches Cassio:

Now will I question Cassio of Bianca,
A hussy that by selling her desires
Buys herself bread and cloth. It is a creature
That dotes on Cassio – as 'tis the strumpet's plague
To beguile many and be beguiled by one.
He, when he hears of her, cannot restrain
From the excess of laughter. Here he comes.
As he shall smile, Othello shall go mad;

And his unbookish jealousy must conster
Poor Cassio's smiles, gesture and light behaviors
Quite in the wrong.

(4.1.91–101)

In *Macbeth*, the witches' *"show of eight kings, last with a glass in his hand; and Banquo"* terrifies him with the aid of a mirror: "Thou art too like the spirit of Banquo. Down! Thy crown does sear mine eyeballs" (4.1.128–9). Plays-within-the-play like *The Mousetrap* also enable Shakespeare's players to double their counterfeiting. Given the two induction scenes in *The Taming of the Shrew*, the entire presentation of Petruchio and Kate is an inset play for Christopher Sly at the hands of an unnamed lord, his fellow huntsmen, and his page Bartholomew. *1 Henry IV* has two plays-within-the-play: the robbery at Gadshill (2.3) and the tavern scene where Prince Hal and Falstaff exchange roles as king and prince (2.5). Other insets are more masque-like: the Pageant of the Nine Worthies in *Love's Labor's Lost* (5.1); the wedding masque in *The Tempest* (4.1).

Such counterfeiting, however, whatever form it took, had to be stored in the players' memories: they had two or three dozen plays at the ready in the company's repertory. To help them prepare plays quickly – even new plays had at the most two or three weeks of rehearsals while other plays were being performed – they may have established certain practices, such as the use of particular doors to mark their entrances and certain places on the stage to play public and private scenes. There were also standardized gestures by which to counterfeit situations and emotions that could signal equally prompt understanding among playgoers. These were taken from cultural practices, such as doffing a hat when meeting someone, using customary greetings (as in *Troilus and Cressida*, 4.5) or kneeling before superiors (*All's Well That Ends Well*, 1.2; *Coriolanus*, 2.1; *Pericles*, 1.4). In *Chirologia* and *Chironomia* (1644), John Bulwer, a teacher of the deaf, published a record of many of these cultural signs. Abraham Fraunce supplies other material practices in his *Arcadian Rhetorike* (1588): "the holding down of the head, and casting down of the eyes betokeneth modesty." Elsewhere he notes that the eyes "express lively even any conceit or passion of the mind." Gestures must "follow the change and variety of the voice," so that the right arm, when extended, can reinforce the flow of speech, and hands and fingers rather "follow than go before and express the words." Striking the breast for Fraunce acknowledges grief, striking the thigh conveys indignation, and striking the ground denotes vehemency.[27] For Bulwer, "To strike another's palm is

Figure 9   John Bulwer, *Chirologia, or the Natural Language of the Hand*, 1644, p. 155.

A. *Munero* (I provide); B. *Auxilium fero* (I bring aid); C. *Irascor* (I am angry); D. *Demonstro non habere* (I show that I do not have [anything]; E. *Castigo* (I chastise); F. *Pugno* (I fight); G. *Confido* (I confide in); H. *Impedio* (I impede); I. *Recommendo* (I recommend); K. *Officiose duco* (I lead in an official capacity); L. *Impatientiam prodo* (I betray impatience); M. *Sollicite cogito* (I think anxiously); N. *Pudet* (he is ashamed); O. *Adoro* (I adore); P. *Conscienter affirmo* (I affirm in good conscience); Q. *Poenitentiam ostendo* (I display contrition); R. *Indignatione timeo* (I fear with indignation); S. *Data fide promitto* (I pledge my faith); T. *Reconcileo* (I reconcile); V. *Suspicionem et odium noto* (I note suspicion and hate); W. *Honoro* (I honor); X. *Reservatione saluto* (I greet with reservation); Y. *Furacitatem noto* (I show thievery); Z. *Benedico* (I bless).
British Library.

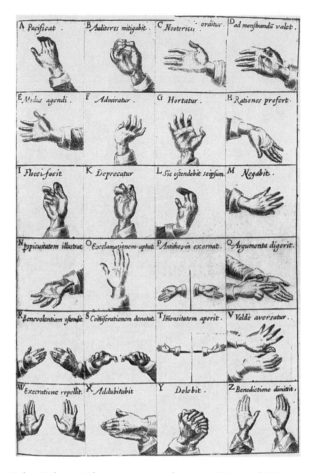

Figure 10   John Bulwer, *Chironomia, or the Art of Manual Rhetoric*, 1644.

A. *Pacificat* (He quiets down [the crowd]); B. *Auditores mitigabit* (He will soothe the audience); C. *Neotericis orditur* (He begins from recent events); D. *Ad monstrandum valet* (He is good for instructing); E. *Modus agendi* (Shows a method); F. *Admiratur* (He admires); G. *Hortatur* (He exhorts); H. *Rationes profert* (He advances arguments); I. *Flocci facit* (He dismisses as trivial); K. *Deprecatur* (He pleads an excuse); L. *Sic ostendebit seipsum* (In this way [the orator] will refer to himself; M. *Negabit* (He will show denial); N. *Perspicuitatem illustrat* (He shows the obvious); O. *Exclamationem aptat* (He furnishes an exclamation); P. *Antithesin exornat* (He illustrates an antithesis); Q. *Argumenta digerit* (He walks through arguments); R. *Benevolentiam ostendit* (He shows good will); S. *Commiserationem denotat* (He denotes sympathy); T. *Immensitatem aperit* (He reveals vastness); V. *Valde aversatur* (He rejects vehemently); W. *Execratione repellit* (He fends off curses); X. *Addubitabit* (He will show doubt); Y. *Dolebit* (He will show grief); Z. *Benedictione dimittit* (He dismisses [the crowd] with a blessing).
British Library.

the habit and expression of those who plight their troth, give a pledge of faith and fidelity, promise, offer truce, confirm a league, buy, sell, grant covenant, bargain, give or take handsell, engage themselves in suretyship, refer their controversies to an arbiter, put to compromise or choose an umpire, engage themselves to be true and trusty, warrant and assure."[28] Polixenes and Hermione striking their palms in *The Winter's Tale* (1.2.117) is what helps arouse Leontes's jealousy.

Shakespeare reinforces expressions and gestures too by description, such as that of Wolsey by Norfolk in *Henry VIII*:

> Some strange commotion
> Is in his brain: he bites his lip and starts,
> Stops on a sudden, looks upon the ground,
> Then lays his finger on his temple; straight
> Springs out into fast gait; then stops again,
> Strikes his breast hard; and anon he casts
> His eye against the moon. In most strange postures
> We have seen him set himself.
>
> (3.2.112–19)

Onstage gestures are often confirmed by those who make them to mean what they signal: "I do defy him and I spit at him" Mowbray says of Bolingbroke in *Richard II* (1.1.60); Samson tells Gregory at the start of *Romeo and Juliet*, "I will bite my thumb at them, which is disgrace to them if they bear it" (1.1.41–2). Tybalt shakes with anger at the Capulet ball when he sees Romeo: "Patience perforce with willful choler meeting Makes my flesh tremble in their different greeting" (1.5.90–1). Brutus prompts Cassius's display of anger as they meet in camp in *Julius Caesar*: "Must I give way and room to your rash choler? Shall I be frighted when a madman stares?" (4.3.39–40). Desdemona points to the "portents" in Othello's attack of epilepsy: "Some bloody passion shakes your very frame" (5.2.45–7). The gesture of the melancholy lover folding his arms displays Don Armado's affectation in *Love's Labor's Lost* and is used by Speed to mock Valentine's symptoms of love in *Two Gentlemen of Verona*. Attending to the imagery of lines, both the playwright and the players can determine where to glance and how to react, as in the well-known scriptings between Romeo and Juliet:

> Juliet   Wilt thou be gone? It is not yet near day.
>   It was the nightingale, and not the lark,
>   That pierced the fearful hollow of thine ear....
> Romeo   It was the lark, the herald of the morn;

No nightingale. Look, love, what envious streaks
Do lace the severing clouds in yonder east.

(3.5.1–8)

All of these were *aides memoire* to players hastily preparing a new play
or remembering an old one.

What appear to us as more artifical parts of Shakespeare's stagecraft
were actually meant to function in the same way and seem to have been
accepted without difficulty by his playgoers. Thus Rumor giving the
Induction to *2 Henry IV* – "Open your ears; for which of you will stop
The vent of hearing when loud Rumor speaks?" – alerts the audience at
the Globe to distrust what may be advocated by the players to follow –
and to question Rumor himself; it sets the scene, characterizes players,
and establishes a theme. No less but no more artificial is the Chorus
opening *Henry V*:

> O for a muse of fire, that would ascend
> The brightest heaven of invention:
> A kingdom for a stage, princes to act,
> And monarchs to behold the swelling scene....
>   But pardon, gentles all,
> The flat unraised spirits that hath dared
> On this unworthy scaffold to bring forth
> So great an object. Can this cock-pit hold
> The vasty fields of France? Or may we cram
> Within this wooden O the very casques
> That did affright the air at Agincourt?
>
> (1–11)

This is not an apology but a proposition and a premise, not only
acknowledging that a crowded stage will counterfeit a whole army, or
even that one or two can, as Falstaff implies in his litany on counterfeiting in *1 Henry IV* (5.4.110–25), but that imaginative reconstructions
of history get things factually wrong if ideologically correct. What it
excuses, if it excuses anything, is Shakespeare's misrepresentation in his
memorial reconstruction of history in this play.

We should likewise reconceive those descriptive passages that, misun-
derstood by us but not by playgoers at the Globe, are also meant to
personate. As B. L. Joseph notes, commenting on *Macbeth* 3.3.5:

> The modern actor is torn two ways by a line such as the First Murderer's
> "The west yet glimmers with some streaks of day," because it is a famous

"poetic" statement and it is put in the mouth of a ruthless desperado concerned not with the beauties of the evening but with revenge. I do not think the Elizabethan actor spoke this line as a beautiful description of the sky, coming out of his character to do so, but that he imagined himself taking up position to kill Banquo, afraid for the moment that he might be too late. Macbeth has insisted the murder must be secret, so the murderers dare not come until it is dark enough for concealment. But if it has got too dark, their prey will already have made his way past this spot. And so, after his first anxiety, the Murderer notices with satisfaction that it is not completely dark, that they have come unnoticed, and they are in time. This is why he takes the trouble to describe the sky.[29]

Soliloquies in *Macbeth* and elsewhere function in the same way, of course; they are not merely inner thoughts passed on to the playgoers at the edge of the stage but forward movements of personation, as Banquo demonstrates:

> Thou hast it now, King, Cawdor, Glamis, all,
> As the weird women promised, and I fear
> Thou play'dst most foully for't: yet it was said
> It should not stand in thy posterity,
> But that myself should be the root and father
> Of many kings. If there come truth from them –
> As upon thee, Macbeth, their speeches shine –
> Why, by the verities on thee made good,
> May they not be my oracles as well,
> And set me up in hope? But hush, no more.
>
> (3.1.1–10)

Asides work the same way; they are not simply artificial confidences, but ways of personating understanding and even motive, as when Speed observes the approaching Silvia in *The Two Gentlemen of Verona* – "O excellent motion...O exceeding puppet...now will [Valentine] interpret her" (2.1.90–1) – or Launcelot Gobbo in *The Merchant of Venice* feels his selfish departure from Shylock's house must itself be counterfeited: "O heavens, this is my true-begotten father" (2.2.32).

Rehearsals

To make remembering simpler, and to make rehearsal time most efficient, players in the Lord Chamberlain's–King's Men did not receive whole scripts. The fair copy was kept by the bookkeeper. Players got parts –

their lines, with a cue, written out from the fair copy and pasted speech by speech into long strips or rolls. This helps to explain why Shakespeare's plays are so full of cues, such as the variety packed into the first scenes of *Hamlet*: "Give you good night"; "Break we our watch up"; "We here dispatch you"; "Come away"; "So fare you well"; "Most humbly do I take my leave, my lord"; "Come your ways"; "Nay, let's follow him"; "Fare thee well at once"; "Nay, come, let's go together."[30] This is the way – the customary way – in which Quince directs preparation of the mechanicals in *A Midsummer Night's Dream*: "masters, here are your parts, and I am to entreat you, request you, and desire you to con them by tomorrow night, and meet me in the palace wood a mile without the town by moonlight. There will we rehearse" (1.2.80–3). There is some evidence the playwright thought this way, too: Hamlet calls not for a scene from the First Player, but for a speech from it – which is what he recalls (2.2.416–18, 436–8). Revisions of playtexts, too, Tiffany Stern has demonstrated, were also most often part-based:

> An example of this happening can perhaps be seen in the two texts of *Othello*, one of which makes "Desdemona" a singing part, the other of which does not. Revisions of a number of different kinds have happened in the play, but the song revision seems to have been made to match playhouse exigencies: depending on the date of the two texts, it was either added because a singing boy had been acquired, or removed because a singing boy's voice had broken. Either way, it is a part revision – a revision along a particular strip of the text. The same seems to have happened in *Twelfth Night*, which was clearly written with a singing Viola in mind: at the play's opening Viola believes that it is her high voice and choral skills that will get her a place in Orsino's house ("Thou shalt present me as an Eunuch to him, It may be worthy thy paines; for I can sing, And speak to him in many sorts of Music" (1.2.52–54)). But in the comedy as we have it, songs have been revised away from Viola (probably, again, because the boy's voice had broken) and given to Feste: a two-part revision, involving the recalling and rewriting of essentially two parts rather than the full play – Orsino's part still involves his request for Viola to sing "one verse" of "That old and Antic song" (2.4.2–3). Specific parts, that is to say, may be found to alter more than others, to meet the specific requirements of the playhouse,[31]

and to be taken up in the part-study of the player(s) before any joint company rehearsal. Stern shows how the revisions of *Hamlet* are also part-based. Hamlet's speech at 3.4.152 has been shortened from that in the second Quarto but without affecting any other of the parts for distribution:

O throwe away the worser part of it,
And leaue the purer with the other halfe,
Good night, but goe not to my Vncles bed,
Assume a vertue if you haue it not,
~~That monster custome, who all sense doth eate~~
~~Of habits deuill, is angell yet in this~~
~~That to the vse of actions faire and good,~~
~~He likewise giues a frock or Liuery~~
~~That aptly is put on to~~ refraine night,
And that shall lend a kind of easines
To the next abstinence, ~~the next more easie:~~
~~For vse almost can change the stamp of nature,~~
~~And either the deuill, or throwe him out~~
~~With wonderous potency:~~ once more good night,
And when you are desirous to be blest,
Ile blessing beg of you, for this same Lord
I doe repent; but heauen hath pleasd it so
To punish me with this, and this with me,
That I must be their scourge and minister,
I will bestowe him and will answere well
The death I gaue him; so againe good night
I must be cruell only to be kinde,
This bad beginnes, and worse remaines behind.
One word more good Lady.[32]

She also finds instances where pairs of speeches are eliminated, as at
1.1.147, so that the cue is not lost:

HORATIO ...this I take it,
         Is the maine motiue of our preparations
         The source of this our watch, and the chiefe head
         Of this post hast and Romeage in the land.
~~BARNADO I thinke it be no other, but enso;~~
         ~~Well may it sort that this portentous figure~~
         ~~Comes armed through our watch so like the King~~
         ~~That was and is the question of these warres.~~
~~HORATIO A moth it is to trouble the mindes eye:~~
         ~~In the most high and palmy state of Rome,~~
         ~~A little ere the mightiest Iulius fell~~
         ~~The graues stood tennatlesse, and the sheeted dead~~
         ~~Did squeake and gibber in the Roman streets~~
         ~~As starres with traines of fier, and dewes of blood~~
         ~~Disasters in the sunne; and the moist starre,~~
         ~~Vpon whose influence Neptunes Empier stands,~~

65

~~Was sicke almost to doomesday with eclipse.~~
~~And euen the like precurse of feare euents~~
~~As harbindgers preceeading still the fates~~
~~And prologue to the Omen comming on~~
~~Haue heauen and earth together demonstrated~~
~~Vnto our Climatures and countrymen~~. [*Enter Ghost*
But soft, behold, loe where it comes againe.[33]

While the players were conning their parts, however, and meant to hold to their cues in entrances and exits, clowns were often allowed (or expected) to improvise. A clown in *Pilgrimage to Parnassus* is put onstage to "say somewhat for thyself, or hang and be *non plus*" (674); at the Red Bull, "it did chance that the Clown... being in the Attiring house, was suddenly called upon the Stage, for it was empty."[34] It is quite possible that some of the longer or extraneous speeches, such as portions of the Porter's speech in *Macbeth* (2.3.1–20) or Lancelot Gobbo's in *Merchant of Venice* (2.2.1–25), were originally the clown's improvisations that were so successful that they remained in the playscript when it was transported as printer's copy for the First Folio.

Multiple Personations

Players – except for the one or two with the largest number of lines – usually got more than one part to con: doubling, even tripling and quadrupling, was necessary in a playing company like the Lord Chamberlain's–King's Men with their twelve men and four boys. (There are, for instance, 47 characters listed in the cast list for *2 Henry VI*; 29 named parts in *Richard II* in addition to "Ladies attending the Queen," "Gardener's Men," "Exton's Men," and the catch-all "Lords, soldiers, attendants.") On occasion, additional actors were hired, although this cut into profits. Alan C. Dessen notes that:

> in *Julius Caesar* only four figures (Brutus, Cassius, Antony, and Lucius) reappear after the assassination (five if one counts Caesar's ghost), so that the many speaking parts after 3.1 had to be taken by the actors who had played the conspirators, Cicero, Artemidorus, the soothsayer, Portia, Calphurnia, and others. On what basis, then, was the decision made as to who came back as whom? Would the players have allotted the roles? Or are we to assume that when Shakespeare killed off a major figure (and hence a major actor) early or midway in a script (e.g., Caesar, Polonius, Duncan)... he somehow planned for the return of that actor?

Scholars have advanced varying formulations about how such necessary doubling or tripling was assigned or conceived. Some of these formulations have been generated by textual oddities (as with the presence of Peto rather than Poins to pick Falstaff's pockets at the end of *1 Henry IV*, 2.4, or the presence of Caius Ligarius but not Cassius in *Julius Caesar* 2.2). Other proposed doubles or triples, however, whether on the page or on the stage, arise from conceptual rather than logistical concerns. For example, in his 1988 Shakespeare Santa Cruz production of *Julius Caesar*, director Michael Edwards had the same actor who had played Julius Caesar reappear not as Octavius (one available hypothesis) but first as Pindarus, then as Strato. In this interpretation, Brutus was correct in more ways than one when he stated: "O Julius Caesar, thou art mighty yet! Thy spirit walks abroad and turns our swords In our own proper entrails" (5.3.94–6), for the Caesar actor, if not Caesar himself, held the swords that killed Cassius and Brutus.[35]

Certain conventions for doubling must have been observed: major parts were not doubled; vague or walk-on parts such as "pages" or "musicians" must have required at least two persons; players who exit could not normally return in another role until they had time to change costume at the least; one character was never taken by two different players; and yet one player could take two or more parts, even alternating them.

Seeing a similarity in humorous parts, Muriel Bradbrook has suggested that the player playing Polonius might also play Osric and even the First Gravedigger.[36] Jennifer Crutcher finds in *The Two Gentlemen of Verona* roles for ten men (Duke, Proteus, Lance, Valentine, Speed, Thurio, Antonio, Panthino, Host, and Eglamour) and three boys (Silvia, Julia, and Lucetta), but a number of these are short enough that they can be doubled as outlaws and even servants and musicians without calling upon gatherers to swell the scene; conversely, the small cast makes the play an excellent choice for touring. Christine Monahan notes that Macbeth has 656 lines, Macduff 177, and Malcolm 185, but they need not be doubled if there are other possible pairings when taking into account entrances, exits, and time for changes of costume (Banquo/Doctor; Ross/Seyton; Duncan/Old Man/?Angus; Donalbain/Menteith; Lennox/Young Siward; Porter/Captain/Caithness). This would allow, with a company of 12 men, for the witches to double as murderers and servants, together suggesting the infernal congregation overpowering Inverness and Dunsinane. Lady Macbeth, with 264 lines, would be a single boy's part, but Macduff's son could be doubled with Fleance (suggesting a continuing need for Macbeth to murder the next generation), Lady Macduff could double with the Gentlewoman, and Hecate, with the next largest number of boy's lines (70), could be a stand-alone part.[37]

Players

The necessity of doubling parts helps to explain the awkwardness in Viola remaining in Cesario's clothing until the end of the play of *Twelfth Night* –

> The captain that did bring me first on shore
> Hath my maid's garments: he upon some action
> Is now in durance at Malvolio's suit.
>
> (5.1.284–6) –

if the Captain and Antonio are doubled, the Captain serving Viola, Antonio serving Sebastian. It may also help to explain the relatively inexplicable disappearance of the Fool in *King Lear* (at 3.6.78) and (more awkwardly) Antigonus, "*pursued by a bear,*" in *The Winter's Tale* (3.3.57). But doubling can also resonate. Nicole Matos notes that the early disappearance of Old Gaunt in *Richard II* (2.1.139), peaceful man that he is, might not be doubled as scholars often suggest with the forceful Bishop of Carlisle but with the other choric character, the Gardener (in 3.4), giving added point to the Duchess of Gloucester's lines concerning:

> Edward's seven sons, whereof thyself art one,
> Were as seven vials of his sacred blood,
> Or seven fair branches springing from one root.
> Some of those seven are dried by nature's course,
> Some of those branches are by destiny cut.
>
> (1.2.11–15)

Other pairings also suggest themselves. The two purveyors of poison in *Romeo and Juliet*, Friar Laurence and the Apothecary, seem a natural doubling. The scene with the Apothecary (5.1) is separated from Friar Laurence's next entrance by only three lines, but the Apothecary only needs to don a loose robe over his other costume; it seems likelier when the Friar arrives on Romeo's line, "O true apothecary, Thy drugs are quick! Thus with a kiss I die" (5.3.119–20). Another probable doubling is revealed with the death of Paris. "Let me peruse thy face," says Romeo; "Mercutio's kinsman, noble County Paris!" (5.3.74–5). Shakespeare might have made much of this earlier, except that by association and alignment, Mercutio and Paris are on opposing sides of the Montague–Capulet divide. Role assignments can cross over plays, too; when Polonius proudly reports to Hamlet that "I did enact Julius Caesar. I was killed i' th' Capitol. Brutus killed me" (3.2.93–4), he is probably referring to roles the two of them were even then playing in *Julius Caesar*, in repertory with *Hamlet* in 1601, but he was also announcing his own death, again, at the hands of Hamlet.

The Use of Plots

Counterfeiting with practiced expressions, gestures, and even places on the *locus* or *platea* would be largely known to actors as they conned their parts. But it still must have been difficult, especially when acting in repertory or performing a revived play, to remember just when to enter and in what role. It is for that reason that the bookkeeper prepared a "plot" or "plat," an outline of the play that listed each entrance (exits, from afar, had to take care of themselves) and posted it near the entry doors at the rear of the stage. Almost no such plots have survived, although fortunately Carol Chillington Rutter has noted one used at the Rose by the Admiral's Men for *Frederick and Basilea*, what she calls "a road map through the production for players."[38] Summary plots permitted the company to keep more secure the fair copy of the full playtext that the bookkeeper had required of his scribe. They also insured stage pictures meant to work visually by guaranteeing who and how many were onstage at key junctures, and in what roles. When Richard II climbs on the ramparts at Flint Castle, the appropriate and necessary members of Bolingbroke's forces are below. Lear's entire court crowds onto the stage to witness the division of the kingdom at the play's outset, and the same large cast of players (except for Gonerli Regan, Gloucester and France) return a second time to observe the outcome of that act. Conversely, when the separated groups of players in *The Tempest* are reunited at the end, Prospero's magic and dreams have also reached their conclusion: the tale he is about to tell Alonso, Antonio, and Sebastian ("the story of my life," 5.1.308) will complement and complete the tale he began with Miranda (1.2).

THE PLOTT OF FFREDERICK & BASILEA

Enter Prologue: Richard Alleine

Enter Frederick Kinge: Mr Jubie R Allenn To them
Basilea seruant Black Dick, Dick.

Enter Gouernor Athanasia Moore: Mr Dunstann. Griffen
Charles, To them Heraclius Seruants. Tho: hunt black Dick

Enter Leonora, Sebastian, Theodore, Pedro, Philippo Andreo
Mr Allen, well, Mr Martyn. Ed. Dutton. ledbeter, Pigg:
To them King frederick Basilea Guarde. Mr. Juby. R Allen
Dick Tho. Hunt, black Dick.

Enter Myron=hamec, lords. Tho: Towne. Tho Hunt ledbeter
To them Heraclius, Thamar, Sam Charles.

Enter Gouernor Mr Dunstann, To hym Messenger Th: Hunt
To them Heraclius Sam, To them Myranhamec goliors

Enter ffrederick, Basilea, R Allen Dick, To them Kinge
Mr Jubie To them Messenger Black Dick, To them
Sebastian, Heraclius, Theodore, Pedro, Philippo Andreo
Thamar. Mr Allen, Sam: Mr Martyn. leadb: Dutton Pigg.
To them Leonora, Will,

Enter ffrederick Basilea, R Allen: Dick. To them
Philippo, Duttonn, To her King ffrederick, Mr Jubie
R Allenn:

Enter, Myron=hamec Sebastian, Pedroe lords
Tho: Towne. Mr Allenn, ledbeter. Attendaunts

Enter King Theodore ffrederick, Mr Jubie, Mr Martyn
R Allenn. To them Philipo Basilea E Dutton his boye Guard
Tho: Hunt. [Black Dick] Gatherers. To them messenger
Black Dick. To them Sebastian Myron=hamec
leonora Pedroe Andreo. Mr Allen: Tho Towne
will: Leadbeter Pigg guard gatherers.

Enter ffrederick Basilea To them Pedro confederates
Robt: leadb: Black Dick Gatherers.

Enter ffrederick Guard. Mr Juby R Allen
Th: [Tow] Hunt &c. To them Sebastian [leonora]
Theodore Myranhamec Guard Mr Allen. Martyn
To them Pedro Basilea vpon the walls. come downe
Pedro Basilea. Ledb: Dick.

Enter Theodore Andreo. Mr Martyn Pigg To hym
Thamar Heraclius Sam charles.

Enter ffrederick, Basilea, ffryer, R Allen: Dick
Mr Dunstann.

Enter Heraclius, Thamar, Andreo, Sam. Charles
Pigg. To them ffryer. Mr Dunstann, To them
Theodore Martynn

Enter ffrederick Basilea R Allen. Dick, To them
ffryer Mr Dunstann, To them Heraclius Sam

Enter Leonora Myronhamec, Sebastian Golior*es*
Will: Mr Towne, Mr Allen. Tho Hunt black Dick

To the queen Theodore Martynn.

Enter Heraclius Thamar sam charles To him
Theodore ffryer Dunstan Martynn To them
[. . . line missing . . .]

Enter King Basilea ffrederick messenger
Mr Juby R Allen Dick Black Dick. To them
Sebastian Leonora Myronhamec Thamar Goliors
Mr Allen will Tho Towne Charles. Tho: Hunt
Black Dick gatherers.

Epilogs R Allenn Finis:/

A representative plot for a play called *Frederick and Basilea*.

Reprinted from Rutter, *Documents of the Rose Playhouse*, pp. 112–13.

All would seem to be over, that is, except for the jig. That is what Thomas Platter testifies to at a performance of *Julius Caesar* in 1599 at the Globe:

After dinner on 21 September, at about two o'clock I went with my companions over the water [the Thames] and in the thatched-roof house saw the tragedy of the first Emperor Julius with at least fifteen characters very pleasingly acted. At the end of the comedy, they danced, according to their custom, exceedingly gracefully: two attired in men's clothes and two in women's performed wonderfully with one another.[39]

Will Kempe was known for such jigs and one had been printed: "Kemp's new jig betwixt a soldier and a miser and Sym the clown." Another jig, a farce for four, "Singing Simkin," tells of a housewife who loves a clown and a soldier; when her husband returns, the clown is in hiding and the soldier pretends to hunt for a thief. The wife and husband cause the soldier to leave, the husband follows, the clown comes out of hiding, and is caught when the husband returns; together, the wife and husband beat the clown off the stage. Such incidents have no relationship to the play that preceded the jig, and it is unlikely the jig continued with the Lord Chamberlain's–King's Men much past Kempe's time. The only playhouses named after 1600 for presenting jigs were not in Southwark but in Clerkenwell, north rather than south of the city, outside the city walls: the Fortune, the Curtain, the Red Bull. Shakespeare's players at the Globe, meanwhile, had moved on to playing richer and more powerful tragedies.

Conclusion

Hamlet is a transparent example of the player's art of counterfeiting. As prince of Denmark, he lives a changing series of personations as a disguise upon his return to witness the expected burial of his father and the unexpected remarriage of his mother. He deliberately avoids the stock personations he finds among actors: "He that plays the king shall have tribute of me; the adventurous knight shall use his foil and target; the lover shall not sigh gratis; the humorous man shall end his part in peace; the clown shall make those laugh whose lungs are tickle o'the sere; and the lady shall say her mind freely" (2.2.341–7) – sometimes by combining these roles. He can also be sullen:

> Seems, madam? Nay, it is. I know not "seems."
> 'Tis not alone my inky cloak, good-mother,
> Nor customary suits of solemn black,
> Nor windy suspiration of forced breath,
> No, nor the fruitful river in the eye,
> Nor the dejected haviour of the visage,
> Together with all forms, moods, shows of grief
> That can denote me truly,
>
> (1.2.76–83)

he claims, with a theatrical emphasis on "forced breath," "dejected haviour," "shows of grief." He can be bewildered before Ophelia – "with his head over his shoulder turned, He seemed to find his way without his eyes, For out o'doors he went without their help, And to the last bended their light on me" (2.1.98–101) – as well as cynical – "the power of beauty will sooner transform honesty from what it is to a bawd than the force of honesty can translate beauty into his likeness" (3.1.113–15), suspicious – "Where's your father?...Let the doors be shut upon him, that he may play the fool nowhere but in 's own house" (3.1.132–3) – and damning: "I'll give thee this plague for thy dowry: be thou as chaste as ice, as pure as snow, thou shalt not escape calumny" (3.1.155–7). He can be jealous too:

> 'Swounds, show me what thou'lt do.
> Woot weep, woot fight, woot fast, woot tear thyself,
> Woot drink up eisel, eat a crocodile?
> Be buried quick with her, and so will I.
> And if thou prate of mountains, let them throw
> Millions of acres on us, till our ground,
> Singeing his pate against the burning zone,
> Make Ossa like a wart. Nay, an thou'lt mouth,
> I'll rant as well as thou.
>
> (5.1.259–68)

His feigned madness before Polonius (2.2) and Claudius (4.3) counterfeits counterfeiting, conning yet another personation.

Yet Hamlet also personates himself by distancing himself from other personations. He distinguishes his call for responsible action from the bookish understanding of Horatio (1.5.168–9). He scorns Rosenkrantz as his foolish antithesis, seeing him as a mere sponge:

> Ay, sir, that soaks up the King's countenance, his rewards, his authorities. But such officers do the King best service in the end. He keeps them, like an ape an apple, in the corner of his jaw, first mouthed to be last swallowed. When he needs what you have gleaned, it is but squeezing you, and, spenge, you shall be dry again. (4.2.12–19)

He cannot duplicate his father's achievement, which he holds as his ideal: "So excellent a king, that was to this Hyperion..., so loving to my mother That he might not beteem the winds of heaven Visit her face too roughly!" (1.2.139–42). He likewise admires "The rugged Pyrrhus" who avenged his father (2.2). Pyrrhus' position, in fact, as a military

73

leader who retaliated for the misfortune and defeat of his father, is repeated by Hamlet's enemy Fortinbras, out to reinstate his father's reputation by winning back lost lands. Fortinbras's mission enables Hamlet to admire him at last, too, as he gives the Norwegian commander his support for the Danish throne: "I do prophesy th'election lights On Fortinbras. He has my dying voice" (5.2.297–8). But that that life finally amounts to personation seems clear to him when he asks Horatio to "Absent thee from felicity a while, And in this harsh world draw thy breath in pain To tell my story" (5.2.289–91).

Understanding the art of playing in Shakespeare's Globe as the art of counterfeiting, of representation and not embodiment, helps us to anticipate Hamlet's swift changes of roles and helps us to sense in his declared and undeclared relationships to other young men in the play what other representations might have been – perhaps should have been – open to him. This is the way the players would have played their parts and the way in which the playgoers would have understood them. Now let us see just who those playgoers were to whom Shakespeare addressed his plays.

3

Playgoers

Truth sayes, of old, the art of making plaies
    Was to content the people; & their praise
    Was to the Poet money, wine, and bayes.
But in this age, a sect of writers are,
    That, onely, for particular likings care,
    And will taste nothing that is populare.
With such we mingle neither braines, nor brests:
    Our wishes, like to those (make publique feasts)
    Are not to please the cookes tastes, but the guests.
                  Ben Jonson, Prologue to *Epicoene*

The tastes, demands, and choices of playgoers were a condition that had material results for everyone connected to Shakespeare's theater – playwrights, players, bookkeepers, and gatherers – and it affected every performance: at the Globe, at the second Blackfriars, at court, on tour. While no two performances and no two audiences are ever identical, of course, expectations at public playhouses like the Globe evolved out of their origins in the market squares and streets of towns and villages long accustomed to plays and entertainments. There temporary stages were surrounded on three sides and all social classes might be in attendance with commoners crowding down toward the front, predecessors of Shakespeare's groundlings. Various estimates have been made of the size of a capacity crowd at the Globe, from 2,000 all the way to 3,500, but 2,500 or so seems reasonable. Nor were all the available spaces usually filled; it is thought that perhaps half to 60 percent capacity held true for most performances. And they, too, were subject to weather; in the first decade of the seventeenth century, winters were especially cold, even brutal, so that in 1612 John Webster was excusing poor showings at his play entitled *The White Devil* at the Red Bull because "it was acted, in so dull a time of Winter, presented in so open and black a theater, that it wanted...a full and understanding auditory."[1] But nothing except epidemics of plague and the 40 days of Lent could stop performances for long – not even, it seems, the restriction against playing on the Sabbath, which was more honored in the breach than in the observance. The *Annals of English Drama, 975–1700* list the titles of 1,056 plays performed between 1560 and 1642 by the established playing companies. During the chief decades of Shakespeare's career, 1590–1610, 449 new titles were registered or referred to, and 181 playtexts survive,[2] but Andrew Gurr estimates that "The total number of playscripts written between 1560 and 1642 was probably at least three times the thousand or so titles that survive and at least six times the number of surviving texts."[3] Their constant and uninterrupted popularity began with provincial players but it was enhanced when Edmund Tilney, as the Queen's Master of the Revels, in charge of organizing court entertainments, found in the 1580s that the customary masques performed for the court at Christmas, with all their scenery, music, and dancing, were considerably more costly, and somewhat less reliable, than the performances of playing companies. This led in turn to the queen's privy councillors patronizing companies and protecting the players against opposition. In a Minute of the Privy Council for December 3, 1581, the first priority after protecting the country in times of plague was, in Gurr's words, "to safeguard the royal pleasure against the opposition of the city fathers [of London] to public playing."[4] For somewhat different reasons than most playgoers, they, too, openly registered their support of plays.

A Playgoing Season

We have no extant record of playgoing at Shakespeare's Globe, but Carol Chillington Rutter has published the receipts for the Rose playhouse during the winter season of 1592 – from February to June. Philip Henslowe, the entrepreneurial manager of the Lord Strange's Men, the playing company at the Rose, has meticulously listed all the fees he paid in pounds, shillings, and pence (*L*, *S*, and *d*) to the Master of the Revels to license plays for performance:

Itm pd vnto mr tyllnes man the 26 of febreary 1591	vs
Itm pd vnto mr tyllnes man the 4 of marche 1591	vs
Itm pd vnto mr tyllenes man the 10 of marche 1591	vs
Itm pd vnto mr tyll*nes* man the 17 of marche 1591	vs
Itm pd vnto mr tyllnes man the 24 of marche 1591	vs
Itm pd vnto mr tyllenes man the 28 of marche 1591	vs
Itm pd vnto mr tyllnes man the 7 of aprell 1591	vs
Itm pd vnto mr tyllnes man the 14 of aprell 1591	vs
Itm pd vnto mr tyllnes man the 21 of aprell 1591	vs
Itm pd vnto mr tyllnes man the 28 of aprell 1591	vs
Itm pd vnto mr tyllenes man the 5 of maye 1592	vs
Itm pd vnto mr tyllnes man the 10 of maye 1592	vs
Itm pd vnto mr tyllnes man the 13 of maye 1592	xij s
Itm pd vnto mr tyllnes man the 20 of maye 1592	vj s 8 d
Itm pd vnto mr tyllnes man th 9 of June 1592	vj s 8 d
Itm pd vnto mr tyllnes man the 14 June 1592	vj s 8 d[5]

as well as the takings for each day, marking the plays new to the repertory "ne" and putting in dashes to indicate new weeks:

—— Rd at clorys & orgasto the 28 of febreary 1591	xviij s
Rd at mvlamvlluco the 29 of febrearye 1591	xxxiiijs
Rd at poope Jone the 1 of marche 1591	xv s
Rd at matchavell the 2 of marche 1591	xiiij s
ne— Rd at harey the vj the 3 of marche 1591	iij li xvj s 8 d
Rd at bendo & Richardo the 4 of marche 1591	xvj s
—— Rd at iiij playes in one the 6 of marche 1591	xxxj s vj d
Rd at harey the vj the 7 of marche 1591	iij li
Rd at the lockinglasse the 8 of marche 1591	vij s
Rd at senobia the 9 of marche 1591	xxij s vj d
Rd at the Jewe of malta the 10 of marche 1591	lvj s
Rd at harey the vj the 11 of marche 1591	xxxxvij s vj d
—— Rd at the comodey of doneoracio the 13 march 1591	xxviiijs[6]

Twenty-three plays are listed for the season, five of them new productions, giving Henslowe an income of £181 9s 11d as his share of the takings. Shakespeare's only play here is *Henry VI*, new on March 3, with later performances scattered representatively through the repertory in the next months. While it brought Henslowe £3 16s 8d on opening night, some fifteen performances later it was still bringing in £1 11s. The continually changing repertory, which is also customary, suggests that

regular playgoers wanted changing fare – some seven plays were performed only once in this period; conversely, popular plays were more
frequently played (such as *Henry VI*). Both *The Jew of Malta* by Christopher Marlowe and *Jeronimo* (*The Spanish Tragedy*) by Thomas Kyd
were old plays in revival; they would still be playing on public stages, in
the case of Kyd revised by Ben Jonson, in 1600 and beyond.

But Henslowe did not merely keep staging popular plays; he kept
performing right through the season of Lent, stopping only for Good
Friday (March 24) and "Ester" the following Sunday. Such church feast
days and holidays were always good business days for plays. Harbage has
averaged Henslowe's receipts of three to five holidays to get earnings
greater than the 30.16 shillings on an average day: he took in 52.5
shillings on New Year's Day; 53.75 shillings on Epiphany (January 6);
41 shillings on Shrove Tuesday; 44.33 shillings on Ash Wednesday; 42.25
shillings on Easter Monday; 43.33 shillings on May Day; 46.33 shillings
on Allhallows Day; and 56.75 shillings, 61.25 shillings, and 50 shillings
on the first, second, and third weekdays after Christmas. Harbage has
also averaged receipts to learn the sums taken in on an ordinary day
(28.18 shillings), on opening day – usually the best – (54.49 shillings), the
last weekday of the month (19.94 shillings), and the days of the week:
Monday, 31.38s; Tuesday, 29.17s; Wednesday, 25.41s; Thursday, 27.41s;
Friday, 27.69s; and Saturday, 21.30s.[7] They represent average days with
1,249 in attendance, supposing 436 in the yard, 705 in the first gallery,
and 108 in the second gallery. At the Globe, meantime, the income for
actors was £8 12s 5d daily exclusive of seats in the Lords Rooms – the

		1594–95	
July	(31.67)	————————	⎫
August	(26.79)	———————	⎬ Long Vacation
September	(25.54)	——————	
October	(26.50)	—————	⎭
November	(23.59)	——————	Michaelmas Term
December	(20.79)	————	⎫ Vacation
January	(28.57)	———————	⎬ Hilary Term
February	(33.33)	————————	⎭
March	(25.14)	——————	⎫ Vacation
April	(37.50)	———————————	⎬ Easter Term
May	(30.20)	———————	⎭
June	(33.20)	————————	Trinity Term

78

1595–96

July	(No acting is recorded.)	
August	(28.80) ———————————	Long Vacation
September	(33.33) ——————————	
October	(23.25) —————————	
November	(19.76) ——————————	Michaelmas Term
December	(23.36) ———————	Vacation
January	(24.68) ———————	Hilary Term
February	(31.63) ———————	
March	(Lent)	Vacation
April	(21.46) —————	
	(The Swan has opened?)	Easter Term
May	(22.38) —————	
June	(25.79) ——————————	Trinity Term

1596–97

July	(19.78) —————————	
August		
September	(Inhibition, *re Isle of Dogs*.)	Long Vacation
October		
November	(15.93) ———————	Michaelmas Term
December	(19.17) ————————	Vacation
January	(18.71) ———————	Hilary Term
February	(28.71) ————————	Vacation
March	(22.33) ———————	
April	(17.14) ——————	Easter Term
May	(22.25) ——————	
June	(23.15) —————————	Trinity Term

Three years of Henslowe's receipts at the Rose given in shillings.
From Alfred Harbage, *Shakespeare's Audience* (New York: Columbia University Press, 1941), pp. 176–7.

Strange's Men – February 19, 1592, to February 1, 1593

Old
- Spanish Tragedy (602)
- Jew of Malta (568)
- Battle of Alcazar (481)
- Friar Bacon and Friar Bungay (126.75)
- Looking Glass for London and England (115)

| New | { Henry VI, Part I (344.9) | } First Seven |
| | Knack to Know a Knave (265) | Performances |

Admiral's Men – June 15 [17], 1594, to July 28, 1597

Old	{ Doctor Faustus (584)
	Tamburlaine, Part I (480)
	Jew of Malta (475.6)
	Spanish Tragedy (282)
	Tamburlaine, Part II (270)
	Massacre at Paris (258.5)

New	{ Humorous Day's Mirth (562)	}
	John a Kent? "Wise Man of West	
	Chester" (515)	} First Ten
	Blind Beggar of Alexandria (479)	Performances
	Captain Thomas Stukeley (279)	}

Henslowe's comparative receipts in shillings for old plays revived and new plays.

From Alfred Harbage, *Shakespeare's Audience* (New York, Columbia University Press, 1941), p. 178.

seating above the rear of the platform – or £1724 3s 4d for an annual playing season of 200 days; the Lords Rooms would add 37s 6d daily, or an annual yield of £375. In addition, the Lord Chamberlain's–King's Men received £873 from Elizabeth I and James I between 1599 and 1609, £70 as relief during plague time in 1608, and £30 for reimbursement for expenses incurred for unusually lengthy travel to and from the court.[8] (This, compared to the annual wages of £20 for Shakespeare's schoolmaster in Stratford or £17 a year for a London artisan, shows Shakespeare's success as a player, playwright, and shareholder was exceptional: he paid £320 for 107 acres of arable land in Old Stratford in 1602 and £440 for leases of tithes in and around Stratford in 1605.)

Who Went to Plays

The Lords Rooms had more expensive seats than the second gallery, which was more expensive than the first gallery; all seating charged more for admission than the standing room in the yard, whose occupants are called "the rabblement" in *Julius Caesar* (1.2.243). (But this does not indicate strict social demarcations, just as today persons of varying incomes sit in the end zone of football games.) Nor should we assume that the cost of admission to the playhouse was the playgoer's only expense. According to Ann Jennalie Cook:

> peripheral evidence cautions against presuming that most in the audience had only modest means, even at the large open-air structures. For boat hire across the Thames, reportedly "three or four thousand people" daily paid a waterman from three pence to six pence so they could attend plays on the south bank (where the major playhouses, including the Globe, were located). Food and drink sold in or brought to the theaters could easily cost more than the price of admission, as could the tobacco so often smoked there and the customary tavern dinner after the entertainment ended. Only the prospect of spectators with fat purses would have led whores and thieves to pay to get into the playhouses. The sale of pamphlets and printed plays at performances points toward literate theatergoers who could afford anywhere from two pence to two shillings to read the latest texts at leisure. Players routinely encouraged patrons to "arraign playes dailie" and many did so, despite the expense.[9]

Yet contemporary witnesses testify otherwise. Thomas Dekker notes in *The Gull's Hornbook* (1609) that "The Theatre is your poet's Royal Exchange" where "your Gallant, your Courtier, your Captain had wont to be the soundest paymasters"; like Sir Thomas Gresham's large mart in central London, the public playhouses allowed anyone to trade:

> Withence then the place is so free in entertainment, allowing a stool as well to the farmer's son as to your templar: that your stinkard has the self-same liberty to be there in his tobacco fumes, which your sweet courtier hath: and that your carman and tinker claim as strong a voice in their suffrage, and wit to give judgement on the play's life and death, as well as the proudest Momus among the tribe of critics.[10]

Women, too, were welcome, including servants; Stephen Gosson is anxious for their welfare in his *School of Abuse* (1579), while in the collapse of Paris Garden in 1583, two of the casualties were women servants: "Alice White, servant to a pursemaker" and Marie Harrison, the daughter of a waterbearer.[11] The foreigner Thomas Platter notices this non-discrimination in 1599: "With these and many more amusements, the English pass their time, learning at the play what is happening abroad;

indeed men and womenfolk visit such places without scruple."[12] In fact, despite the distinct differences in cost, playgoers who could pay the price could sit wherever their payment put them. (Stratification by social and economic class did not necessarily, or always, deny accessibility.)

Until very recently – and in some scholarly circles still today – it has been argued that the working class – the journeymen, apprentices, and men and women servants sometimes known as subalterns – had neither the money nor the liberty to attend plays. There is strong documentary evidence that this is not so. Many of the journeymen and apprentices may have attended Merchant Taylors School, so that they were well educated; Thomas Heywood's play on *The Four Prentices of London* (1594) is dedicated to "the honest and high-spirited Prentises." But some of the members of the working class could be seen as troublemakers. Edmund Gayton reports that:

> on holy days, when sailors, watermen, shoemakers, butchers and appren-
> tices are at leisure, then it is good policy to amaze those violent spirits, with
> some tearing Tragedy...the spectators frequently mounting the stage, and
> making a more bloody catastrophe amongst themselves than the players
> did....And unless this were done, and the popular humor satisfied, as
> sometimes it so fortuned, that the players were refractory; the benches,
> the tiles, the laths, the stones, oranges, apples, nuts, flew about most
> liberally, and as there were mechanics of all professions, who fell every
> one to his own trade, and dissolved a house in an instant, and made a ruin
> of a stately fabric.[13]

Henry Chettle concurs: in *Kind-Harts Dream* (1593), the playwright reports that thieves would create fights between servants and apprentices so as to distract their victims.[14] A disgruntled master writes to the Carpenters Company in November 1600 concerning his apprentice, who "will work nowhere but by drinking at the alehouse and roams to plays all the day long."[15] Even Dekker, who seemed to admire the mixed audience as another Royal Exchange, was of a different mind in 1611 concerning a play at the Red Bull by Heywood:

> A Play whose *Rudeness*, *Indians* would abhor,
> If't fill a house with Fishwives, *Rare, They All Roar.*
> It is not Praise is sought for (Now) but *Pence*,
> Tho' dropped, from Greasy-apron *Audience.*[16]

Recent work by Ilana Ben-Amos and Paul Griffiths provides a great deal of evidence that not all subalterns were unruly, however, and that a great many had access to public playhouses, either when given time off during the week for seeking out recreation or in periods between jobs or indentures.[17] Steve Rappaport cites an entry in the bakers' court minutes for 1589 that "Diverse Journeymen and other Servants in this Company have heretofore accustomed on the Thursdays and other work days, to go abroad to gaming houses, taverns, plays or other such like places."[18] But in 1591 the company put an end to such activity. Charles Whitney has found a similar attitude in an ordinance of the plasterers company in 1586/7, although it seems fundamentally concerned with behavior of servants on the Sabbath and on holiday: Those found:

> haunting of alehouses, taverns, plays, unlawful games or such like upon pain that every householder so offending contrary to this ordinance shall forfeit and pay for every such offense the sum of 2s. 6d. of lawful English money. And it is further ordered that every apprentice offending contrary to this ordinance shall receive such corporal punishment as the said Master and wardens for the time being shall think meet and appoint to the example of others in like case offending.[19]

Whitney has also found similar ordinances, passed at about the same time, by the cloth workers' and tallow-chandlers' companies.[20]

But subalterns were not the only troublesome playgoers. Apparently the gallants sitting on the stage at Blackfriars were irritating, too, enough so that Dekker sees them as a perfect target for burlesque in his *Gull's Hornbook*:

> let our Gallant ... presently advance himself up to the throne of the stage. I mean not the Lord's room (which is now but the stage's suburbs): no, those boxes, by the iniquity of custom, conspiracy of waiting-women and gentle-men-ushers, that there sweat together, and the covetousness of sharers, are contemptibly thrust into the rear, and much new satin is there damped, by being smothered to death in darkness. But on the very rushes where the comedy is to dance, yea, and under the state [canopied throne] of Cambises himself, must our feathered ostrich, like a piece of ordnance, be planted valiantly (because impudently) beating down the mews and hisses of the opposed rascality. . . .
>
> Present not yourself on the stage (especially at a new play) until the quaking prologue hath (by rubbing) got color into his cheeks, and is ready to give the trumpets their cue, that he's upon point to enter: for then it is time, as though you were one of the properties, or that you dropped out of the hangings, to creep from behind the arras, with your tripos or three-footed stool in one hand, and a teston mounted between a forefinger and a thumb in the other: for if you should bestow your person upon the vulgar,

when the belly of the house is but half-full, your apparel is quite eaten up, the fashion lost, and the proportion of your body in more danger to be devoured than if it were served up in the Counter amongst the Poultry [that is, jail]. Avoid that as you would the bastome [cudgel]. It shall crown you with rich commendation, to laugh aloud in the midst of the most serious and saddest scene of the terriblest tragedy. And to let that lapper (your tongue) be tossed so high, that all the house may ring of it. Your Lords use it; your Knights are apes to the Lords, and do so too. Your Inns-a-court-man is Zany to the Knights and (marry, very scurvily) comes likewise limping after it. Be thou a beagle to them all, and never lin [cease] snuffing, till you have scented them.[21]

It is always difficult to judge the degree of exaggeration in a satire of another period, but Dekker's account may seem somewhat less far-fetched when placed alongside the account by Antimo Galli, a Florentine, reporting on the Venetian ambassador's attendance at the Curtain in August 1613:

he went the other day to a playhouse called the Curtain, which is out beyond his house. It is an infamous place in which no good citizen or gentleman would show his face. And what was worse, in order not to pay a royal, or a scudo, to go in one of the little rooms, nor even to sit in the degrees [galleries] that are there, he insisted on standing in the middle down below among the gang of porters and carters, giving as his excuse that he was hard of hearing – as if he could have understood the language anyway! But it didn't end there because, at the end of the performance, having received permission from one of the actors, he invited the public to the play for the next day, and named one. But the people, who wanted a different one, began to call out "Friars, Friars" because they wanted one that they called "Friars." Then, turning to his interpreter, my Tambalone [punning on pantalone, a fool] asked what they were saying. The inter-preter replied that it was the name of a play about friars. Then he, bursting out of his cloak, began to clap his hands as the people were doing and to yell "Friars, Friars." But at this racket the people turned on him, thinking him to be a Spaniard, and began to whistle at him in such a fashion that I don't think he'll ever want to go back there again. But that doesn't stop him frequenting the other theaters, and almost always with just one servant.[22]

Given such evidence as we now possess, then, Shakespeare's playhouse attracted men and women from all the social strata.

Indeed, it was not only economically feasible for the gentry class – the "gentles" – and citizens but an attractive bargain for the working class, too: it was within anyone's means (especially if they did not mind standing in the yard). To give some sense of how possible (and how appealing) it was to journeymen and hired servants, Rutter has published portions of a statute regulating (and thereby stating) wages in London issued from Westminster on July 1, 1588, and again in 1589 and 1590:

To the best and most skilful workmen Journeymen and hired *serv*ants of any the companyes herevnder named

Clothworkers by the yeare with meate and drinke	*v li*
ffullers by the yeare with meate and drinke	*v li*
Sheremen by the yeare with meate and drinke	*v li*
Diers by the yeare with meate and drinke	vj *li* xiij *s* iiij *d*
Taylours hosiers by the yeare with meate and drinke	iiij *li*
Drap*ers* being hosiers by the yeare with meate and drinke	iiij *li*
Shoemakers by the yeare with meate and drinke	iiij *li*[23]

The value of such money was inconstant, of course. From 1580 to 1600, the population of London doubled. These were also years of drought, failing crops, and extensive food shortages (as well as deliberate hoarding and engrossing); outbreaks of plague; and preparation for frequently expected Spanish invasion. Consequently, there were serious cycles of inflation and depression.

Leo Salinger has pointed especially to the inflation of the 1590s:

We are told that after the years of dearth culminating in 1597 the buying-power of a London building worker's wages stood at the lowest point for 200 years; and over the next forty years, punctuated as they were by economic depressions, the recovery of wages in London and the provinces was both uneven and slight. No doubt the effects of this economic hardship can be read in the records of acting throughout the provinces, where the number of players' companies and the number of their known visits had been rising steadily since the time of Shakespeare's childhood, only to fall away just as steadily soon after 1595. If we could have statistical records about the middling and poorer classes' playgoing in London, I presume they would tell a very similar tale.[24]

Perhaps. But such matters are contemporaneously relative, and the penny admission for the playhouse yard would cost the playgoer the same as a quart of the cheapest ale, one-third the cost of a small pipeload of tobacco, and one-third the price of a meal in the cheapest ordinary (the average ordinary meal cost 6d). By comparison, Alfred Harbage writes:

A penny fee would admit one to a puppet show, a conducted tour of the monuments in Westminster Abbey, a view from the roof of St. Paul's Cathedral, a glimpse of a six-legged calf, or other "monster," or of the lions in the tower; by 1641, at least, it would purchase a stroll in a private garden where a nosegay was given as a souvenir. But these were evanescent joys, to be tasted now and then, whereas beer, ballads, plays, and animal fights were staples. A play meant over two hours' entertainment in impressive surroundings – entertainment of a quality not to be found in the beer and ballads. Craftsmen, then, with their families, journeymen, and apprentices, must have composed the vast majority of "groundlings."[25]

Still, Nashe, for one, finds the money going to playhouses and players money that could go to other trades: "As for the hindrance of trades and traders of the city by them, that is an article foisted in by the vintners, alewives, and victuallers, who surmise, if there were no plays, they should have all the company resort to them, lie bowzing and beer-bathing in their houses every afternoon."[26] But if many London merchants lost business, the watermen who ferried people across the Thames between the city and Bankside may well have flourished.

Sound and Sight

We do not merely know who could be playgoers; we know some who actually were. Andrew Gurr has taken up the task of ferreting out all references to actual playgoers in the period and has found records for 162 of them between 1567 and 1642. Of these, 46 persons are recorded for the years that Shakespeare was active as a playwright, player, and sharer. If, however, we discount those who were attending playhouses other than the Theatre, Curtain, Globe, or Blackfriars during Shakespeare's connections with them, we are left with records for only 21. Of these, seven – Sir Christopher Blount, the younger brother of the earl of Devonshire; Edward Bushell; Sir John Davis, of the Tower of London; Captain Ellis Jones; Captain Thomas Lea; Sir Gilly Merrick, secretary to the earl of Essex; and William Parker, fourth Baron Monteagle – were conspirators with Essex when he called for the playing of *Richard II* and saw it on the eve of the rebellion. Those remaining are: Sir John Davies, a gallant connected to the Inns of Court; Simon Forman, an astrologer, who saw *Macbeth*, *The Winter's Tale*, and *Cymbeline*; John Gee, a student of Brasenose College, Oxford, who knew *Hamlet* and *A Midsummer Night's Dream*; Giustinian, the ambassador from Venice, who saw *Pericles*; the satirist Everard Guilpin, whose work alludes to *Romeo and Juliet* and

Hamlet; the writer from Cambridge and Saffron-on-Walden Gabriel Harvey, who refers to *Hamlet*; the earl of Holland, who saw *Henry VIII*; Prince Frederick Lewis of Württenberg, who saw *Othello* on a visit to London; the playwright John Marston, whose *Antonio's Revenge* seems indebted to *Hamlet*; Francis Meres, whose critical treatise *Palladis Tamia* (1598) lists *Two Gentlemen of Verona*, *The Comedy of Errors*, *A Midsummer Night's Dream*, and *King John*; Thomas Platter, a Swiss scholar and writer who saw *Julius Caesar*; Antony Scoloker, whose *Daiphantus* (1604) echoes *Hamlet*; Robert Tofte, gentleman, who saw *Love's Labor's Lost*; and Leonard Digges, a writer who saw many of Shakespeare's plays.[27]

This is an extraordinary range: a gallant, an astrologer, a student, an ambassador, a nobleman, a prince, a scholar, a gentleman, and five writers including a fellow playwright; only names for the middling class and subalterns are missing, or those least likely to have left any records. Thomas Middleton acknowledges the difficulty of writing for such a mixed audience in his prologue to *No Wit, No Help Like a Woman's*:

> How is't possible to suffice
> So many ears, so many eyes?
> Some in wit, some in shows
> Take delight, and some in clothes:
> Some for mirth they chiefly come,
> Some for passion – for both some;
> Some for lascivious meetings, that's their errand –
> Some to detract, and ignorance their warrant.
> How is it possible to please
> Opinion toss'd in such wild seas?
> Yet I doubt not, if attention
> Seize you above, and apprehension
> You below, to take things quickly,
> We shall both make you sad and tickle ye.[28]

His verse, however, concludes with confidence, not dismay. This is because playwrights like Middleton and Shakespeare seem to have responded with an awareness that as poets they gave playgoers both poetry and spectacle, something other forms of entertainment did not offer. Indeed, "There is no English term which acknowledges the full experience of both hearing and seeing the complete 'action' of a play," Andrew Gurr writes, and continues:

> This lack is a simple consequence of the fact that all the relevant terms in Latin and English relate to specific senses. From the Latin *audire*, to listen,

come *audiens*, hearing, *audientia*, an audience or the act of giving a hearing to something, and *auditor*, a hearer or student. From *specere*, to see, and *spectare*, to watch, come *spectaculum*, a show or play, or theatre, and *spectator*, a spectator or critic. English kept these Latin roots, despite a campaign for English alternatives waged in the later sixteenth century when the drama was beginning to demand a new vocabulary. Even then all that George Puttenham and the enemies of "inkhorn terms" could come up with were "hearers" and "beholders."[29]

Thomas Gainsford subscribes to the importance of the playwright as poet in 1616 when he notes that "as an Orator was most forcible in his elocution; so was an actor in his gesture and personated action."[30] "For a while," Gurr writes:

> "auditor" was more current than "audience," in Gosson and others of the more academically-trained writers. Shakespeare also used the word through the 1590s. In *A Midsummer Night's Dream* III.i.79–80 Puck applies it precisely: "What, a play toward? I'll be an auditor, / An actor too perhaps." In *Love's Labour's Lost* V.i.138 and *A Midsummer Night's Dream* I.ii.26 the royal playgoers are quite properly called the "audience," in a combination of their judicial and playgoing functions.[31]

John Marston calls the playgoers at Paul's "select, and most respected Auditours" in *Antonio and Mellida* (1600); in 1603 Thomas Middleton refers to "a dull Audience of Stinkards sitting in the Penny Galleries of a Theater" in *Father Hubburd's Tale*, while in 1605 George Chapman refers to "many a moist auditor" in *The Widow's Tears*. In his prologue to *The Isle of Gulls* (1606), John Day disclaims any "bawdy and scurill jests, which neither becomes his modestie to write, nor the eare of a generous Auditory to heare," while a foolish gallant speaks of presenting speech "fit to the ears of my auditorie" (3.2). Again and again Shakespeare stops action and spectacle to concentrate on the sounds of language: in the battles between Petruchio and Kate (2.1, 4.1, 4.3, 4.6); with the opening soliloquy of Richard III ("Now is the winter of our discontent," 1.1.1–40); with the moving tale of Egeon that must hold its significance throughout the subsequent farce of *The Comedy of Errors* (1.1.31–95); the King of Navarre's eloquent but unrealistic covenant (1.1.1–23); Juliet's confrontation with the Friar's potion (4.3); Richard II's return to England ("Dear earth, I do salute thee with my hand," 3.2.6), his magnificent confrontation with Bolingbroke ("What must the King do now? Must he submit?," 3.3.142), and his final soliloquy ("I have been studying how I may compare This prison where I live unto the world," 5.5.1–2). There is Portia's sheer reliance on the words of a song (3.2.63–6) and Shylock's "I am a Jew. Hath not a Jew eyes?" (3.1.49–50). There is King Harry's speech before Harfleur (3.3), and his concerns (4.1.211–66) and his battlecry (4.3.20–67) before Agincourt. There are the funeral orations of Brutus and Antony for the assassinated Caesar (3.2) and the third funeral oration, as brief as Brutus', as rhetorical as Antony's, which Antony delivers on Brutus at the end of the play (5.5.67–74). All these crucial dramatic moments depend heavily on the poetry of the lines and the hearing of the auditors, although doubtless gestures reinforced them.

Yet the authority of Aristotle and Galen taught otherwise, as Andreas du Laurens makes clear in his *Discourse of the Preservation of the Sight*, translated by Richard Surphlet in 1599:

> Amongst all the senses, that of the sight, in the common judgment of all the Philosophers, hath been accounted the most noble, perfect, and admirable. The excellency thereof is to be perceived in an infinite sort of things: but more principally in four: as first, in respect of the variety of the objects which it representeth unto the soul: secondly, in respect of the means of his operation, which is (as it were) altogether spiritual: thirdly, in respect of his particular object, which is the light, which is the most noble and perfect quality that ever God created: and lastly, in respect of the certainty of his action.

As early as 1592 Nashe writes in *Pierce Penilesse* of young men "seeing a Playe" and describes Shakespeare's Talbot as "new embalmed with the tears of ten thousand spectators." Shakespeare was also experimenting with the effect of sight in his work of the 1590s, if less so than with the appeal of the sound of poetry, in the ghosts that haunt Richard III (5.5), the use of twins in *Comedy of Errors*, the eavesdropping in *Love's Labor's Lost* and *Much Ado About Nothing*. But sight and sound begin to gain equal, even on occasion counterbalancing, authority by 1599 – the bloody corpse of Caesar accompanies Antony's oration; the appearance of the Ghost of Hamlet's father underscores the urgency of his narrative request; the appearance of Falstaff in a buckbasket and with the cuckold's antlers as Herne undermine his courtships of Mistresses Ford and Page. Orlando's love poetry is written for a Rosalind clearly in disguise. Orsino's love melancholy and the gulling of Malvolio are both reflected in Feste's song lyrics. Othello needs visible proof for Iago's reports. The sight of Timon's generosity gives way to fierce lines of misanthropy, but Coriolanus' appearance before the senators and his later embracing of Aufidius are never finally answered by the pleading of Virgilia and Volumnia: in one, rhetoric takes over, in the other, spectacle. Indeed, as Gurr notes:

Volumnia gives patrician instructions to her son on how to perform his second attempt at winning the plebian votes, in these terms:

> Thy knee bussing the stone (for in such business
> Action is eloquence, and the eyes of th' ignorant
> More learned than the ears).

Furthermore, when the King's Men moved into the Blackfriars in 1608, Shakespeare emphasized spectacle even more. Gurr tells us that:

In *The Winter's Tale*, where theatre illusion is precisely set out to deceive the eye with bears onstage and statues that come to life, Hermione uses the term for seeing a play as the appropriate one for deception. Her life, she says, was a happy tale and is now sad, "which is More / Than history can pattern, though devis'd / And play'd to take spectators." The same kind of "taking" is there also shortly after, in Time's invitation to the credulous:

> ...imagine me,
> Gentle spectators, that I now may be
> In fair Bohemia.

The ease with which sight can be confused by mere appearance, affirmed in Paulina's declaration about the moving statue, "It *appears* she lives," has been anticipated by the gentleman of the preceding scene when he describes the reunion of Leontes and Camillo:

A notable passion of wonder appear'd in them; but the wisest beholder, that knew no more but seeing, could not say if th' importance were for joy or sorrow.

In later years, as the unexpected spectacles of tragicomedies and the dazzling vision of masques encroached on public performances, Shakespeare increasingly turns to the visual, from the reception of Cressida among the Greeks to Imogen's discovery of a headless corpse in her room to the shipwreck, harpies' banquet, and wedding masque of *The Tempest* and the presentation of the child Elizabeth that closes *Henry VIII*.

Playgoers' Tastes

We have some indication of the reactions of playgoers in Shakespeare's time. Michael Drayton reports "Shouts and Claps at ev'ry little pause,

When the proud round on ev'ry side hath rung," referring to the shape of the public playhouses,[32] while a playgoer in Oxford who saw the King's Men perform *Othello* comments that:

> not only by their speech but also by their deeds they drew tears. – But indeed Desdemona, killed by her husband, although she always acted the matter very well, in her death moved us still more greatly; when lying in bed she implored the pity of those watching with her countenance alone.

John Manningham entered into his diary an account of a performance of *Twelfth Night* he attended at Middle Temple in February 1602:

> At our feast we had a play called "Twelve Night, or What You Will"; much like the Comedy of Errors, or Menechmi in Plautus, but most like and near to that in Italian called Inganni. A good practice in it to make the steward believe his lady widow was in love with him, by counterfeiting a letter, as from his lady, in general terms, telling him what she liked best in him, and prescribing his gesture in smiling, his apparel, etc., and then when he came to practice, making him believe they took him to be mad.[33]

The astrologer Simon Forman writes in his "Book of plays and notes hereof performances for common policy," by which he means lessons for living, concerning his attendance at *The Winter's Tale*, *Cymbeline*, and *Macbeth*. He notes the moral of *The Winter's Tale* is to "Beware of trusting feigned beggars or fawning fellows" and praises *Macbeth* for its spectacles of witches.

The title-pages of published quartos of Shakespeare's plays, used for advertising when pinned up for display on the bookstalls in Paul's churchyard and hung on posts around the city, also give an indication of what was thought important by printers and booksellers, if not playgoers. Gurr cites two of them: the 1597 quarto of *Richard III*:

> The Tragedy of King Richard the Third. Containing his treacherous plots against his brother Clarence: the pitiful murder of his innocent nephews: his tyrannical usurpation: with the whole course of his detested life, and most deserved death. As it hath been lately acted by the Right honorable the Lord Chamberlain his servants

and the 1600 quarto of *The Merchant of Venice*:

> The most excellent History of the *Merchant of Venice*. With the extreme cruelty of *Shylock* the Jew towards the said Merchant, in cutting a just

pound of his flesh; and the obtaining of *Portia* by the choice of three chests. As it hath been diverse times acted by the Lord Chamberlain his Servants. Written by William Shakespeare.[34]

to which we may add, among others, the 1608 quarto of *King Lear*:

> Mr. William Shakespeare: His true chronicle history of the life and death of King Lear, and his three daughters. With the unfortunate life of Edgar, son and heir to the Earl of Gloucester, and his sullen and assumed humor of Tom of Bedlam. As it was played before the King's Majesty at Whitehall upon St. Stephen's Night in Christmas holidays.

Such summaries, however, are designed to attract readers whatever the responses of playgoers.

Shakespeare also writes his sense of playgoers into his plays. Puck addresses the epilogue of *Midsummer Night's Dream* to the gentry, to "gentles" (7); so does the opening Chorus of *Henry V* (8). The Prologue to *Troilus and Cressida* – while "not in confidence Of author's pen or actor's voice" – nevertheless rests with the judgments of the playgoers: "Like or find fault; do as your pleasures are; Now, good or bad, 'tis but the chance of war" (23–4, 30–1). There are playgoers within Shakespeare's plays as well: Christopher Sly; the ducal court of Athens; the royal court of Denmark; the court of Sicily. Here Shakespeare assembles a range of attitudes and responses, both auditory and visual, so that we may take more as characteristic of Hamlet than as general for Shakespeare the prince's rather haughty sense of "a speech once" that he remembers because "'Twas caviare to the general" (2.2.416, 418) but that "pleased not the million" (418), for him "an excellent play" because it was "well digested in the scenes, set down with as much modesty as cunning" (420–2). This refinement of taste agrees with Hamlet's later comment that it offends him "to hear a periwig-pated fellow tear a passion to tatters, to very rags" and his attack on the groundlings as those "who for the most part are capable of nothing but inexplicable dumb shows and noise" (3.2.7–11). This attitude might seem confirmed as Shakespeare's because of his sense of "the rabblement" who "shouted and clapped hands, and threw up their sweaty nightcaps, and uttered such a deal of stinking breath" at the return of Julius Caesar to Rome (1.2.243–5), written at the same time or, later, Coriolanus' view of the mob – "Bid them wash their faces And keep their teeth clean" (2.3.56–7). But these lines are clearly part of the personation, the counterfeiting, of Casca and Coriolanus; we are doubtless on safer ground when we look instead to Shakespeare's own direct addresses to "gentles all."

Shakespeare's Strategies

The best evidence for learning about Shakespeare's playgoers is to see how he strategizes his playtexts and performances to take in the widest sweep of reactions the public playhouses could attract. There are the alluring titles: *As You Like It* and *Twelfth Night, or What You Will*, surely, but also *Much Ado About Nothing*, *The Taming of the Shrew*, *Love's Labor's Lost*, and (given the new emphasis on markets and trade) *The Merchant of Venice*, and even *All Is True* (*Henry VIII*). The risks and tribulations of courtship in the comedies, the focus on family relations (rather than royal prerogatives) in a play like *King Lear* and the domestic issues of marriage in a tragedy like *Othello*, all cast a wide net. Bringing Richard II to a final self-analysis or Prince Hal into the Boar's Head Tavern makes of distant historic characters men more accessible to all the playgoers. The very human issues of adolescence are portrayed by Proteus and Romeo, of the desire for heroism by King Harry and Brutus, of the difficulties of mature love by Beatrice and Benedick, Cleopatra. The broader social issue of jealousy is examined by Proteus, Portia, Othello and Leontes. Yet to remark this is to focus on only one part of a play: *King Lear* has its steward in Oswald and its fool in a madman like Tom; *Othello* has roles for clowns and a serving woman. For the groundlings there are not only clowns but possibilities of upward social and economic mobility: Audrey attracts Touchstone; Jaquenetta (for the moment) has Don Armado. Even those as well-to-do as Helena and Isabella must resort to bed-tricks. With such an array of characters, and with such a multiply-focused story line, Shakespeare's plays are commercial in their box-office appeal. It is not accidental. Sequential scenes show it: Launce's address to the audience at the edge of the *platea* in *The Two Gentlemen of Verona* is set alongside the more formal scene in Julia's house in Verona, upstage on the *locus*. Such scenes can be simultaneous, too, as when Polonius and Claudius share responses to Ophelia's meeting with Hamlet, or when the courtiers of Navarre write heartfelt poems to the comments of those who come before them, or the First Murderer addresses Macbeth, in the *platea*, while up on the *locus* the formal coronation banquet continues. This frequent use of the *platea*, with its addresses, soliloquies, asides, and commentary, forces the complicity of the groundlings especially, but Shakespeare's plays continually arrange the scenes through declamations and disputations, formal speeches and seemingly informal colloquies, so that just as the disguises are known by all the playgoers – of Julia, Portia, Rosalind; of Hal, the Muscovites,

Edgar – the complicity as well as the imagination of those who attend the plays is constantly exercised.

This is also the view of Leonard Digges – the most frequent playgoer of Shakespeare's plays on record – as he registers his reactions, auditory and visual, to characters across the social spectrum:

> I do not wonder when you offer at
> Blackfriars, that you suffer: 'tis the fate
> Of richer veins, prime judgements that have fared
> The worse, with this deceased man compared.
> So have I seen, when Caesar would appear,
> And on the stage at half-sword parley were,
> Brutus and Cassius: oh, how the Audience
> Were ravish'd, with what wonder they went thence...
> Yet these sometimes, even at a friend's desire
> Acted, have scarce defrayed the seacoal fire
> And doorkeepers: when let but Falstaff come,
> Hal, Poins, the rest you scarce shall have a room
> All is so pester'd: let but Beatrice
> And Benedick be seen, lo in a trice
> The Cockpit galleries, boxes, all are full
> To hear Malvolio that cross-gartered Gull.[35]

These lines preface an edition of Shakespeare's *Poems*, published in 1640, but by then Digges had been dead five years. They were probably intended as a tribute joining that of Heminges, Condell, and others of Shakespeare's playing company for the First Folio of 1623. They preserve the first playgoers' reactions to Shakespeare's plays, showing us their variety, and the necessity – commercial and theatrical – to appeal to as many of them, and in as many ways, as possible.

Conclusion

If we examine Shakespeare's plays through the possible reactions of his playgoers, a play like *The Merchant of Venice* can resonate in new ways. For its appeal is clearly multiple. As merchandise itself, it examines the purpose and function of economics. In early retrospect, the opening line is puzzling, for the master merchant Antonio, whose commercial ventures are strategically planned and have resulted in considerable success, finds his life unfulfilled: "In sooth, I know not why I am so sad" (1.1.1). His situation speaks to the nobility in his audience who invested family money, the gentry who made use of it, and the tradesmen and apprentices whose goods were at stake. The use, rather than the earning, of money introduces through a deliberate echo the opening line of the next scene, when Portia says "By my troth, Nerissa, my little body is aweary of this great world" (1.2.1). The heiress of a goodly fortune echoes Antonio. But the play is not as simple as to conclude that money does not buy happiness, because in the end – with Bassanio and Portia, with Lorenzo and Jessica – it does, although success in the world of Elizabethan commerce, as represented in Venice and Belmont, leaves Shylock punished and Antonio solitary.

Portia's first scene looks at money in another way, which is familial and social rather than primarily economic, or so Nerissa says. When Portia complains that "I may neither choose who I would nor refuse who I dislike; so is the will of a living daughter curbed by the will of a dead father" (1.2.20–2), her waiting-woman replies:

> Your father was ever virtuous, and holy men at their death have good inspirations; therefore the lottery that he hath devised in these three chests of gold, silver, and lead, whereof who chooses his meaning chooses you, will no doubt never be chosen by any rightly but one who you shall rightly love. (1.2.24–8)

Nerissa's assurance may seem romantic and optimistic, but we have seen that before, too, in Bassanio's confidence before Antonio that one last financial loan will bring him, as it brought Jason, the Golden Fleece of great fortune (1.1.161–76). Fortune in love is absolutely equated with fortune in property and in gold. The play, then, holds out hope for those without fortune among the playgoers, the underprivileged who, like Bassanio, deserve a better station in life (even, it would appear, without working for it). Thus the financial conditions and their real value which are at the heart of the play can appeal simultaneously to several sorts of playgoers.

Shylock brings to the play another, related set of issues. He too is a father who, like Portia's, may place too heavy a hand on the protection of his daughter. When he locks her up against the temptations of the Gentile world, he is only acting in the same way – and for the same reasons – as Portia's father has. On the one hand, Shylock represents the new capitalism that had arrived with great force in the 1590s with the expanded international commerce out of London, and the usury he practices, while disliked by those required to pay without received goods for their money, is a necessary practice if businesses are to be started up and, from time to time (as now with Antonio), maintained. Shylock is both despised and vital, but insofar as his living is through loans (that is, investments for return), he is only another version of Antonio – and of Portia's father once more. Thus the London economy that is inhabited by many play-goers – and was practiced by them when they paid their admission fees to the gatherers at the playhouse – is under scrutiny. In *The Merchant of Venice*, this is necessarily joined with religion, since Jews alone could be usurers in Shakespeare's London; Christians could not. Rather, Chris-tians were supposed to care little for material goods – the realm of Mammon – and instead to practice "The quality of mercy" (4.1.179). If Shylock represents the old religion of the Old Testament, the book of justice, then Portia's opening lines are foreign and treacherous to him, for she speaks the words of Christ, which he may not know and does not accept. What follows in the great trial scene of 4.1, however, is Portia acting in a way that is anything but merciful: she wins over Shylock, saves Antonio's life, and relieves Bassanio of guilt and shame by exercis-ing Old Testament-like justice. Thus, teaching Shylock the need for mercy, she will not give it.

Just how playgoers saw these turns of events is open to question, but it is possible that Portia emerges as the play's best merchant, able to deal in monetary terms in order to gain new purchase on her husband. This use of money for individual advancement through skill and labor was in Shakespeare's day the trademark not of Jews but of Puritans: the play-goers are not allowed to disjoin the economic and the religious. Nor are they allowed to disjoin the economic and the romantic. To what extent does the love of or dependence on money permit an individual's freedom of choice and chance of happiness? By addressing segments of his audi-ence in *The Merchant of Venice* – merchants and usurers, fathers and children, Christians and Jews – Shakespeare finds a common way to to address them all by finding individually and communally concerns all playgoers would necessarily share.

4

Equipment

I am a wise fellow, and which is more an officer, and which is more, a householder, and which is more, as pretty a piece of flesh as any is in Messina, and one that knows the law, go to, and a rich fellow enough, go to, and a fellow that hath had losses, and one that hath two gowns, and every thing handsome about him.

William Shakespeare's counterfeiting of Dogberry,
Much Ado About Nothing

Material clothes give Constable Dogberry, in charge of the night watch in Messina, his identity, his stature, his role as a player in Shakespeare's *Much Ado About Nothing*. "It was clothing, not the stationers' trade, that was central to the putting on of plays," Ann Jones and Peter Stallybrass write.[1] For some, they remained the most important part of a performance. The chaplain of the Venetian embassy, for instance, attending a play in 1617, could not understand the language, but nevertheless received "amusement . . . from gazing at the very costly dresses of the actors."[2] The Swiss traveller Thomas Platter agreed, and tried to find reasons for it. He notes in his journal for 1599 that "it is the English usage for eminent lords or knights at their decease to bequeath and leave almost the best of their clothes to their serving men, which it is unseemly for the latter to wear, so that they offer them for sale for a small sum to the actors."[3] The actor Edward Alleyn, leading man for the Lord Admiral's company, owned a "black velvet cloak with sleeves embroidered all with silver and gold" that cost him £20 10s 6d. Thus we are not surprised when S. P. Cerasano observes that "The contents of the tiring house of the Rose Playhouse seem to have been worth as much, or slightly more than the cost of the playhouse itself."[4]

As manager of the Lord Admiral's Men at the Rose, Philip Henslowe bought some costumes new and others second-hand from clothing dealers or pawnbrokers such as himself; when neither could supply him, he had them made. In 1600 he paid a tailor £3 for making suits with a Polish cut for a lost play known as *News out of Poland*, but he paid £21 for the velvet, satin, and taffeta fashioned into cardinal's robes for another lost play, *Cardinal Wolsey* (1600). Costumes were the most expensive equipment a playing company owned. When he built the Swan in 1586, Francis Langley put out an initial £300 for new apparel for the players; when Henry Evans established a boys' playing company at the first Blackfriars, he joined with Edward Kirkham, Yeoman of the Revels and in charge of the wardrobe for the Revels, but later paid £200 for costumes. If companies collapsed, they sold what costumes they could to pay off incurred debts. The Earl of Pembroke's Men, in difficulty in 1593, sold off costumes to the amount of £80 which they divided among their six sharers. When Lady Elizabeth's Men fell out with Henslowe (in 1615), it was because Henslowe was accused of selling "ten pounds worth of old apparel" that belonged to the company; of pricing apparel at £63 when it was worth £40; and of withholding from the company arras curtains for which they had paid £40. Two years later, Christopher Beeston was charged by the Queen's Players with embezzling costumes, selling some of them to other playing companies, and converting others for his own use. But these men were not strangers to the clothing trade. Langley was a member of the Drapers Company and was made alnager to the court of aldermen in 1585 to check the quality, size, and weight of woolens. Henslowe was a member of the Dyers Company, manufactured starch, and was a pawnbroker. Shakespeare himself was the son of a glover who also bought and sold wool wholesale.[5] The haberdasher Thomas Giles bought, sold, and perhaps rented costumes, as did the players Edward Alleyn and Christopher Beeston. But Alleyn made an inventory of his extensive wardrobe; besides his black velvet gown he owned a number of the clothes he had used in plays as well as those used by his apprentice and had other costumes he loaned out: suits to Will Kempe the clown, in Shakespeare's playing company, for one. Players also left their costumes to other players in their wills. Thomas Pope, one of Shakespeare's fellow King's Men, in 1604 did "bequeath to Robert Gough and John Edmans all my wearing apparel, and all my arms, to be equally divided between them." William Bird, a player for the Earl of Pembroke's Men and later the Lord Admiral's Men, left "unto my eldest son William Bird my ash-color suit and cloak of cloth laced with satin lace" and to his third son Thomas "my ash-colored suit and cloak trimmed with green silk and silver lace."

Given the heavy investment in costumes, the King's Men like other companies hired tiremen (for the attiring house back of the stage), wardrobe keepers, and perhaps even a tailor to mend, alter, or make costumes. Henslowe paid 6s to repair a coat that was rat-eaten in July 1601; he "appointed a man to the seeing of his accounts in buying of clothes (he being to have 6s a week)." In addition, Jones and Stallybrass note, "Henslowe also made independent payments on behalf of the actors to tailors, mercers, a milliner, lacemakers, and a 'sylke man.' In other words, a labor force grew up around the theater because of the value of its clothes."[6] We can estimate the significance of this if we consider a pair of silk stockings could cost £2 to £4, a woman's gown might cost between £7 and £20 and more. "The Earl of Leicester," says Andrew Gurr, "paid £543 for seven doublets and two cloaks, at an average cost for such items rather higher than the price Shakespeare paid for a house in Stratford."[7] Little wonder, then, that clothing and cloth were recycled. Jean MacIntyre has reported that cloth woven with gold or silver was valuable no matter what its state: for "fees" for the Revels employees, green cloth of silver was transformed into linings for German slops, baggy breeches, and then cut again into pieces for fishermen's slops, then into a masque of mariners, then for torch

---

27 August 1595

Sold unto James Donstall, player, the 27th of August 1595, a man's gown of purple color cloth faced with coney and laid on the sleeves with buttons for 43s 4d to be paid 20s in hand and 23s 4d at Michaelmas next coming after the date above written, I say for:

43s 4d

Rd in part of payment the same day being the 27 of August 1595 of James Tunstall the sum of:

10s

Rd in part of payment the 28 of August 1595 in money of James Tunstall the sum of:

10s

Rest to pay:

23s 4d

An entry in Philip Henslowe's account book showing his practice of selling gowns to his players.

Reprinted from Glynne Wickham, Herbert Berry, and William Ingram, eds, *English Professional Theatre, 1530–1660* (Cambridge: Cambridge University Press, 2000), p. 236.

---

bearers for a second masque of Turks, and so eventually into gowns of cloth of gold blue velvet with raised roses to gold. Rich fabrics might be recycled without being cut up. Going through two or three alterations by court maskers, they would pass down to torchbearers and then on down to players, but this was the last usage made of the material. Yet in spite of the fact that a costume might be made from material used in many previous guises, it was still part of the most valuable items in a playing company's inventory of equipment.[8]

The Use of Costumes

Costumes are important because, in a time of little scenery and often just a bare platform, the identification and relationship of characters could rest solely on their dress. As Andrew Gurr and Mariko Ichikawa have pointed out:

> The deception of playing was very largely a matter of dress, and of audiences accepting appearances as, however transient, the theatrical reality. In *Twelfth Night* Viola and Sebastian were made into identical twins not by their faces but by their similar dress [as are the twin Antipholi and Dromios of *The Comedy of Errors*]. In 4.4 of *The Taming of the Shrew* the Pedant when disguised as Vincentio simply wears a different hat to confirm which role he is assuming. The changing dress of the victimized characters in *King Lear*, from Lear himself to Edgar as Poor Tom, showed how their status shrank. Lear starts with his crown and regalia, reappears in more casual clothes as a huntsman, loses even that when he rages bareheaded in the storm, and finally stands crowned with flowers as a mad parody of his original kingly status. Edgar moves from noble dress to the material deprivation of nakedness under a blanket.[9]

Tom's initial disguise is to appear to be a madman such as those on display at Bethlem Hospital in London, the hospital for the incurably insane, but he transforms himself beyond that before the playgoers at the Globe so that he is virtually naked:

> No port is free; no place,
> That guard, and most unusual vigilance,
> Does not attend my taking. Whiles I may 'scape,
> I will preserve myself; and am bethought
> To take the basest and most poorest shape
> That ever penury, in contempt of man,

Brought near to beast. My face I'll grime with filth,
Blanket my loins, elf all my hair in knots,
And with presented nakedness out-face
The winds and persecutions of the sky.

(2.3.3–12)

His thoughts, reinforced by his costuming and appearance, are reflected in short order by Lear himself:

Why, thou wert better in thy grave than to answer with thy uncovered body this extremity of the skies. Is man no more than this? Consider him well. Thou owest the worm no silk, the beast no hide, the sheep no wool, that cat no perfume. Ha! here's three on's are sophisticated! Thou art the thing itself; unaccommodated man is no more but such a poor, bare, forked animal as thou art. (3.4.94–100)

Seeing his condition, and therefore himself, mirrored in Poor Tom, Lear attempts to make himself alike by undressing himself, too: "Off, off, you lendings! Come unbutton here" (3.4.100–1). He attempts, through costume or the lack of it, to twin himself to Tom o' Bedlam. It is a powerful stage spectacle that asks the playgoers whether Lear's philosophy has struck new insights into the nature of man, and his own nature, or whether he is truly mad. Or, twinned to Tom, is he a wise fool?

Costumes, then, are crucial signifiers of meaning that reinforce the dialogue and are an essential element in the players' presentation. We witness and then remember characters by their costumes: Caesar's bloodied toga; Macbeth's armor; Malvolio's nightgown and (before and after) his robes of office; Coriolanus' gown of humility; Prospero's magic robes. So do Shakespeare's characters. Troilus expresses his anxious concern for Cressida's well-being when she is called early from their bed to depart to the Grecian camp: "You will catch cold and curse me" (4.2.17). Troilus and Cressida give testimony to their love – so as to remember each other – by part of their costumes given in pledges to each other: her glove, his sleeve (4.5). But signifying costumes can also precede dialogue, as when Solinus, Duke of Ephesus, and Egeon, a merchant of Syracuse, open *The Comedy of Errors* in costumes that display a discrepant distinction in both country and status. Costume can undermine a personation, as with Malvolio's anachronistically outdated cross-garters. Costumes can contradict a character, as does Hal's clothing at the Boar's Head Tavern, or ostracize one, as Shylock's Jewish gaberdine does. That is one purpose they serve. But perhaps most important was initial definition of place. "The scattered evidence," Alan C. Dessen writes:

suggests that, at the Globe or Fortune or Blackfriars, place was signaled primarily by means of costume. For example, a prison would be signaled not by a grate or by onstage objects comparable to our sense of a "set" but rather by the presence of a [jailer] along with manacled prisoners. Similarly, a forester or woodsman would signal a forest; a host or vintner, an inn; figures in nautical costume, a ship. In such an onstage vocabulary, distinctive properties or costumes serve as visual clues: the [jailer's] keys; the forester's green garments or weapons; the vintner's apron or handheld glasses.[10]

Once introduced, however, they take on their own weight in meaning. Friar Laurence tells Juliet to put on her "best robes" when she takes his potion so she will be prepared to be carried to the family tomb (4.1.109–12), but these must surely be the clothes she also wears at the Capulets' masked ball and, therefore, is wearing when she appears in the first balcony scene shortly thereafter (1.5; 2.1), linking visually the scenes of her forbidden love with Romeo to her death. *Hamlet* is in part about the threat of war from the invasion of Denmark by Norway, but the only named characters who appear in armor are the Ghost in act 1 and Fortinbras in act 5, linking the two. They are linked to a third in the play's closing speech by Fortinbras:

> Let four captains
> Bear Hamlet like a soldier to the stage,
> For he was likely, had he been put on,
> To have proved most royally; and for his passage,
> The soldiers' music and the rites of war
> Speak loudly for him.
> Take up the body. Such a sight as this
> Becomes the field, but here shows much amiss.
> Go, bid the soldiers shoot.
> (5.2.339–47)

Hamlet will receive the funeral of a soldier because he would have made a good one, like the two soldiers in battle gear that are (or will be) called kings of Denmark. If this is not a mockery – and it is unlikely, since Hamlet supports Fortinbras's succession – then playgoers have a somewhat different idea of what Hamlet lacks or what Denmark needs than much of the play has seemed to emphasize.

Dessen finds nightgowns to be the costumes that lead to visual meaning in *Othello*:

In *Othello*, the Folio stage directions mention no nightgowns, but the 1622 Quarto has Brabantio first appear in the opening scene "*at a window*" and

102

then enter to Roderigo, "*in his night gown*" accompanied by servants "*with Torches.*" The nightgown and the torches confirm that the scene takes place at night, a fact already established in the dialogue. More important, Shakespeare is here setting up a Brabantio "*as newly come out of Bed*" (*A Woman Killed with Kindness*, II.141) or "*as newly risen*" (*Dick of Devonshire*, 1286), with the awakening of this "unready" figure caused by a plot set up by Iago (and using Roderigo as a tool) that leads to accusations against Desdemona and her lover, Othello.

No equivalent stage direction survives for 2.3, but as a result of Cassio's brawling, Othello (rather than Brabantio) is awakened from sleep, again as part of a plot instigated by Iago with Roderigo as a tool, a plot that soon leads to accusations against Desdemona and a supposed lover, this time Cassio, with the willing ear being lent not by Brabantio but by Othello. Although neither the Quarto nor the Folio specifically calls for a night-gown, when Desdemona enters, Othello remarks: "Look if my gentle love be not raised up!"; then tells her: "All's well now, sweeting; come away to bed"; and concludes at his exit: "Come, Desdemona, 'tis the soldiers' life / To have their balmy slumbers waked with strife" (2.3.240–8). Brabantio's sleep, interrupted and poisoned by Iago, has now become Othello's inter-rupted wedding night, again affected by Iago's pestilence, with the two moments linked (perhaps) by both the nightgown and, equally important, by the associations that garment carried – here unreadiness, vulnerability.[11]

In 4.3 Desdemona, preparing for night, is again in the same nightgown; she awaits Othello. We know she is vulnerable; but the question, given what happens, is how prepared she is for the outcome of this meeting.

The Duke's costume as Friar in *Measure for Measure* must have been unusually significant on the Jacobean stage when the King's Men staged the play, because the two costumes embodied by a single character com-bined state and church as James I and VI insisted was a cornerstone of his own rule; in a way, the play tests the efficacy of state rule without church support. That Angelo, probably dressed like a Puritan, is moralistic but ineffective suggests, however, that the Church of England, with its tolerant understanding of the people, was a far better choice; and it may not be beside the point that, at the play's end, Isabella is invited to marry the secular Duke, surrendering her novitiate's robes for the Catholic Order of the Sisters of St Clare. But besides the Duke, there is no major costume change, isolating and emphasizing his. "Other characters," Jean MacIn-tyre observes, "put on and remove gowns, cloaks, hats, and veils, but noth-ing indicates that anyone else changes a basic costume." But, she continues:

> In *Measure for Measure* fixed costume is not mere economy. Unchanging dress symbolizes the rigid fixations of most of the characters, whether

Angelo's absolute enforcement of the law's letter, Isabella's absolute certainty that her morality applies to everyone, Barnardine's absolute refusal to obey anybody, or Pompey's absolute confidence that his job in a bawdy house will continue despite the law. The costumes thus function, like verbal images, visual correlatives to the play's many walls and locked doors.[12]

The Duke's disguise leads to comedy with Lucio in 5.1, but his comment, when the Friar tells him he has slandered the Duke – "You must, sir, change persons with me ere you make that my report" (5.1.333–4) – shows that personation relies on costume. Properties play a role in this scene as well: the last manacled prisoner – after seeing Barnardine manacled – is Angelo: a potentially telling condemnation of his kind of rule.

Costumes as Signs

Costume does not only denote a particular role – duke, friar – but social class generally: "What is thy name?" Henry V asks the French envoy Mountjoy; "I know thy quality" (3.6.137). Class was clearly marked because the Elizabethans upheld a statute which regulated the dress for each social rank, a statute reinforced by Elizabeth I on July 6, 1597 (although eventually repealed in 1604). Only the players were allowed to dress in garments inappropriate to their station, something that especially bothered the player and playwright Stephen Gosson after he had left the stage for a career in the church:

> Overlashing in apparel is so common a fault, that the very hirelings of some of our players, which stand at reversion of 6s by the week, jet under gentlemen's noses in suits of silk, exercising themselves to prating on the stage, and common scoffing when they come abroad, where they look askance over the shoulder at every man, of whom the Sunday before they begged an alms.[13]

For Men's Apparell Her Maiestie doeth straightly charge and commaund, that None shall weare in his Apparell Cloth of gold or siluer tissued, Silke of colour Purple, vnder the degree of an Earle, except Knights of the Garter in their purple Mantels onely.

Cloth of gold or siluer, tincelled Sattin, Silke or cloth mixed or imbrodered with Pearle, Gold, or Siluer, woollen Cloth made out of the Realme, vnder the degree of a Baron, except Knights of the Garter, Privy Counsellors to The Queenes Maiestie.

Equipment

Passemaine lace or any other lace of gold or siluer or mixed with gold &
siluer, with gold and silke, with siluer and silke, Spurres, Swordes, Rapiers,
Daggers, Skaines, Woodkniues, Hangers, Buckles, or studs or girdles, Gilt or
Damasked with gold or siluer, Siluered, Under the degree of a Barons sonne,
except Gentlemen in ordinarie Office, attending upon her Maiestie in her
house or chamber: Such as haue bin imploied in Ambassage to forren Princes
Such as may dispend v. C. [500] marks by the yeere, for terme of life in
possession aboue all charges. And Knights for wearing onely of Spurres,
Swordes, Rapiers, and Daggers, and those other things therewith ensuing.
And likewise Captaines being in her Maiesties pay.

Veluet in Gownes, Cloakes, Coates, or other vppermost Garments, Embrod-
eries with silke, Netherstocks of silke, Under the degree of a Knight, except
Gentlemen in ordinarie Office, attending vpon her Maiestie in her house or
chamber; Such as haue bin imploied in Ambassage to foreine Princes. The
sonne and heire apparant of a Knight. Captaines in her maiesties pay: and such
as may dispend CC.*li.* [£200] by the yeere for terme of life in possession aboue
all charges.

Veluet in Jerkins, Hose, Doublets: Sattin, Damaske, Taffata, Grogeran in
Gownes, Cloakes, Coates or other vppermost Garments. Under the degree
of a Knights eldest sonne, except Gentlemen in ordinarie Office, attending
vpon her maiestie in her house or chamber: Such as haue bene imploied in
Ambassage to forein Princes: And such as may dispend C. *li* [£100] by the
yeere for terme of life in possession aboue all charges.

Sattin, Damaske, Grogeran, Taffata in Hose, Doublet, Under the degree of a
Gentleman bearing Armes, except Gentlemen in ordinarie Office, attending
vpon her maiestie in her house or chamber: Such as have bene imploied in
Ambassage to forein Princes: And such as may dispend xx.*li* [£20] by *the*
yeere for terme of life in possession aboue all charges.

Extracts from statutes and proclamations enforcing the regulations on apparel
(the "sumptuary laws") issued by Elizabeth I from Greenwich on July 6, 1597.

Reprinted from Carol Chillington Rutter, ed., *Documents of the Rose Playhouse* (rev.
edn) (Manchester and New York: Manchester University Press, 1999), pp. 231–2.

This criticism held because – except possibly for Venetian gentlemen who
were known to wear gowns of black from neck to ankle, senators and
doctors who dressed in gowns of scarlet, Jews who wore dark red with
yellow caps and the Prince of Morocco who, in the stage direction, is
dressed all in white in *The Merchant of Venice* (2.7) – all of Shakespeare's

players wore English dress. This must be so, for instance, in the case of *Julius Caesar*, where Lucius tells Brutus the conspirators have arrived with "hats...pluck'd about their ears And half their faces buried in their cloaks" (2.1.73–4). Portia accuses Brutus of risking his health because he "walk[s] unbraced and suck[s] up the humours Of the dank morning" (2.1.261–2), Ligarius carries a kerchief (2.1.314), Caesar appears in a "*nightgown*" (stage direction for 2.2), and Brutus puts on a gown for bed, finding a book in its pocket (4.2.291, 303–4). Edmond Malone found at Dulwich College an inventory of the costumes belonging to Philip Henslowe's company drawn up in 1598. According to MacIntyre's count:

> the "sewtes," hose, doublets, and jerkins listed in the inventory gives something over eighty complete men's outfits not identified with any role or play and presumably usable in many parts.
>
> These outfits seem mostly for one social class, the gentry. Partly this is because of the variety of styles and still more the rapid changes of fashion worn by this class, compared with the conservative dress of countrymen and, in theory, of citizens. In January 1602/03, Henslowe lent 50s "to by a sytyzen [citizen] cotte & sleves" [coat and sleeves], which needed no further specifics of cloth or cut. The costume of an apprentice, servant, or rustic could appear in play after play, since its cut and color represented what was fitting, even established by law, for the status of the character it clothed and was therefore not in itself very memorable. A gallant's doublet, hose, cloak, and hat, however, were subject to whimsical changes in the fashion, and so would become stale if shown too often....
>
> For a company with twelve adult actors, the eighty or more complete men's costumes represented by the inventory give each man in the company six or seven suits, more if doublets and jerkins were mixed-and-matched with the hose and each other. Besides these, there were specialty outfits like the six jerkins and hats for the clown, the seven "anteckes cootes," and the costumes for priests, soldiers, heralds, and so forth, which have "minor role" written all over them. Obviously one role would rarely if ever call for six or more costume changes, though, allowing one costume per role in each play, the wardrobe the inventory represents could be shown entire to a regular playgoer in little more than a fortnight, especially with doubling. The more costume change in individual plays, the sooner all of the wardrobe would be seen. Many of the 1590s plays suggest that the actors seldom got more than one costume per role unless that role demanded a traditional reason for a costume change, and that experienced playwrights, especially if company members like Shakespeare, took some care to keep the changes few and functional. Such care would prevent too quick a familiarity with a company's apparel, and help prevent the rapid wear of its costumes.[14]

The booke of the Inventary of the goods of my Lord Admeralles men, tacken the 10 of Marche in the yeare 1598.

Gone and loste.

Item, j orenge taney satten dublet, layd thycke with gowld lace.
Item, j blew tafetie sewt.
Item, j payr of carnatyon satten Venesyons, layd with gold lace.
Item, j longe-shanckes sewte.
Item, j Sponnes dublet pyncket.
Item, j Spanerd gyrcken.
Item, Harey the fyftes dublet.
Item, Harey the fyftes vellet gowne.
Item, j fryers gowne.
Item, j lyttell dublet for boye.

The Enventary of the Clownes Sewtes and Hermetes Sewtes, with dievers other sewtes, as followeth, 1598, the 10 of March.
Item, j senetores gowne, j hoode and 5 senetores capes.
Item, j sewtte for Nepton; Fierdrackes sewtes for Dobe.
Item, iiij genesareyes gownes, and iiij torchberers sewtes.
Item, iij payer of red strasers, and iij fares gowne of buckrome.
Item, iiij Herwodes cottes, and iij sogers cottes, and j green gown for Maryan.
Item, vj grene cottes for Roben Hoode, and iiij knaves sewtes.
Item, ij payer of grene hosse and Andersones sewte. j whitt shepen clocke.
Item, ij rosset cottes, and j black frese cotte, and iiij prestes cottes.
Item, ij whitt sheperdes cottes, and ij Danes sewtes, and j payer of Danes hosse.
Item, The Mores lymes, and Hercolles lymes, and Will. Sommers sewtte.
Item, ij Orlates sewtes, hates and gorgetts, and vij anteckes cootes.
Item, Cathemer sewte, j payer of cloth whitte stockens, iiij Turckes hedes.
Item, iiij freyers gownes and iiij hoodes to them, and j fooles coate, cape, and babell, and branhowlttes bodeyes, and merlen gowne and cape.
Item, ij black saye gownes, and ij cotton gownes, and j rede saye gowne.
Item, j mawe gowne of calleco for the quene, j carnowll hatte.
Item, j red sewt of cloth for pyge, layed with whitt lace.

Item, v payer of hosse for the clowne, and v gerkenes for them.
Item, iij payer of canvas hosse for asane, ij payer of black strocers.
Item, j yelow leather dublett for a clowne, j Whittcomes dublett poke.
Item, Eves bodeyes, j pedante trusser, and iij donnes hattes.
Item, j payer of yelow cotton sleves, j gostes sewt, and j gostes bodeyes.
Item, xviij copes and hattes, Verones sonnes hosse.
Item, iij trumpettes and a drum, and a trebel viall, a basse viall, a bandore, a sytteren, j anshente, j whitt hatte.
Item, j hatte for Robin Hoode, j hobihorse.
Item, v shertes, and j serpelowes, iiij ferdingalles.
Item, vj head-tiers, j fane, iiij rebatos, ij gyrketruses.
Item, j longe sorde.

The Enventary of all the apparell for my Lord Admiralles men, tacken the 10 of marche 1598. – Leaft above in the tier-house in the cheast.

Item, My Lord Caffes gercken, & his hoosse.
Item, j payer of hosse for the Dowlfen.
Item, j murey lether gyrcken, & j white lether gercken.
Item, j black lether gearken, & Nabesathe sewte.
Item, j payer of hosse, & a gercken for Valteger.
Item, ij leather anteckes cottes with basses, for Fayeton.
Item, j payer of bodeyes for Alles Pearce.

Inventory of goods by Philip Henslowe

Reprinted from Rutter, *Documents of the Rose Playhouse*, pp. 65–6.

Moreover, diminished wardrobes might be taken on tour, and playwrights such as Shakespeare, therefore, would be highly conscious of the company's supplies when fashioning scenes.

Shakespeare's culture practiced its own kind of costuming in the ritual known as breeching. Up until the age of seven, boys and girls dressed alike, in gowns and aprons; but at the age of seven a boy was breeched – changed into doublet and hose to establish that second period of childhood when he was separated from his mother and taught manly discipline. Bianca refers to this when choosing between her disguised tutor Lucentio and her lutemaster Hortensio, also her suitor, in *The Taming of the Shrew*:

Why, gentlemen, you do me double wrong
To strive for that which resteth in my choice.
I am no breeching scholar in the schools,
I'll not be tied to hours nor 'pointed times,
But learn my lessons as I please myself;
And to cut off all strife, here sit we down.

(3.1.16–21)

When Julia in *The Two Gentlemen of Verona* decides to go on a pilgrimage to be with Proteus, her maid is aware of breeching and how it marks gender:

Lucetta	But in what habit will you go along?
Julia	Not like a woman, for I would prevent
	The loose encounters of lascivious men.
	Gentle Lucetta, fit me with such weeds
	As may beseem some well-reputed page.
Lucetta	Why then, your ladyship must cut your hair.
Julia	No, girl, I'll knit it up in silken strings
	With twenty odd-conceited true-love knots.
	To be fantastic may become a youth
	Of greater time than I shall show to be.
Lucetta	What fashion, madam, shall I make your breeches?
Julia	That fits as well as "Tell me, good my lord,
	What compass will you wear your farthingale?"
	Why, e'en what fashion thou best likes, Lucetta.
Lucetta	You must needs have them with a codpiece, madam.
Julia	Out, out, Lucetta. That will be ill- favoured.
Lucetta	A round hose, madam, now's not worth a pin
	Unless you have a codpiece to stick pins on.
Julia	Lucetta, as thou lov'st me let me have
	What thou think'st meet and is most mannerly.
	But tell me, wench, how will the world repute me
	For undertaking so unstaid a journey?
	I fear me it will make me scandalized.
Lucetta	If you think so, then stay at home, and go not.

(2.7.39–62)[15]

Gender may be transformed on the stage by means of costuming, but when such a disguise is introduced into a play, Shakespeare tells the playgoers, often in advance as here, or as the disguises of gender for Rosalind and Celia in *As You Like It* (1.3), or for Viola when she becomes Cesario in *Twelfth Night* (1.2). This happens twice in *King Lear*, not as a matter of gender but as a matter of identity or station: "banished Kent" "razed [his] likeness" to become Caius (1.4.4); Edgar describes his disguise to the playgoers at considerable length (2.3). This also happens when roles are exhanged: it is often done onstage, as in *The Winter's Tale*, when Perdita puts on Florizel's hat and Florizel trades clothes with Autolycus to enable them to escape Bohemia (4.4); as matters turn out, Perdita's identity is restored by the discovery of her mother's mantle and her mother's jewel around her neck as well as by the letters of Antigonus (5.2.32–5). Such disguises are likewise used in the history plays – in *1 Henry IV*, when Hal proposes to Poins that they use "cases of buckram" to rob Falstaff and his men of the money they rob of travellers at Gadshill (1.2.159); the battle of Shrewsbury is partly won by King Henry's forces when some of them dress up as the king (5.4). In *Henry V*, King Harry visits his troops on the eve of Agincourt unrecognized because he wears the cloak of Sir Thomas Erpingham: "Lend me thy cloak, Sir Thomas. Brothers both" (4.1.24). So simple a matter as a cloak can change identities; and so simple a matter as a beard. Bottom has a whole stock of them, he tells Quince, to help him play the part of Pyramus: "I will discharge it in either your straw-colour beard, your orange-tawny beard, your purple-in-grain beard, or your French-crown-colour beard, your perfect yellow" (1.2.76–8). Beatrice judges men by their beards in *Much Ado About Nothing* (2.1.27–31). In *1 Henry IV* Douglas tells Hotspur that only bearded men are worthy opponents (4.1.11–12).

Costumes, then, are used by players to distinguish gender and sex, rank, occupation, even age and marital status. Because this is so fixed a material practice, *As You Like It* realizes its comic title, MacIntyre comments, by giving "much attention to characters in the wrong clothes for sex or status, and some characters in clothes wrong for their social situation": Jaques, Corin, Rosalind, Celia. MacIntyre continues:

> Orlando in his first shabby clothes is unfitly clad for a knight's son, while Duke Senior and his followers in their "Robin Hood" array are unfitly clad for nobles and gentlemen. In fact, the only characters properly dressed for sex, station, and place are on the one hand the wicked Duke Frederick and Oliver, and on the other the lower-class Adam, Corin, Silvius, Phoebe, Audrey, and William.[16]

Such a distinction between unnatural and natural dress underscores the artificial and transitory nature of court transferred to the forest. Costumes meant to identify characters also judge them.

Othello uses costumes to distinguish four very different military men: Othello, Cassio, Iago, Roderigo. Much is made of military terms to heighten the sense of war in *Troilus and Cressida* – harness, mail, gorget, helm, beaver, vambrace, crest, plume, casque – yet it is a somewhat more domestic garment – Troilus' sleeve that he gives Cressida as a token of his loyalty and their pledge to one another – that carries charged significance in the later acts.[17] MacIntyre suggests that Shakespeare wrote his plays so that different characters in different works could share the same costumes. She finds, for instance, that Falstaff and Sir Toby Belch, in plays some distance in time and performance, could have shared the same stuffed and bulky outfit. The clown Robert Armin could have used the same clown outfit for Touchstone and for Feste, again with playing seasons dividing the plays. Feste's disguise as Sir Topas – a plain curate's gown – might have been used earlier by Sir Hugh Evans and Sir Oliver Martext. The King of France wears a sick man's gown and coif in *All's Well That Ends Well* (2.1) when he is carried in on a sick chair, but here Shakespeare is writing to the material conditions he had already employed with the sick King Henry IV (in *2 Henry IV* 4.3). The same costume is given to Caius Ligarius in *Julius Caesar* (2.1), who is also ailing. (The chair might be used later to seat Antony when he is pulled up, dying, to the presence of Cleopatra [4.16] in *Antony and Cleopatra*.) For MacIntyre, the use (and reuse) of costumes can also lead to a more reliable representation of what actually happened in the Globe playhouse:

> The "cases of buckram" which Poins supplies "to immask our noted outward garments" (1.2.175) are quick (and inexpensive) diguise costumes. His lines suggest that, except for his buckram guise, Hal is meant to remain in one costume until he and Westmoreland meet Falstaff on the road to Shrewsbury. This seems a better place to show Hal armed as a hero-prince than the earlier scene where he and Poins enter "*marching*" and "*Falstaff meets him, playing upon his truncheon like a fife*" (III.iii.SD 86). With the rest of the Boar's Head crew, Poins disappears after this scene which recalls the tavern highjinks of Act II, for none of them has a place in the heroic world where Hal kills Hotspur.[18]

Similarly the two tetralogies could share costumes among them, both for kings and for parts in more than one play, such as Richard, Duke of York; Prince Hal; Falstaff; Lady Percy; Poins; and Bardolph.

Costume Changes

The possibilities and limitations of the Lord Chamberlain's–King's Men inventory allowed Shakespeare to write certain parts that could be doubled because of the change of identity by the change of costume,

Figure 11 The tiring-room at the Globe by C. Walter Hodges. This shows costumes and properties kept near at hand for the play in progress, costumes being mended, and, on the bookkeeper's desk, the plot of the play doubtless just consulted by the two actors about to go on stage.

but in doing so, he had to write plays that allowed a player time to change. He had some help (which may be seen in his plays) from introducing fights, songs, or clown scenes that could be extended if necessary while a character was putting off one disguise and putting on another. Egeon could re-enter as First Merchant (1.2), Balthasar (3.1), and Pinch (4.4) before returning as Egeon well into 5.1 (at line 130) in *The Comedy of Errors*. Christopher Sly may disappear after the Induction of *The Taming of the Shrew* in order to play his counterpart Petruchio (who does not enter until 1.2), and therefore is not able to appear again at the play's end. The roles of Mowbray and Gaunt are freed by act 2 of *Richard II* so as to reappear in new dress as new personations. Indeed, York calls Richard "plume-plucked" (4.1.99); when he reappears (at 4.1.152) he has been offstage some 269 lines, more than time to remove his royal garments. In The *Merchant of Venice*, Shakespeare not only inserts a scene among Lancelot, Jessica, and Lorenzo (3.5) before Portia and Nerissa must reappear disguised as Doctor Balthazar and his clerk in 4.1, but also manages to delay their entrance in that scene until line 117 (for Nerissa) and line 161 (for Portia), leaving them considerable time to don new robes; and he begins act 5 with Lorenzo and Jessica (5.1.1–88) so as to give them time to change back to their earlier costumes. Hamlet bids the travelling players to "Go make you ready" for performing *The Murder of Gonzago* at 3.2.40, but then confers with Horatio, observes the royal progress into the play, and banters with Ophelia, giving the players time to prepare for their re-entrance at 3.2.122 for the dumb show. Rosalind and Celia exit in *As You Like It* at 5.4.25 and there follows a speech by Touchstone on the seven degrees of quarrelling before Rosalind and Celia need to re-enter dressed for their weddings at 5.4.96, and then ceremoniously preceded by Hymen, who may improvise if they are not yet ready. The first scene of *King Lear* shows extraordinary orchestration: Kent exits first because he will be the first to reappear in a different guise (1.4) while France leaves shortly after – MacIntyre thinks to reappear doubled as Edgar.[19] The most complicated changes for Macbeth, from battlefield armor to royal robes in act 1, and later from travelling gear to informal royal robes in acts 4 and 5, are separated by Lady Macbeth's soliloquy and by the long scene in England between Macduff and Malcolm respectively. *Coriolanus* relies heavily on changes in costumes, transforming citizens into senators and distinguishing Romans from Volscians. But where most characters have two costumes, Coriolanus' story is made more prominent by his five costume changes. Leontes and Hermione appear in informal costumes in the first two acts of *The Winter's Tale*, but when they put on their crowns for the trial scene (3.2) their sudden change of appearance underscores Leontes' tyranny and Hermione's suffering. Polixenes' plan to observe Florizel disguised – "I fear the angle that plucks our son thither," he tells Camillo; "we will, not appearing what we are, have some question of the shepherd" (4.2.39–42) – is followed by an entire scene with Autolycus and the clown (4.3) in which he can prepare for his eavesdropping (4.4.54).

MacIntyre contends that "As well as any play of its time, *Romeo and Juliet* demonstrates how costume conventions might be squared with realistic social decorum and as much economy as possible." There are not many costume changes for some characters, such as Mercutio, Tybalt, and Romeo, who wear masks at the ball by holding them over their faces; or for other dancers who were probably gatherers who have finished taking in money (the ball is delayed until 1.5). The Nurse and Friar likely never change costumes either. However, others do:

> After the balcony scene Juliet is off for two long scenes before her reentry in Act II. The senior Capulets (and all the players of minor roles) are likewise absent until after Mercutio's and Tybalt's deaths in the first scene of Act III. These absences give the Capulets time enough to resume their "work day" costumes. But during the later scenes of Act III and throughout Act IV, the Capulets are onstage a great deal, with only brief absences. Though they might be expected to put on festive clothing for Juliet's wedding to Paris, Capulet's embarrassment when Paris arrives so early in the morning suggests that they are still in their "workday" apparel. When they enter Juliet's chamber expecting to lead her to church, they carry, as tokens of festivity, "bridal flowers" and "*rosemary*" (used at both weddings and funerals) which they cast upon her "corpse" before closing the curtains of her bed. But it is unlikely that they have made any other changes in their appearance,

reinforcing, in their informality, the failure of the wedding to take place. MacIntyre also conjectures the way in which *A Midsummer Night's Dream* works a small cast through doubling and costuming:

> With no disguises and no changes of status or inward state, the reasons for costume change . . . are confined to the doubling of parts between Athenians and fairy characters, to the decorum of best apparel for the wedding feast in Act V, and, for their play, the appareling of the mechanicals. Most of the doubling among the twenty-two speaking parts is straightforward. The players of the four lovers and Bottom double with no one. Philostrate and Puck (each a master of revels in his world) were likely played by one man, and the elderly Egeus could double the elderly Peter Quince; the five mechanicals (Bottom excluded) match five speaking parts for minor fairies. Costume change with the roles of the lovers probably consisted of cloaks; in the woodland, boots may have been added to the Athenian apparel, and for Hippolyta and Theseus something suitable for a hunt at dawn over their Athenian costumes.

As for *All is True*, MacIntyre sees the old form of the mask performed at Wolsey's feast (1.4) while Katherine's vision (4.2) represents the new form, suggesting the progress of history; this is reinforced by parallel processions – those to Queen Katherine's trial (2.4), Anne Boleyn's coronation (4.1), and the christening of Princess Elizabeth (5.4) – that take us through part of the chronology of Henry VIII's reign.[20]

Properties

Identification was established for Shakespeare's players, as Dessen has noted, not only by costumes but by properties. Often they were conventional enough: Lawrence Danson reminds us that *A Warning for Fair Women*, played by the Lord Chamberlain's Men in 1599 at the Globe, featured an argument among History, carrying a drum and martial banner, Tragedy with a knife, and Comedy with a fiddle.[21] While changes in costumes were fairly frequent, following the fashions adopted by various social classes, properties remain comparably stable as signifiers: crowns and scepters indicated royalty; axes were carried by executioners; tradesmen carried tools; peddlers, packs of goods: Henslowe's inventory lists 140 large and small properties, but many were standard – weapons,

Item, one scarlet cloak faced with green velvet and silver lace ... £3
Item, one scarlet cloak caped with blue velvet and with gold lace ... £4 10s
Item, *Charlemagne's* cloak with fur ... £1 6s 8d
Item, a Spanish cape cloak ... £1 6s 8d
Item, a short cloak with bugle ... 10s
Item, one orange tawney velvet pee with [g]old lace ... 20s
Item, one black velvet pee with gold lace and blue satin sleeves ... £3 10s
Item, one green satin doublet ... 15s
Item, one white satin doublet ... 40s
Item, one white satin suit, hose and doublet ... 40s
Item, one antic coat ... 10s
Item, a red scaffler ...
Item, a pair of old purple velvet hose, laced ... 15s
Item, a pair of embroidered paned hose scaled with red velvet ... 15s
Item, a pair of embroidered paned hose scaled with murrey satin ... 30s
Item, a pair of embroidered paned hose scaled with black taffeta ... 13s 4d

Item, a pair of silver paned hose scaled with yellow damask . . . 20s
Item, a pair of gold paned hose scaled with peach-coloured velvet . . . 35s
Item, a woman's gown of cloth of gold . . . 50s
Item, a hermit's gray gown
Item, a parasite's suit for a boy
Item, a clown's suit
Item, six beards *Item*, a white hair and cap, two yellow hairs . . . 13s 4d
Item, two head-tires (*Item*, two rebatos. *Item*, two hairs) . . . 6s 8d
Item, waggon, and waggon cloth . . . £4
Item, two rebatos . . . 23s 4d
Item, two periwigs . . . 6s
Item, a trunk . . . 6s
Item, *Saul and David. Charlemagne* . . . £4
Item, a hair and beard for *Charlemagne* and *Saul and David* . . . 10s

An Elizabethan theatrical stock list from a manuscript (Thr. 276) in the Harvard College Library, transcribed by G. Blakemore Evans.

Reprinted from *Elizabethan–Jacobean Drama: A New Mermaid Background Book*, ed. G. Blakemore Evans, (London, A. & C. Black Ltd, 1987), p. 76.

books, candles, lanterns, jewelry – while others were clearly meant for individual characters in particular but popular plays, such as Neptune's fork, Mercury's wings, Mahomet's head, a frame for *Black Joan*, a cauldron for *The Jew*. Many of the properties were what Frances Teague has called objects with "dislocated function" – that is, weapons that do not harm, letters that may be blank, cards or dice played without anyone winning or losing, lanterns or torches lit when no light is needed.[22]

The primary, unavoidable properties, in a sense, were the physical features of the stage itself: the area over the stage which could be used for scenes of long perspective, eavesdropping, or solitude; the stage posts which could act as a place of refuge or hiding or as shelter, or as posts to

Item, one rock, one cage, one tomb, one Hell mouth.
Item, one tomb of Guido, one tomb of Dido, one bedstead.
Item, eight lances, one pair of stairs for *Phaëton*.
Item, two steeples and one chime of bells and one beacon.
Item, one heckfer [i.e. heifer] for the play of *Phaëton*, the limbs dead.
Item, one globe and one golden sceptre; three clubs.

Item, two marchpanes and the city of Rome.

Item, one golden fleece; two rackets; one bay tree.

Item, one wooden hatchet; one leather hatchet.

Item, one wooden canopy; old Mahomet's head.

Item, one lion skin; one bear's skin; and Phaëton's limbs, and Phaëton['s] charet [i.e. chariot]; and Argus' head.

Item, Neptune['s] fork and garland.

Item, one croser's staff [i.e. cross-staff or bishop's crosier]; Kent's wooden leg.

Item, Iras's head and rainbow; one little altar.

Item, eight vizards; Tamburlaine['s] bridal; one wooden mattock.

Item, Cupid's bow and quiver; the cloth of the Sun and Moon.

Item, one boar's head and Cerberus' three heads.

Item, one caduceus; two moss banks and one snake.

Item, two fans of feathers; Belin Dun's stable; one tree of golden apples; Tantalus' tree; nine iron targets [i.e. light round shields].

Item, one copper target and seventeen foils.

Item, four wooden targets; one greave armour [i.e. armour for the legs].

Item, one sign for Mother Redcap; one buckler [i.e. small round shield].

Item, Mercury's wings; Tasso['s] picture; one helmet with a dragon; one shield with three lions; one elm bowl.

Item, a chayne [i.e. chain?] of dragons [i.e. snakes?]; one gilt spear.

Item, two coffins; one bull's head; and one vylter [i.e. philtre? or vulture?].

Item, three timbrels; one dragon in *Faustus*.

Item, one lion; two lion heads; one great horse with his legs; one sackbut.

Item, one wheel and frame in the *Siege of London*.

Item, one pair of rough gloves.

Item, one Pope's mitre.

Item, three imperial crowns; one plain crown.

Item, one ghost's crown; one crown with a sun.

Item, one frame for the heading in *Black Joan*.

Item, one black dog.

Item, one cauldron for *The Jew*.

Philip Henslowe's inventory of properties belonging to the Lord Admiral's Men made on March 10, 1598.

Reprinted from Evans, *Elizabethan–Jacobean Drama*, pp. 76–7.

which players might be bound for torture or punishment. The creaking winch above the canopy or roof of the stage could slowly lower Juno in *The Tempest* or Jupiter in *Cymbeline* – "*Jupiter descends in Thunder and Lightning, sitting uppon an Eagle. Hee throws a thunderbolt*" – doubtless a firecracker, for Sicilius subsequently remarks, "He came in thunder. His celestial breath Was sulphurous to smell" (5.5.208–9).[23] There was not only a sick chair, but, far more imposing, a throne or chair of state, often with an accompanying dais used at court, at the trial by combat in *Richard II* (1.1, 1.3), and in senate rooms (*Othello*, 1.1): the throne Lear enjoys in 1.1 might reappear, empty, in 5.3. Beds are crucial to *Romeo and Juliet*, to *Richard II* (for Old Gaunt), to *2 Henry IV*, to *Othello*. Bernard Beckerman notes chairs, counting 22 instances where characters are seated in Shakespeare's plays, as well as the simple joint-stool used by Lear when he substitutes it for Goneril in his arraignment of her on the heath (3.6), by Banquo at the coronation banquet in *Macbeth* (3.4), and by Volumnia and Virgilia as they sit sewing in *Coriolanus* (1.3). Tables are used in the Boar's Head tavern, for spreading out a map in *1 Henry IV*, and for Miranda and Ferdinand to play chess in *The Tempest*.[24] Some are used less frequently, like the chariot and ladder in *Titus Andronicus* (although the ladder was probably reused to scale the walls of Harfleur in *Henry V*).

There were smaller, hand-held properties, too. Jewels, letters, and swords are crucial to *Twelfth Night* – as is Malvolio's chain of office. Battle-axes and shields and bucklers were used in battle in *Cymbeline* as well as the history plays; the broadsword or wide cutting-sword is probably what Hal, Douglas, and Hotspur use in *1 Henry IV* and Macbeth and Macduff employ in *Macbeth*; this was applied in long sweeps, so that Pistol's reference to its point (*Henry V*, 4.4.9) suggests he is inexperienced. Toward the end of the sixteenth century, in the 1580s, Italians opened fencing-schools in London and the rapier began to replace the broadsword; this made fighting more personal and combat much closer; it is what Hamlet and Laertes use at the end of *Hamlet*, increasing the tension and the danger, underpinning the force of their convictions. Pikes or long staffs are what Edgar and Oswald use in battle in *Lear*, and what Posthumus, Iachimo, Belarius, and the two boys use against the Romans in *Cymbeline*.[25] Bladders or sponges with vinegar or pig's blood were held in the armpit and squeezed to counterfeit human blood when used in battle, although in less violent scenes, such as the blood ritual in *Julius Caesar* (with the conspirators, 3.1; in the forum, 3.2), costumes were probably rolled up so as not to stain them before the next performance for which they were employed.

Property	Plays	Scenes	Method of Introduction
Tables	Othello	I, iii	probably discovered
	Pericles	II, iii	no indication
	Antony and Cleopatra	II, vii	brought on
	Antony and Cleopatra	I, ii	brought on
	Timon	I, ii	brought on
	Timon	III, vi	brought on
	Macbeth	III, iv	probably brought on
	As You Like It	II, v	probably brought on
	Hamlet	V, ii	brought on
	Macbeth	V, i	use uncertain
	Julius Caesar	IV, iii	use uncertain
Seats	Antony and Cleopatra	II, vii	brought on (stool)
	Coriolanus	II, ii	brought on (stool)
	Othello	V, ii	brought on
	King Lear	IV, vii	brought on
	Julius Caesar	III, i	probably brought on
	Hamlet	I, i	probably brought on
	Measure for Measure	V, i	probably brought on
	All's Well	II, i	probably brought on
	Pericles	V, i	probably brought on
	Pericles	V, i	probably discovered
	Antony and Cleopatra	III, x	probably brought on
	Coriolanus	I, iii	probably brought on
	Hamlet	III, iv	no indication
	King Lear	III, vi	no indication
	Julius Caesar	IV, iii	no indication
	Pericles	I, ii	no indication
	All's Well	II, iii	no indication
	Coriolanus	V, iii	no indication
	Antony and Cleopatra	II, ii	no indication
	Macbeth	III, iv	probably discovered
	Hamlet	III, ii	no indication
	King Lear	III, vii	no indication
Beds	Antony and Cleopatra	V, ii	taken off
	Pericles	III, i	probably discovered
	Othello	V, ii	probably discovered
	Julius Caesar	IV, iii	no indication (cushions)

Property	Plays	Scenes	Method of Introduction
	King Lear	III, vii	probably discovered (cushions)
	Pericles	V, i	discovered
Scaffold	Antony and Cleopatra	IV, xvi	probably brought on
	Julius Caesar	III, ii	brought on
	Troilus and Cressida	I, ii	probably brought on
Tombs	Timon	V, iii	no indication
	Pericles	IV, iv	no indication
Tents	Julius Caesar	IV, ii	use uncertain
	All's Well	III, vi	use uncertain
	Troilus and Cressida	I, iii	use uncertain
Trees,	As You Like It	III, ii	use uncertain
Rocks,	All's Well	IV, i	use uncertain
etc.	As You Like It	II, v	use uncertain
	King Lear	V, ii	use uncertain
	Antony and Cleopatra	IV, xiii	use uncertain
	Timon	IV, iii	use uncertain
	Twelfth Night	II, v	no indication
	Hamlet	III, ii	no indication
Straw	King Lear	III, iv	discovered
	Julius Caesar	V, v	no indication
	Julius Caesar	V, iii	use uncertain
	Merry Wives of Windsor	V, vi	use uncertain
Statue	Julius Caesar	III, i	use uncertain
Desk	Merry Wives of Windsor	I, iv	use uncertain
Stocks	King Lear	II, ii	brought on
Cauldron	Macbeth	IV, i	taken off
Chest	Pericles	III, ii	brought on
Corpses	Pericles	I, i	probably discovered

Total number of properties..65
Less properties whose use is uncertain........................15
Total number of properties used...............................50

Properties brought on......................................12 24%
Properties probably brought on........................11 22% } 50%
Properties taken off...2   4%

Equipment

Properties discovered...2 4% ⎫
Properties probably discovered.........................7 14% ⎬ 18%
Properties for whom method of introduction
  is not indicated...16 32%

Properties required by texts for the Globe.

Reprinted from Bernard Beckerman, *Shakespeare at the Globe* (New York: The Macmillan Company / Simon & Schuster Inc, 1962), pp. 221–2.

Large cups or "stoups" (II.iii.14)
  for wine   I.iii. and II.iii.
Pipe and tabor for Feste   (I.v.) and III.i.
Ring (presumably not the
  Lucrece seal-ring)   I.v. and II.ii.
Veil for Olivia   I.v.
(? Cithern) for Feste   II.iii. and V.i.
Chain of office for Malvolio as steward   II.iii. and passim.
Purses (for Orsino, Viola, and Antonio)   II.iv., III.i., III.iii.
                                              and V.i.
Jewel for Orsino to give to Viola to give
  to Olivia   II.iv.
Sealed letter thrown in Malvolio's path   II.v.
Written challenge (brought on by
  Sir Andrew)   III.iv.
Jewel containing Olivia's portrait   III.iv.
Dagger for Sebastian   IV.i.
Gown and beard to disguise Feste   IV.ii.
Letter (written by Malvolio)   V.i.
Swords
(Yellow stockings and cross-garters would be the responsibility of
  the tireman.)

A listing of properties for *Twelfth Night*.

Reprinted from Peter Thomson, *Shakespeare's Theatre* (London, Routledge and Kegan Paul, 1992), p. 95.

Another hand-held prop was the mirror, most notably used in the deposition scene in *Richard II*:

121

Give me that glass, and therein will I read. . . .
No deeper wrinkles yet? Hath sorrow struck
So many blows upon this face of mine
And made no deeper wounds? O flatt'ring glass,
Like to my followers in prosperity,
Thou dost beguile me! . . .
    there it is, cracked in an hundred shivers.
Mark, silent King, the moral of this sport:
How soon my sorrow hath destroyed my face.
(4.1.266–81)

Shakespeare may be anticipating Hamlet's comment that players "hold as 'twere the mirror up to nature" (3.2.20), reflecting what is, but the poetic and imaginative Richard may also be referring back to the writer and dramatist George Gascoigne's sense of a glass (as opposed to a steel) mirror which shows the viewer just what the viewer wanted to see, or back further yet to the Catholic poet John Skelton's "Phylyp Sparowe" and the earlier understanding of the mirror as the body's soul. But the theatrical Richard will also make much of surrendering his crown, "the hollow crown That rounds the mortal temples of a king [where] Keeps Death his court" (3.2.156–8). It is the same "troublesome bedfellow . . . polished perturbation, golden care" that Prince Hal discovers left behind on his father's bed (*2 Henry IV*, 4.3.153–4). (Both look forward to the imperial crown Macbeth will usurp.) Even the simplest properties need to be watched carefully. Katherine Duncan-Jones has suggested that the "happy dagger" which Juliet finds appropriate as a means to end her life and join Romeo in act 5 is probably not taken from the dying Romeo but is her own weapon with which she prepares herself, one she has earlier shown to Friar Laurence:

And with this knife I'll help it presently.
God joined my heart and Romeo's, thou our hands,
And ere this hand, by thee to Romeo's sealed,
Shall be the label to another deed . . .
'Twixt my extremes and me this bloody knife
Shall play the umpire, arbitrating that
Which the commission of thy years and art
Could to no issue of true honor bring.
(4.1.54–65)

That she carries a knife might well startle the playgoers at the Globe, but they would not be allowed to forget: in 4.2, about to take the potion, she

122

draws it forth again: "Lie thou there" (22). It is this single property that allows us to realize that Juliet is prepared to die long before she awakens to find the dying Romeo, and then dies at her own hand, with her own weapon, not his.

Hamlet holds two properties – a book which has been thought to be Timothy Bright's *Treatise of Melancholy* of 1586, and Yorick's skull, another occasion for melancholy and thoughts of death (3.1.58–90, 5.1.170). Both are held at moments of considerable change in the prince: having learned that "Alexander died, Alexander was buried, Alexander returneth into dust, the dust is earth, of earth we make loam, and why of that loam whereto he was converted might they not stop a beer-barrel?" (5.1.191–5), he is enabled to leap into Yorick's grave, now become Ophelia's (5.1.242); the Reformation philosophy he was learning in Luther's Wittenberg prepares him to accept God's providence whatever it might be (5.2.157–60). Out of tune with the other players onstage around him, he thus moves toward the condition of Ophelia, if only temporarily: that of acknowledging disharmony in the world, the awful and inexplicable. Dessen has thought of this, too:

> Consider Ophelia's lute. . . . the first or "bad" quarto calls for Ophelia's entrance *"playing on a Lute, and her hair down singing."* . . . the presence of a musical instrument can add to a spectator's sense of harmony violated (as signaled also by Ophelia's disheveled hair or by her terms earlier: "sweet bells jangled, out of time and harsh" (3.1.158).[26]

In *Othello* it is a matter of a handkerchief, a prop representing a luxury article of fashion in Shakespeare's culture, related to such other personal items as gloves and fans, used as an object for individual portraits and, quite commonly, as a marriage accessory or wedding gift. This "trifle" (5.2.235), "Spotted with strawberries" (3.3.440), has "magic in the web of it" (3.4.68), blown out of all proportion by the obsession of Othello with his wife's infideilty and so, strikingly incommensurate with the meaning he projects on it, a way Shakespeare has of personating his fits of madness and jealousy. There is also the property head – of Suffolk in *2 Henry VI*, of Lord Saye and Jack Cade; and then, much later, of Macbeth proudly held out to the new King Malcolm by a loyal Macduff, about to announce his coronation: "Hail, King, for so thou art. Behold where stands Th'usurper's cursed head. The time is free" (5.11.20–1).

One of Portia's train sings out in *The Merchant of Venice* that hopes and realities are "With gazing fed" (3.2.68), that the words outside the three caskets collate with the images inside them, the auditory with the spectacle, and Portia reinforces the commitment she makes to Bassanio with a pledge of rings, when he chooses the right casket, her own bond (3.2.171–4). It links her more to Shylock than she ever knows, although her literal treatment of his bond with Antonio matches the literal treatment she puts on her bond with Bassanio (4.1.319–27, 5.1.198–205). The two plots, never far apart in the play, come together soundly at the end. At the same time, Shakespeare was writing *Richard II* with the use of properties to marry words and things: Richard's invitation to Aumerle and Scrope – "Let's talk of graves, of worms and epitaphs" (3.2.141) – is realized with the property that ends the play: "*Exeunt [with the coffin]*" (5.6.52). The final powerful conveyance of meaning in *Richard II* lies not in poetry – the king of poetry is dead – but in a property from the inventory of the Lord Chamberlain's Men in the tiring room of the playhouse.

Conclusion

Twelfth Night, like other of Shakespeare's plays, utilizes the wardrobe and properties kept in the tiring room at the Globe. Costumes, as we have seen, align Viola and Sebastian as twins whether or not they actually are similar in appearance, and so permits the wonderfully comic scene of resolution at the play's end: "One face, one voice, one habit, and two persons, A natural perspective, that is and is not" (5.1.208–9); "Most wonderful!" (5.1.218). But the lines are richly suggestive elsewhere, too: when Viola suggests to the captain that she wishes to dress in his clothes – "Conceal me what I am, and be my aid For such disguise as haply shall become The form of my intent" (1.2.49–51) – she makes him complicit. *Disguising* was a particular word in Shakespeare's time – it was a specific form of entertainment by masking – as it was the chief activity of Twelfth Night ceremonies on January 6, celebrating the Epiphany and the end of the Christmas season when everyone tried on different "guises," pretending to be someone else. If Viola first announces such an intention, it is a speech that reflects backwards to Orsino's first appearance as an artificially lovesick man – "If music be the food of love, play on, Give me excess of it that, surfeiting, The appetite may sicken and so die" (1.1.1–3). The line equally looks forward to Olivia's disguise of excessive (and prolonged) mourning by dressing, veiled, in black: "The element itself till seven years' heat Shall not behold her face at ample view" (1.1.25–6). This is a play in which everyone is, in some sense, disguising himself (or herself): Sir Toby Belch is a landless knight sponging off Olivia but acting as if he still had the authority of a landed knight; Maria is withholding the fact that she leaves her mistress to join the revelers to win Sir Toby for her husband; while Sir Andrew, a knight who does have land and money still, is being milked by Sir Toby on the false grounds that Toby will win for him Olivia's hand in marriage. Sir Andrew's dreams are echoed in Malvolio's desire quite explicitly, yet reflect on Cesario's desire for Orsino and Olivia's desire for Cesario (not to mention Antonio's desire for Sebastian). The costumes of the Lord Chamberlain's–King's Men are what allowed such a play of disguisings to be written and performed.

But the play is also a study *in* disguising: the characters need to hide their secret feelings (in the cases of Cesario and Malvolio) because they seem to cross lines of gender and class. Their dreams survive because of the disguise, and the improbability of its long-time extension, like the impossibility of Twelfth Night continuing, is what gives to the play its psychological and dramatic edge. Like the mistaken impression deliberately given to Sir Andrew and like the revelry of midnight in 2.3, such conditions cannot last. The enemy is time. Yet in the fleeting passage of time when dreams are dreamt, life and its values are measured out. Malvolio's comeuppance anticipates Sir Toby's; the excorism of Malvolio only makes literal the exorcism to a new state of being – a liberty freed of disguise – that Viola, Olivia, Orsino, and Maria are about to enjoy. The central portion of the play is at midnight – that cusp between disguise and exposure, fantasy and reality – which all of us at one time or another experience. And disguise is signalled to us through costumes.

Disguises wear thin when Cesario and Sir Andrew are told to fight a duel to determine who shall have the hand of Olivia in marriage. Until then, properties have reinforced disguises: the lute has allowed Orsino to extend his lovesickness through mournful songs; Olivia's ring is employed to lure Cesario's return (1.5); Maria writes a letter to trick Malvolio – such properties embed the themes of love and the comic mode as they extend disguising and role-playing. But they also acknowledge excess, as the useless swords in the hands of Sir Andrew and Cesario do. Feste's costume, as a clown, indicates his ability to see more deeply, but he betrays this costume with that of Sir Topas, in his disguise as a curate, and becomes excessive himself as the agent for Malvolio's cure – what Malvolio tells Olivia is a "Notorious wrong" (5.1.318). Those who escape in the revelry of Twelfth Night – leaning heavily here on costumes and on properties – must live to see the dawn of the workaday world of reality. The result is bittersweet as Feste recognizes in his final song, the play's final lines: "For the rain it raineth every day" (5.1.379, 383, 387, 391).

5

Reactions

The daily abuse of Stage Plays is such an offence to the godly, and so great a hindrance to the gospel, as the papists do exceedingly rejoice at the blemish thereof, and not without cause. For every day in the week the players' bills are set up in sundry places of the City, some in the name of Her Majesty's men, some the Earl of Leicester's, some the Earl of Oxford's, the Lord Admiral's and divers others...The playhouses are pestered when churches are naked ...It is a woeful sight to see two hundred proud players get in their silks, where five hundred poor people starve in the streets.... Now, me thinks, I see your honour smile, and say to yourself, these things are fitter for the pulpit than a soldier's pen: but God (who searches the heart and [kidneys]) knoweth that I write not hypocritically, but from the very sorrow of my soul.

> Letter of an anonymous army officer to Sir Francis
> Walsingham, secretary to Elizabeth I, January 25, 1587

Shakespeare often wrote his plays under adverse conditions, despite their popularity, and always under the continuing surveillance prompted by morally outraged preachers, the opposition of the lord mayor and aldermen of London, the regulations of the Privy Council, even the potential censorship of the Master of the Revels. The City fathers were largely concerned with unrest – they frequently complained that the crowds drawn to plays were likely to be disruptive and even riotous and that such congestion brought chance of the plague, which they were certain was spread by human contact – and it is clear that they were concerned

126

about matters of governance. Since the city was ruled by a lord mayor and twelve aldermen drawn from the city guilds, there was also the unspoken concern that the players, who were not allied to any guild, somehow escaped their jurisdiction and might even set up an alternative means of commerce. Their protests began with the introduction of public playing early in the reign of Elizabeth I. On March 2, 1574, the lord mayor and aldermen wrote to the lord chamberlain objecting to the application of "one Holmes...that he might have the appointment of places for plays and interludes within this city"; while "it may please your Lord to retain undoubted assurance of our readiness to gratify, in any thing that we reasonably may, any person whom your Lord shall favor and recommend," it was quite clear to Mayor John Rivers and his associates that this was not true of the present instance. So there were other more significant issues:

> this case is such, and so near touching the governance of this city in one of the greatest matters thereof, namely the assemblies of multitudes of the Queen's people, and regard to be had to sundry inconveniences, whereof the peril is continually, upon every occasion, to be foreseen by the rulers of this city, that we cannot, with our duties, beside the precedent far extending to the heart of our liberties, well assent that the said appointment of places be committed to any private person.[1]

Thus emboldened, on December 6 of that year, Sir James Hawes, now the lord mayor, after a petition to play from the Queen's Men in November, issued an Act of Common Council that adds anticipated consequences in graphic detail:

> Whereas heretofore sundry great disorders and inconveniences have been found to ensue to the city by the inordinate haunting of great multitudes of people, specially youth...occasion of frays and quarrels, evil practices of incontinency in great inns, having chambers and secret places adjoining to their open stages and galleries, inveigling and alluring of maids, specially orphans and good citizens' children under age, to privy and unmeet contracts, the publishing of unchaste, uncomely, and unshamefast speeches and doings...unthrifty waste of the money of the poor..., sundry robberies by picking and cutting of purses, [and] uttering of sundry popular busy and seditious matters.

Such "corruptions could result in sundry slaughters and mayhemings of the Queen's subjects."[2] The Act attempted to regulate plays outside the city walls in the liberties and ordered fourteen days' imprisonment for all those uttering words of unchastity or sedition, as well as a fine of £5 for each offense. In 1583 the lord mayor wrote Francis Walsingham urging him to restrain playing in the liberties because they attracted base people infected with running sores. But every lord mayor in the 1570s and 1580s was writing to the Privy Council asking that plays be banned from the city. In turn, the Privy Council stoutly resisted, for they wished to protect the professional playing companies so that they could perform for the queen – and it did not help the city fathers any that the lord chamberlain, who oversaw such royal performances, was a cousin of the queen.

Players first responded by escaping the lord mayor's jurisdiction, building their playhouses in the suburbs: to the north of the city in Shoreditch, to the east of the city in Stepney, to the south of the city, across the Thames, in Southwark. No playhouse was erected within the city walls, but players still managed to perform there: at St Paul's and at Blackfriars between the 1570s and 1590. They also performed in a handful of inns such as the Bel Savage, near St Paul's, or the Bull and the Cross Keys in Gracechurch Street, because they were not officially recognized as playhouses. But concession was made by the Privy Council: while they would not allow playing inside the city, they would allow two companies of professional players and those under their direct patronage and supervision, along with the supervision of the Queen's Master of the Revels, Edmund Tilney. The two companies, organized in 1594, were the Lord Chamberlain's Company, playing successively at the Theatre, the Curtain, and the Globe, and the Lord Admiral's Company, playing at the Rose.

But clearly the city fathers' minds were not put completely to rest. On July 28, 1597, they were applying for total suppression of plays again, this time advancing first the charge of sedition, appealing to statutory legislation against rogues, vagabonds, and sturdy beggars that represented masterless men. Surprisingly, the Privy Council now agreed. In a letter of the same date to the magistrates in Middlesex and Surrey, the councillors apparently reversed direction and rescinded the earlier ruling by the lord chamberlain, writing that:

> Her Majesty being informed that there are very great disorders committed in the common playhouses, both by lewd matters that are handled on the stages and by resort and confluence of bad people, hath given direction that not only no plays shall be used within London or about the City, or in any public place during this time of summer, but that also those playhouses that are erected and built only for such purposes shall be plucked down – namely the Curtain and the Theatre near to Shoreditch, or any other within that County.[3]

This has surprised some historians, left without an explanation, but there are some things we can note. The Council goes on to ban all plays "until All Hallowtide next," not indefinitely. Moreover, 1597 was a year of particularly poor harvests and bad weather and there may have been danger of riots among those protesting uneven distribution of food and high unemployment. Richard Dutton also conjectures that "They presumably intended to reinforce the bad impression which had been made shortly before by 'a lewd plaie that was plaied in one of the plaiehouses on the Bancke Side, contanynge very sedition and sclanderous matter' – *The Isle of Dogs* staged at the new Swan Theatre by Pembroke's Men."[4] On August 15, the Privy Council ordered the arrest of members of the company and their co-author, Thomas Nashe, for interrogation; there is a warrant dated October 3 that three of the company – Gabriel Spencer, Robert Shaa (or Shaw), and Ben Jonson – were released from Marshalsea Prison. On October 11, 1597, Henslowe records that "my Lord Admiral's and my Lord of Pembroke's men [began] to play at my house, 1597."[5] Apparently theaters were not plucked down, not at once, anyway, because a new and much the firmest order of the Privy Council, dated June 22, 1600, reduced playing companies to two once again, ordered one to play at the Fortune (which had replaced the Rose) and the other at the Globe (which had replaced the Theatre and Curtain). Once more the Lord Chamberlain's Company and the Lord Admiral's Company were permitted to play at their own playhouses, again under the supervision of the council and the Master of the Revels. In 1603, James ascended the throne, renamed Shakespeare's company the King's Men, and put them under royal patronage. He reinforced their professionalism as a trade and their continuing performances as a royal service. He created the post of Master of Ceremonies, with an annual fee of £200. And in 1608 the King's Men were allowed to purchase the Blackfriars within the city walls and restore it as their indoor playhouse for the winter season.

A Matter of Morality

Argument over jurisdiction, dependent on incipient riot or contagion, was not the only opposition the Lord Chamberlain's–King's Men faced. There were also frequent expressions of moral indignation and censure by preachers, by the devout, and by a growing Puritan sect. The best-known attack, and the most comprehensive, was *The Anatomy of Abuses*, which went through five editions between 1583 and 1595. It was written by Philip Stubbes, an Anglican pamphleteer whose chief concern was the self-indulgence unleashed by the growing atmosphere of commerce. He disliked excessive apparel and the cozening tricks of butchers and drapers and was deeply distressed about the condition of the poor. But he had no patience with plays, either, finding that "the arguments of tragedies is anger, wrath, immunity [from the law], cruelty, injury, incest, murder, and such like, the persons or actors are gods, goddesses, furies, fiends, hags, kings, queens, or potentates; of comedies the matter and ground is love, bawdry, cosenage [cheating], flattery, whoredom, adultery; the persons or agents, whores, queans [prostitutes], bawds, scullions, knaves, courtesans, lecherous old men, amorous young men, with such like of infinite variety." He adds that:

> you shall have them flock thither, thick and threefold, when the church of God shall be bare and empty. Do they not... renew the remembrance of heathen idolatry? ... Then, these goodly pageants being done, every mate sorts to his mate, everyone brings another homeward of their way very friendly and in their secret conclaves (covert) they play the sodomites, or worse.[6]

Some of these ideas and even some of the language are drawn from Stephen Gosson's earlier *School of Abuse* (1579) where, a disappointed player and playwright, he had turned on plays as inciting immorality and effeminacy. In *Plays Confuted in Five Actions*, the most learned treatise against plays in the time of Shakespeare, Gosson defines plays by the four Aristotelian causes taken from *Physics* 194–5: the efficient cause of plays is the devil; the material cause of plays is players, who counterfeit; the formal cause of plays is the use of dramatic convention to violate nature; and the final cause of plays is the overflow of powerful passions. To these, he adds a fifth, that of unification, showing how each of the four causes reinforces the others.

For William Rankins, writing in 1587, players were "monsters," "painted sepulchres," because while they incited interest and passion by their outer show they were nothing but "a mass of rotten bones" within – that is, in counterfeiting, players were actually no real persons at all. They merely imitated people to seduce playgoers.[7] In a letter by Samuel Cox written in January of 1590, players were too commercial; they were profiteers. He is quite willing to return to the old days when there were only three types of players: those before the king at holidays, those who performed in noblemen's houses, and the artisans who performed at certain holidays "in their town halls, or some time in churches, to make the people merry," "shoemakers, tailors, and such like." Now, however, he witnesses "rich men [who] give more to a player for a song, which he shall sing in one hour, than to their faithful servants for serving them a whole year," to "infinite numbers of poor people [who] go a begging about the streets for penury, when players and parasites wax rich by juggling and jesting."[8] Nor did such arguments cease under James I. In *Vertues Common-wealth* (1603), Henry Crosse is still making the same arguments:

> If a man will learn to be proud, fantastic, humorous, to make love, swear, swagger, and in a word closely do any villainy, for a two-penny alms he may be thoroughly taught and made a perfect good scholar. . . . And as these copper-lace gentlemen grow rich, purchase lands by adulterous plays, and not few of them usurers and extortioners, which they exhaust out of the purses of their haunters, so are they puffed up in such pride and self-love, as they envy their equals, and scorn their inferiors.[9]

William Crashaw, the father of the poet Richard Crashaw and the preacher at the Inner Temple, says more forcefully in a sermon preached at Paul's Cross, a pulpit under the direct supervision of the bishop of London, "The ungodly plays and interludes so rife in this nation: what are they but a bastard of Babylon, a daughter of error and confusion, a hellish device (the devil's own recreation to mock at holy things) by him delivered to the heathen, from them to the papists, and from them to us?"[10] The sermon was preached on February 14, 1608, just as the affluent sharers of the King's Men, Shakespeare among them, were contracting to purchase the second Blackfriars under royal patronage.

In Defense of Plays

The critics' voices were more shrill than the defenders', yet even in *The School of Abuse*, Gosson is able to say it is the abuse of the form, its ill use, rather than the form itself, that is to blame and that good plays get written and performed:

> The two prose books played at the Bel Savage, where you shall find never a word without wit, never a line without pith, never a letter placed in vain. The *Jew* and *Ptolome*, shown at the Bull, the one representing the greediness of worldly choosers, and bloody minds of usurers; the other very lively describing how seditious estates, with their own devises, false friends, with their own swords, and rebellious commons in their own snares are

overthrown, neither with amorous gesture wounding the eye nor with slovenly talk hurting the ears of the chaste hearers.[11]

In 1592, Thomas Nashe, not yet a playwright although praising the work of Robert Greene, uses the same defense of morality in *Pierce Peniless*:

> In plays, all cosenages, all cunning drifts overgilded with outward holiness, all stratagems of war, all the cankerworms that breed on the rust of peace, are most lively anatomized: they show the ill success of treason, the fall of hasty climbers, the wretched end of usurpers, the misery of civil dissension, and how just God is evermore in punishing of murder.... Whereas some petitioners of the Council against them object, they corrupt the youth of the city, and withdraw apprentices from their work, they heartily wish they might be troubled with none of their youth nor their apprentices; for some of them (I mean the ruder handicrafts servants) never come abroad, but they are in danger of undoing [losing their jobs], and as for corrupting them when they come, this is false, for no play they have encourageth any man to tumult or rebellion, but lays before such the halter [rope] and the gallows; or praiseth or approveth pride, lust, whoredom, prodigality, or drunkenness, but beats them down utterly.[12]

In counterpoint to Stubbes, the player and playwright Thomas Heywood wrote a comprehensive *Apology for Actors* published in 1612. He meant to exonerate his fellow players, in part by drawing on their classical history and legacy, ancient dignity, and the true functions they performed; and, like Gosson, he provided an insider's view:

> what English blood seeing the person of any bold Englishman presented and doth not hug his fame, and honey at his valour, ... as if the personator were the man personated, so bewitching a thing is lively and well-spirited action, that it hath power to new mould the hearts of the spectators and fashion them to the shape of any noble and notable attempt.... [Ancient philosophers] that lived (as I may say) in the childhood and infancy of the world, before it knew how to speak perfectly, thought even in those days that action was the nearest way to plant understanding in the hearts of the ignorant.
>
> Yea (but say some) you ought not to confound the habits of either sex, as to let your boys wear the attires of virgins, etc. [as forbidden in Deuteronomy]. To which I answer: the Scriptures are not always to be expounded merely according to the letter... Besides, it is not probable that plays were meant in that text, because we read not of any plays known in that time that Deuteronomy was writ, among the children of Israel.

Furthermore, "playing is an ornament to the City, which strangers of all nations, repairing hither, report of in their countries, beholding them here with some admiration: for what variety of entertainment can there be in any city of Christendom more than in London?" He provides eyewitness testimony for the moral effects of playgoing: "At Lynn, in Norfolk, the then Earl of Sussex's players acting the old 'History of Friar Francis' drove a townswoman to confess the murder of her husband in circumstances parallel to those of the play." Another, "out of the trouble of her afflicted conscience," confessed a murder she had committed years before.[13] Hamlet, it seems, was not the first or last to realize that "The play's the thing Wherein I'll catch the conscience of the King" (2.2.581–2).

Heywood's arguments are not random: he directly answers the common charges against playing and against players. As early as 1580, Anthony Munday's anti-theatrical polemic was charging that the "bewitching" Heywood denies was caused by stimulating and seducing playgoers as both spectators and auditors:

> Are not our eyes (there) carried away with the pride of vanity? Our ears abused with amorous, that is lecherous, filthy and abominable speech? Is not our tongue there employed to the blaspheming of God's holy Name; or the commendation of that is wicked? Are not our hearts through the pleasure of the flesh, the delight of the eye, and the fond motions of the mind, withdrawn from the service of the Lord and meditation of his goodness?[14]

Stock phrases combined the ear and eye: "painted shows" and "painted eloquence," "colors of rhetoric," "polished words," "filed phrases."[15] This reveals what the restless criticism of the stage does not deal with so openly (and what Sir Philip Sidney's *Defense of Poetrie* in response to Gosson's attack could not answer): that human nature could not be trusted. God-given senses could betray – could betray the heart and the mind, according to Munday. The problem with plays was that they not only showed villainy in the course of their plots; they made it attractive (given man's fallen nature): Cassius' seduction of Brutus, Iago's seduction of Othello, the effect of the sight and sound of the weird sisters and Lady Macbeth on Macbeth are all, in miniature, representations of what the critics feared. Worse yet, actors were seen as protean, as shape-shifters whose values were fluid and whose actions could be swiftly transformed. The only protection fallen man would have (or so the critics imply) is the word of God, but if people attend theaters on the Sabbath, they cannot hear the word of the Lord or see its effect on their fellow worshippers.

Proteus has something like this in mind when, in *Two Gentlemen of Verona*, he asks Valentine, "Was this the idol that you worship so?" Valentine replies, "Even she; and is she not a heavenly saint?"; "if not divine, Yet let her be a principality, Sovereign to all the creatures on the earth" (2.4.137–8, 144–6). But Proteus becomes idolatrous, too. He dismisses Julia, who is now seen as "thawed, Which like a waxen image 'gainst a fire Bears no impression of the thing it was" (2.4. 193–5). But Proteus, the image of the false lover for Shakespeare's playgoers, is repulsed by Sylvia – "I am betrothed" (4.2.104) – and in turn asks for her image:

> Madam, if your heart be so obdurate,
> Vouchsafe me yet your picture for my love,
> The picture that is hanging in your chamber.
> To that I'll speak, to that I'll sigh and weep;
> For since the substance of your perfect self
> Is else devoted, I am but a shadow,
> And to your shadow will I make true love.
> (4.2.113–19)

Proteus is Shakespeare's false lover because he betrays Julia; but he is also a false lover because he loves an image of Sylvia when he cannot love Sylvia herself, asks the disguised Julia to carry the image, and is exposed. It is as if, early in his career, Shakespeare was thinking of anti-theatrical criticism about the distrust of images.

This strategy becomes commonplace in his work. At the first balcony scene, Juliet asks Romeo to "swear by thy gracious self, Which is the god of my idolatry, And I'll believe thee" (2.1.155–6), prelude to their tragic entanglement; Claudio's eyes are deceived by Margaret when he thinks she is Hero; in the letter Polonius reads to Claudius and Gertrude, Hamlet refers to Ophelia as "my soul's idol" (2.2.100). Antonio tells Cesario of rescuing Sebastian, confusing the two; he resists arrest, telling the officer of Illyria:

> Let me speak a little. This youth that you see here
> I snatched one half out of the jaws of death,
> Relieved him with such sanctity of love,
> And to his image, which methought did promise
> Most venerable worth, did I devotion.
> (4.1.324–8):

his misplaced devotion is not likely to fool playgoers who have seen Viola disguise herself, but it will betray him, Shakespeare thus using the anti-theatrical charge to overcome it. Bottom's confusion of spectacle and sound in *A Midsummer Night's Dream*, then, is not surprising, but in his inability to report his dream, the misunderstanding and misapplication of the senses by playgoers are made farcical: "The eye of man hath not heard, the ear of man hath not seen, man's hand is not able to taste, his tongue to conceive, nor his heart to report what my dream was" (4.1.204–8).

Heywood's reference to the scriptures and his denial that it was written in a period of drama – what he has in mind is Deuteronomy 22.5: "A woman shall not wear anything that pertains to a man, nor shall a man put on a woman's garment; for whoever does these things is an abomination to the Lord your God" – is a response to the anti-theatricalists' insistence that here the Word of God itself expressly forbids playing. What is at issue is the ease with which boys can change gender, acting as women – the kind of easy slippage of Viola into Cesario, Rosalind into Ganymede, Portia into Balthazar, Imogen into Fidele – so that sexual identity was dependent on clothing and fashion. It betrays an unease among those opposing plays that men might be effeminate, as Sir Andrew Aguecheek is when he is forced to challenge Cesario to a duel (3.4) or women might seem masculine as with the weird sisters in *Macbeth*: "You should be women," Banquo observes, "And yet your beards forbid me to interpret That you are so" (1.3.43–5). Shakespeare responds to such anxieties by having the sex of his players seen and discussed; Viola, Rosalind, Portia, and Imogen all first appear as themselves and return to their initial appearances. He even flaunts this openly when Cleopatra refuses to "see Some squeaking Cleopatra boy my greatness I'th'posture of a whore" (5.2. 215–17). But the threat the anti-theatricalists address runs deeper than gender, sexuality, effeminacy, even sodomy; it also reveals the fixed social order by which Shakespeare's society regulated itself. "Acting threatened to reveal the artificial and arbitrary nature of social being," David Scott Kastan writes. "The constitutive role-playing of the theater demystifies the idealization of the social order that the ideology of degree would produce. The successful counterfeiting of social rank raises the unnerving possibility that social rank is a counterfeit."[16] The anti-theatricalists expose this anxiety when they worry, as they consistently do, over players walking about in suits of silk; dressed better than what is thought to be their station in life, what is disclosed is that they have no station in life; their station is constantly redefined by the parts they play. Doubling only exacerbates the problem, yet without it there could be no play. Shakespeare may well be responding to this in *Henry V* in the scene where King Harry, disguised in Sir Thomas Erpingham's cloak, walks unrecognized among his men, becoming one of them on the eve of

Agincourt: "I am a gentleman of a company," he tells Pistol (4.1.40). Shakespeare uses such a disguise to praise the loyalty and courage of the English troops, outnumbered as they are against the French.

The Dangers of Counterfeiting

But any counterfeiting of royalty could be seen as an act of subversion or sedition. One of Elizabeth I's first proclamations, issued on May 16, 1559, declares that no play would be permitted:

> Wherein either matters of religion or of the governance of the estate of the commonweal shall be handled, or treated, being no meet matters to be written or treated upon but by men of authority, learning and wisdom, nor to be handled before any audience, but of grave and discreet persons: All which parts of this proclamation, Her Majesty chargeth to be inviolably kept. And if any shall attempt to the contrary, Her Majesty giveth all manner of officers that have authority to see common peace kept in commandment, to arrest and imprison the parties so offending, for the space of fourteen days or more, as cause shall need. And further also until good assurance may be found and given, that they shall be of good behavior, and no more to offend in the likes.[17]

Elizabeth knew the power of staging: her coronation progression in January of that year, from the Tower of London to Westminster Abbey, was marked by little pageants along the way that asked boy players to join with her in brief scenes of her heritage, her love of peace, and her acceptance of the Protestant Bible. As the procession's recorder has it, "If a man should say well, he could not better term the city of London that time, than a stage wherein was showed the wonderful spectacle, of a noble hearted princess toward her most loving people, and the people's exceeding comfort in beholding so worthy a sovereign, and hearing so princelike a voice."[18] Playing the roles of queen and also Diana, Astraea, even Juno, Elizabeth was no stranger to performance and to playgoing. She encouraged plays at court at Christmas and masques and entertainments on her progresses through the Midlands. But "Although she drew considerable 'solace and pleasure' from the theater," Kastan comments:

> Elizabeth was quick to smell a fault. She never would permit her passions openly to be sported with or made a May-game to the beholder – unless, of course, it was her May-game. "Sometimes Kings are content in Playes and Maskes to be admonished of divers things," wrote Thomas Scott in 1622;

but this was rarely true of Elizabeth. She was often sensitive to being subjected to her subject's representations. In 1565, Guzman de Silva, the Spanish ambassador, wrote to Philip that, at a dramatic debate between Juno and Diana on the virtues of marriage and chastity, Elizabeth angrily asserted, "This is all against me." However obscure the text, Elizabeth was able to find evidence of a personal application. At an entertainment put on by Essex in 1595, there was much discussion of the meaning of his device. "The World makes many vntrue Constructions of these Speaches," wrote Rowland Whyte, but Elizabeth was sure of the proper one. Though from the description Whyte supplies, Elizabeth was not portrayed and was mentioned only flatteringly (as the source of "Vertue which made all his [Essex's] thoughts Deuine, whose Wisdom taught him all true Policy, whose Beauty and Worth, were at all Times able to make him fitt to comand armies"). Nonetheless, Whyte reports, "the Queen said, if she had thought their had bene so much said of her, she wold not haue bene their that Night, and soe went to Bed." Burghley's remark about a similar episode earlier that same year seems shrewd: "I thinke never a ladye besides her, nor a decipherer in the court, would have dissolved the figure to have found the sense as her Majestie hath done."[19]

Her knowledge and use of drama and disguisings could make her edgy about them.

Yet under her rule (and under the lord chamberlain's patronage), Shakespeare's company would perform *Richard III*, which opens with the duke of York, Richard, moving from the *locus* to the *platea* in a conspiratorial soliloquy with the playgoers:

> Now is the winter of our discontent
> Made glorious summer by this son of York [King Edward],
> And all the clouds that loured upon our house
> In the deep bosom of the ocean buried....
> He capers nimbly in a lady's chamber
> To the lascivious pleasing of a lute....
> Plots have I laid, inductions dangerous,
> By drunken prophecies, libels and dreams
> To set my brother Clarence and the King
> In deadly hate the one against the other.
> And if King Edward be as true and just
> As I am subtle false and treacherous,
> This day should Clarence closely be mewed [caged] up
> About a prophecy which says that "G"
> Of Edward's heirs the murderer shall be.
>
> (1.1.1–4, 12–13, 32–40)

It is the same duke of York who proudly asserts in *3 Henry VI*, "I can smile, and murder whiles I smile" (3.2.182) – a villain in the Elizabethan chronicles of Holinshed and the accounts of Edward Hall and Sir Thomas More, but yet an ancestor of Shakespeare's queen. Shakespeare would seem immune, and answerable to the anti-theatrical prejudice: "A substitute shines brightly as a king Until a king be by," Portia tells Nerissa on their return to Belmont (5.1.93–4), while at Shrewsbury, Douglas dispatches a number of counterfeit kings, peopling the stage with them, and then finds he is unable to tell the real king himself (*1 Henry IV*, 5.4.34–7). In his accepted personations of King John and King Henry VI, Shakespeare shows English kings inadequate to their task. Later, Hamlet will find Elsinore theatrical and present a play of a king which he has scripted himself.

Such scenes are, however, set off by others. There are the deaths of the Talbots at Bordeaux, the dying father cradling the dying son:

> Thou antic death, which laugh'st us here to scorn,
> Anon from thy insulting tyranny,
> Coupled in bonds of perpetuity,
> Two Talbots winged through the lither [yielding] sky
> In thy despite shall scape mortality.
>
> (*1 Henry VI*, 4.7.18–22)

There is the ignominious end of the rebel Jack Cade:

> Fie on ambitions; fie on myself that have a sword and yet am ready to famish. These five days have I hid me in these woods and durst not peep out, for all the country is laid for me. But now am I so hungry that if I might have a lease of my life for a thousand years, I could stay no longer. Wherefore o'er a brick wall have I climbed into this garden to see if I can eat grass or pick a sallet [salad] another while. (*2 Henry VI*, 4.9.1–7)

There is Prince Hal, anxious to tell us in confidence that he remains loyal to the court of his father, not to that of Falstaff:

> My reformation, glitt'ring o'er my fault,
> Shall show more goodly and attract more eyes
> Than that which hath no foil to set it off.
> I'll so offend to make offence a skill,
> Redeeming time when men think least I will.
>
> (*1 Henry IV*, 1.2.191–5)

On the whole, following the polemical chronicles of his time, Shake-speare's history plays uphold the monarchy inherited by Elizabeth: the long sweep of eight joined history plays, from *Richard II*, in which the Yorkist king is betrayed by the Lancastrian Bolingbroke, through the War of the Roses to the conclusion of *Richard III* and the crowning of Henry VII, Elizabeth I's grandfather, and on to her own christening in *All Is True* ("She shall be, to the happiness of England, An aged princess," Cranmer tells Henry VIII [5.4.56–7]). And what is true of the history plays runs deeply through Shakespeare's other plays. The usurpation by Henry IV, the assassination committed by Brutus and Cassius, Lear's division of the kingdom, Coriolanus' brutality – his son would tear butterflies to death with his teeth (1.3.54–61) – are brought to stabilizing judgment. The totally selfish, proud, and immoral world of *Troilus and Cressida* does not escape the cynicism and bitterness of its twin commentators, Thersites and Pandarus. Even in the comedies, Shakespeare uses the abrupt entrance of Mercade and the death of the Princess's father to bring the King of Navarre and his courtiers to an overdue, sobering sense of responsibility in *Love's Labor's Lost*.

But all the comedies assure the restoration of proper social status at their close. In her acceptance of Orsino, Cesario restores not only her rightful gender, but her proper social position. In attracting Florizel, Perdita will in due course learn she is not a shepherdess but the daughter of a King. In arranging the courtship of Ferdinand with Miranda, Prospero plans the continuation of his rule with a more suitable marriage than Claribel found in Tunis. As landed gentry, Petruchio is a proper suitor for Kate the cursed. Such marriages not only insure the Tudor state but on occasion employ the words of the Established Church. In *The Comedy of Errors*, Luciana instructs her sister Adriana to have patience with Antipholus of Ephesus, her husband, with words drawn directly from the church's Homily on Obedience:

> There's nothing situate under heaven's eye
> But hath his bound in earth, in sea, in sky.
> The beasts, the fishes, and the wingèd fowls
> Are their males' subjects and at their controls.
> Man, more divine, the master of all these,
> Lord of the wide world and wild wat'ry seas,
> Indued with intellectual sense and souls,
> Or more pre-eminence than fish and fowls,
> Are masters to their females, and their lords.
> Then let your will attend on their accords.
>   (2.1.16–25)

Unlike Bianca and the Widow, but instructing them, too, Kate makes her responsibility to Petruchio public knowledge at the end of *The Taming of the Shrew* in her conversion, by drawing on the same church homily (5.2.150–8). The Church of England runs underneath many of the plays: the Abbess leaves the Catholic church in Ephesus at the end of *Errors*; Isabella presumably leaves the convent at the close of *Measure for Measure* (and the Duke disrobes as the Friar); even Antonio requires that the alien Jew Shylock "become a Christian" (4.1.382). The other social and political aliens – Othello in Venice; Coriolanus among the Volscians – do not survive, either; the Venetian Lodovico closes Othello by referring to him as "the Moor," whose fortunes are transferred to Cassio (5.2.376–7).

The playwright's conventional beliefs are nowhere more evident than in the denouement of *Cymbeline* – the longest denouement in Shakespeare. Cymbeline learns of the death of his wife and how much she really hated him; he finds again his two lost sons, Guiderius and Arviragus, long presumed dead, and forgives Belarius for stealing them; he discovers that Fidele, page to the Roman ambassador, is his daughter Imogen; he listens to the confession of the villain Iachimo; he listens to the remorse of Posthumus and sees Imogen reunited with him; he makes friends with the Roman ambassador; and he promises peace and plenty between Rome and Britain:

> Laud we the gods,
> And let our crooked smokes climb to their nostrils
> From our blest altars. Publish we this peace
> To all our subjects. Set we forward, let
> A Roman and a British ensign wave
> Friendly together. So through Lud's town march,
> And in the temple of great Jupiter
> Our peace we'll ratify, seal it with feasts.
> Set on there. Never was a war did cease,
> Ere bloody hands were washed, with such a peace.
> (5.6.476–85)

What Cymbeline does not mention, but Shakespeare has arranged, is the succession of Cymbeline's sons to the throne so that his daughter, once thought his only heir but one who married a commoner, will not bring him into direct succession. Consciously or not, Shakespeare and the Lord Chamberlain's–King's Men performed plays that accounted for the opposition to public playing while making certain any of their works would be transferable to court presentation.

The Master of the Revels

Court presentations were arranged by the Master of the Revels. Originally the Revels office confined itself to selecting royal entertainments, in the course of their activity collecting a "great store"[20] of costumes, properties, weapons, and sets. But on December 24, 1581, in the midst of the Christmas season, a new patent of commission was issued to Edmund Tilney, the Master of the Revels, that was, virtually without change, issued to Sir George Buc in 1603 and again to Sir John Astley in 1622. Tilney was given authority to hire "as many painters, embroiderers, tailors, cappers, haberdashers, joiners, carders, glaziers, armorers, basketmakers, skinners, saddlers, wagon makers, plasterers, feathermakers, and all other property makers and cunning artificers and laborers whatsoever," all "at competent wages," but, more importantly, he was:

> to warn, command, and appoint, in all places within this our realm of England, as well within franchises and liberties as without, all and every player or players, with their playmakers, either belonging to any noble man, or otherwise bearing the name or names of using the faculty of playmakers or players of comedies, tragedies, interludes, or what other shows soever, from time to time, and at all times, to appear before him with all such plays, tragedies, comedies, or shows as they shall have in readiness, or mean to set forth; and them to present and recite before our said servant, or his sufficient deputy,...all shows, plays, players, and playmakers, together with their playing places, to order and reform, authorize and put down, as shall be thought meet or unmeet unto himself, or his said deputy in that behalf. And also...that in case if any of them, whatsoever they be, will obstinately refuse upon warning unto them given by the said Edmund, or his sufficient deputy, to accomplish and obey our commandment in this behalf, then it shall be lawful to the said Edmund, or his sufficient deputy, to attach the party or parties so offending, and him or them to commit to ward, to remain without bail or mainprise until such time as the said Edmund Tilney, or his sufficient deputy, shall think the time of his or their imprisonment to be punishment sufficient.[21]

The Master of the Revels was given absolute authority to regulate Shakespeare, the Lord Chamberlain's–King's Men, and the Globe, and he was never subject to recourse.

It is this position that Philostrate holds in *A Midsummer Night's Dream* when Theseus asks:

Come now, what masques, what dances shall we have
To wear away this long age of three hours
Between our after-supper and bed-time?
Where is our usual manager of mirth?
What revels are in hand? Is there no play
To ease the anguish of a torturing hour?

(5.1.32–8)

and the job he performs when he advises the Athenian Duke, concerning the mechanicals' "Pyramus and Thisbe":

It is not for you. I have heard it over,
And it is nothing, nothing in the world,
Unless you can find sport in their intents
Extremely stretched, and conned with cruel pain
To do you service.

(5.1.77–81)

Philostrate collects no money for his services for the mechanicals, but Henslowe records his payments to Tilney, collected by his deputy. He paid 5s a week for permission to operate his theater in the early months of 1592; by the end of the year, he was paying 6s 8d; late in the decade and early in the next, he was paying 40s and then £3 a month. He also paid out money to license each play deemed acceptable by the Revels office:

Laid out for my Lord Admiral's men as followeth, 1597

Lent unto Thomas Downton for the company to pay to the Master of the Revels for licensing of 2 books 14 shillings, abated to Downton 5 shillings and so rest . . . 9s.

Paid unto the Master of the Revels's man for the licensing of a book called the Four Kings . . . 7s.

Paid unto the Master of the Revels's man for licensing of a book called Beech's Tragedy the sum of . . . 7s.

Paid unto the Master of the Revels's man for licensing of a book called Damon and Pithias the 16 of May, 1600, the sum of . . . 7s.[22]

Because no play could be performed without the authority of Tilney or his office, Shakespeare had to write plays that would meet his approval. But that may not have been difficult; it is not altogether clear whether the

Revels office saw itself as a regulator of drama on behalf of the queen and the Privy Council or a negotiator concerning what was permissible on behalf of the players. Dutton maintains that Tilney "also emerged as a protector"[23] of the playing companies.

As for the licensing of plays, Tilney's usual process, according to Dutton, was:

> to "peruse" a script (rather than see a rehearsal), insist on any changes he felt necessary, then append his "allowance" to the corrected version, which thereafter was the "allowed copy" – the only version to be used as the basis for performance. The "allowance" was to the company that was to perform the play, and it was entered as such in the office-book, rather than to the author or as constituting an open license. It thus served as a form of copyright, which must have helped to tie the actors into this structure of control.[24]

In time, though, Tilney relaxed, allowing the companies themselves to report on the suitability of a playscript. Tilney must have relaxed the rule against playing in Lent, too; although the Privy Council renewed the restriction in 1600, 1601, and 1604, the Admiral's Men had played through 12 days of Lent in 1597, and as the Prince's Men they played at Whitehall during Lent 1605, while the King's Men played before James I during Lent in 1607.

Censorship

The minutes of the Privy Council for November 12, 1589, register letters sent to the archbishop of Canterbury, the lord mayor of London, and the Master of the Revels establishing a Commission of Censorship. The letter to Tilney's office reads, in part, that the officers or such "men of learning and judgment" are to:

> call before them the several companies of players (whose servants soever they be) and to require them, by authority hereof to deliver unto them their books, that they may consider of the matters of their comedies and traged-ies, and thereupon to strike out or reform such parts and matters as they shall find unfit and undecent to be handled in plays, both for divinity and state, commanding the said companies of players, in Her Majesty's name, that they forebear to present and play publicly any comedy or tragedy other than such as they three shall have seen and allowed, which if they shall not observe, they shall then know from their Lordships that they shall be not

only severely punished, but made [in]capable of the exercise of their profession forever hereafter.[25]

Dutton thinks little came of this, for the Commission is never heard of again,[26] but censorship is notoriously difficult to discover since its very traces are what have been eliminated. Analyzing "scattered surviving records of censorship, reprimand, and punishment of the players for offenses in their plays" led Gerald Eades Bentley to distinguish five types:

1. Critical comments on the policies or conduct of the government
2. Unfavorable presentations of *friendly* foreign powers or their sovereigns, great nobles, or subjects
3. Comment on religious controversy
4. Profanity (after 1606)
5. Personal satire of *influential* people.[27]

Shakespeare's *Richard II* seems to have fallen under the first injunction. This is the play that the Essex conspirators wished to see on the eve of their rebellion against Elizabeth I in 1601; later Elizabeth compared herself to Richard II and decried the fact that it was played some 40 times in the streets. The crux seems to be the deposition scene (4.1) and the evidence that it was censored is that it does not appear in the first three quarto editions of the play published in 1597 and again twice in 1598; it does not appear in print until the fourth quarto of 1608 and the folio of 1623. Heminges seems to have been unwilling at first to perform the play when he told the conspirators it was an old one – it was hardly old by company standards if it had been printed as recently as 1598, and then twice – but in time the company performed it anyway. The assumption has always been that the performance contained the deposition scene, but we have no clear indication that the scene was ever performed in Elizabeth's time. The play itself, which deals with what is thought to be a reasonable cause for usurpation, does not need a deposition scene to make its point, of course; and the play is a reminder that Elizabeth's ancestry included both the ineffectual Richard II and the rebellious Bolingbroke – both the houses of York and Lancaster that had married (with Henry VII and Elizabeth of York, namesake for Elizabeth I) to become the House of Tudor.

Shakespeare may well be aware of the second possibility for censorship – matter dealing with foreign powers – for his portrayals of France (*Henry VI*; *King John*; *Henry V*; *Love's Labor's Lost*; *As You Like It*; *All's Well That Ends Well*) are in the end in no way critical, while the portraits of Morocco and Aragon (Spain) in *The Merchant of Venice* are caricatures

and the portrait of the Spaniard Don Armado in *Love's Labor's Lost* is that
of a buffoon. But *The Play of Sir Thomas More*, in which Shakespeare is
thought by many to have had a hand, is another case altogether. Tilney
took strong exception to parts of it and insisted on changes. "The most
striking feature of the play," Richard Dutton writes, "is that it was written
at all: that practitioners of the theatre thought there was a realistic possibility of staging a play about Sir Thomas More, who had gone to the block
for denying (or, at least, refusing to support) Henry VIII's claim to suprem-
acy over the Pope and who was widely regarded as a Roman Catholic
martyr."[28] But in the play More is treated evenhandedly; King Henry VIII
does not appear. The poet Surrey says of More's death, "A very learned
woorthie Gentleman Seales errour with his blood" (lines 1983–4). Tilney
ignores this, but insists on altering or deleting the passage where More and
the bishop of Rochester refuse to sign the Oath, while Surrey and Shrewsbury do so (1247–75). Instead, Tilney's greater concern is the "Ill May
Day" riots, directed against foreigners then living in London, the subject of
scenes iii–vii. Tilney again crossed out the text and wrote "Leave out the
insurrection wholy & the Cause ther off & begin with Sr Tho: Moore att
the mayors sessions with a reportt afterwardes off his good service don
being Shrive [Sheriff] of London uppon a mutiny Agaynst the Lumbardes
only by A shortt reporte & nott otherwise att your own perrilles. E.
Tyllney." In connection with this, he crosses out two passages: "It is hard
when Englishmens pacience must be thus jetted on by straungers and they
dare not revendge their owne wrongs" (24–5) and "Will this geere never be
otherwise? must these wrongs be thus endured?", "Let us step in, and help
to revendge their injurie" (30–1). In another speech, in scene iii:

> My Lord of Surrey, and Sir Thomas Palmer,
> might I with pacience tempte your grave advise.
> I tell ye true, that in these daungerous times,
> I doe not like this frowning vulgare brow.
> My searching eye did never entertaine,
> a more distracted countenaunce of greefe
> then I have late observ'de
> in the displeased commons of the Cittie,
>   (316–23)

Tilney writes, "Mend it." In lines that follow, Tilney changes "Englishe"
to "man," "straunger" and "ffrenchman" to "Lombard," and orders that
"Englishe blood" and "saucie Aliens" be struck out. Adding up the
evidence, Dutton concludes that we must infer:

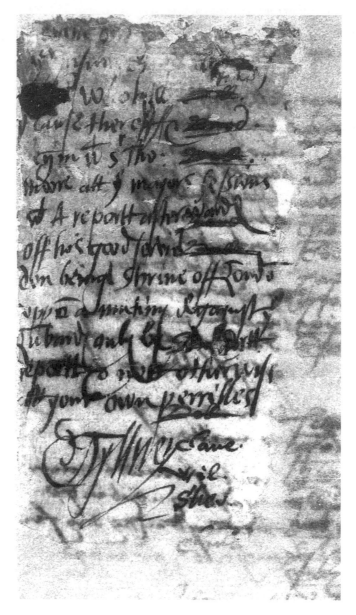

Figure 12 Tilney's orders to revise the insurrection scene in *The Play of Sir Thomas More*.

British Library, BL MS Harley 7368, front sheet of manuscript.

Tilney was concerned by the whole subject and depiction of riot, especially when it was directed at "aliens" in the name of patriotism, and particularly if the French were the target. Lombards, of whom there were doubtless far fewer in London at the time, were apparently an acceptable substitute. Reasons for such concern would not be hard to find. In June 1592 there was "a great disorder & tumult" in the Borough of Southwark, rioting led by feltmakers' apprentices, which was only subdued by the forceful intervention of Sir William Webbe, the Lord Mayor. In 1593 there were specifically anti-alien riots, when in 1595 there were extensive riots which resulted in reprisals by the authorities so savage that A. W. Pollard argued no one could even have thought of performing the opening scenes of *Sir Thomas More* after them.[29]

There are, however, no indications extant of censorship on religious grounds in Shakespeare's plays, and we have seen how he avoids this not only in the futures of the Abbess Emelia in *The Comedy of Errors* and Isabella in *Measure for Measure*, but in the quotations from a fundamental church homily in both *Shrew* and *Errors*, plays written during our only evidence of Tilney's intervention into the content of playtexts.

Profanity was another matter as well. Commonplace oaths such as "Zounds," a contraction of "God's wounds" (upon the cross), occur frequently in Shakespeare's early plays; the word comes quickly and often to Falstaff – "What, upon compulsion? Zounds, an I were at the strappado, or all the racks in the world, I would not tell you on compulsion" (*1 Henry IV*, 2.5.218–20), anticipated by Poins, "Zounds, ye fat paunch, an ye call me coward, by the Lord I'll stab thee" (2.5.151–2) – but the seriousness of such oaths seems to have been in the minds of the beholder or listener, for it does not concern the Revels office. But then, in 1606, Parliament passed "An Act to Restrain Abuses of Players" attempting to eliminate such language:

> For the preventing and avoiding of the great abuse of the holy name of God in stage plays, interludes, Maygames, shows, and such like; be it enacted by our sovereign Lord the King's majesty and by the Lords spiritual and temporal, and Commons in this present Parliament assembled and by the authority of the same, that if at any time or times, after the end of this present session of Parliament, any person or persons do or shall in any stage play, interlude, show, May-game or pageant jestingly or profanely speak or use the name of God or Christ Jesus, or of the Holy Ghost or of the Trinity, which are not to be spoken but with fear and reverence, shall forfeit for every such offense by him or them committed ten pounds, the one moiety thereof to the King's majesty, his heirs and successors, the other

moiety thereof to him, or them that will sue for the same in any court of record at Westminster, wherein no essoigne, protection, or wager of law shall be allowed.[30]

Since any playgoer could make £5 by reporting the offense to court, it may explain the oaths to Hecate (1.1.110), to Apollo (1.1.160), and to Nature (1.4.252) by Lear and the ease of oaths in the Roman plays following the passing of this statute. But there is also clear evidence of how this censorship changed Shakespeare's plays in the case of *Othello*. The 1622 quarto of the play is thought to be based on a fair copy or transcription of the play as it was performed before the king before the statute on oaths; the 1623 folio is a revised text which takes the statute into account:

	1622	1623
1.2.35	And I, God blesse the marke	And I (blesse the marke)
1.1.94	Zounds [God's wounds] sir you are robd.	Sir, y'are rob'd
2.2.91	Fore God an excellent song	Fore Heaven: an excellent song
2.2.167	Zouns, you rogue, you rascal	You rogue; you rascal
3.3.180	Zouns	What dost thou mean?
3.3.203	Good God, the souls of all	Good Heaven, the souls of all
3.4.92	Then would to God	Then would to Heaven
4.3.114	God me such usage send	Heaven me such uses send
5.2.105	O Lord, Lord, Lord.	[Line omitted]
5.2.148	O Lord, what cry is that?	Alas! what cry is that?
5.2.270	O God, O heavenly God. Zouns, hold your peace.	Oh Heaven! O heavenly Powers! Come, hold your peace.[31]

Such changes reach their climax in the descent of Jupiter in *Cymbeline* (5.5) and of Juno in *The Tempest* (4.1).

Bentley's final classification of censorship activities is that of personal satire. It might be easy to slip satire past the Revels Office with the playtext if it were the costuming and gestures in performance that made the point or if the satire was performed in an interlude or jig.

Such occasions might be lost to us, too. This seems to have been the case at the Curtain in Shoreditch, according to a letter sent to the justices of the peace in Middlesex from the Privy Council dated May 10, 1601:

> We do understand that certain players that use to recite their plays at the Curtain in Moorfields do represent upon the stage in their interludes the persons of gentlemen of good desert and quality that are yet alive under obscure manner, but yet in such sort as all the hearers may take notice of both the matter and the persons that are meant thereby. This being a thing very unfit, offensive, and contrary to such direction as have been heretofore taken that no plays should be openly showed but such as first were perused and allowed and that might minister to occasion of offense or scandal we do hereby require you that you do forthwith forbid those players to whomsoever they appertain, that do play at the Curtain in Moorfields to represent any such play and that you will examine them who made that play and to show the same unto you, and as you in your discretion shall think the same unfit to be publicly showed to forbid them from henceforth to play the same, either privately or publicly, and if upon view of the said play you shall find the subject so odious and inconvenient as is informed, we require you to take bond of the chiefest of them to answer their rash and indiscreet behavior before us.[32]

Station thus mattered: "gentlemen of good desert" and their superiors were not to be satirized, but those of lower status could – like the playwrights Thomas Dekker and Ben Jonson and others in the parodies and counter-parodies in plays of the late 1590s. Moreover, gentlemen could be played onstage if they were played favorably, a point which seems to be made by Rowland Whyte in a letter from the Strand to Sir Robert Sidney on October 26, 1599:

> Two days ago, the overthrow of *Turnholt* [Turnhout] was acted upon a stage, and all your names used that were at it; especially Sir *Fra. Veres*, and he that played that part got a beard resembling his, and a watchet Satin Doublet, with Hose trimmed with silver lace. You was also introduced, killing, slaying, and overthrowing the *Spaniards*, and honorable mention made of your service, in seconding Sir *Francis Vere*, being engaged.[33]

It is tempting to find contemporary originals for Sir Toby Belch or Sir Andrew Aguecheek (*Twelfth Night*), Osric (*Hamlet*) or Oswald (*Lear*), but the only evidence we now have indisputably is Shakespeare's satire of the deceased Sir John Oldcastle in *1 Henry IV*. We still do not know why. The play was written when Oldcastle's descendant, William Brook, the seventh Lord Cobham, was not only living but, from August 1596 to March 1597, was lord chamberlain, the patron of Shakespeare's company; and he took offense. The character's name was changed to Falstaff, although a trace of the earlier script remains in the line where Falstaff is referred to as "my old lad of the castle" (1.2.37). Perhaps it was a dare or a joke; perhaps it was a misplaced tribute, for Falstaff remains one of Shakespeare's most memorable counterfeits. There are, in addition, traces that Peto was originally named "Harvey," the name of the stepfather of the earl of Southampton, Shakespeare's patron, and Bardolph was originally "Russell," the family name of the prominent earls of Bedford. In any event, those references to actual persons were scripted well before the Privy Council letter of 1601; and, anyway, they do not remain.

Indeterminacy of final meaning in Shakespeare's plays may be a result of the possibility, if not the fact, of censorship. Janet Clare has noted that "*Richard II* depicts resistance to tyranny, while articulating passive resistance, particularly in the words of John of Gaunt" (1.2.37–41), at the same time.[34] As Roslyn Lander Knutson has recently observed, "In a political environment where an innocuous passage in one play might be taken on a Tuesday as welcome praise of an adored public figure and on a Saturday as treason, [Shakespeare and his fellow playwrights] shared the need to exercise as much control as possible over long-established protocols of pointing at topical events and persons"[35] even as they made such references continually central to their plays.

Conclusion

What does remain are constant reminders of the material conditions under which, and to which, Shakespeare wrote his plays and the players played them. In writing *Macbeth*, his only Scottish play shortly after the Scottish King James I and VI took the throne, Shakespeare must have been unusually conscious of writing a script especially subject to scrutiny. It has been argued that by making Banquo, James's ancestor, an early victim of Macbeth's tyranny, the playwright insured his work against censorship. But surely that is too simple an interpretation of the text we have, for in his silence about the witches' prophecy just after the assassination of Duncan, Banquo becomes a silent co-conspirator of the act. Nor is the portrait of Macbeth an unrelieved criticism. In the early scenes of the play, Macbeth's conscience is torn between believing the witches and denying any efforts to foster their statements, unlike the insistent promptings of his wife:

> Was the hope drunk
> Wherein you dressed yourself? Hath it slept since?
> And wakes it now to look so green and pale
> At what it did so freely? From this time
> Such I account thy love. Art thou afeard
> To be the same in thine own act and valour
> As thou art in desire? Wouldst thou have that
> Which thou esteem'st the ornament of life,
> And live a coward in thine own esteem,
> Letting "I dare not" wait upon "I would,"
> Like the poor cat i'th'adage?
>
> (1.7.35–44)

Blaming first the witches for their seditious suggestions – although it is Macbeth who makes the application, not the witches – and then deflecting blame on to Lady Macbeth, Shakespeare would seem to navigate past the dangers of censorship.

If so, he steers close to censorship once more when he develops Macbeth as an absolute ruler who brooks no opposition, for the king as absolute ruler of his people, given the divine right of rule by God, was a political principle King James was arguing in his handbook of rule, the *Basilicon Doron*, published in London and distributed widely in 1603, three years or so before Shakespeare's play. James was also known as the author of a book on the dangers of witchcraft entitled *Demonologie*, and Macbeth's analogous association with the witches might be seen to flatter James – or run the risk of seeming to condemn him, since Macbeth's belief in the witches is the play's inciting incident. King James also at first refused to practice the King's Touch as the royal cure for scrofula, again directly linking him with the Macbeth found wanting by Malcolm, who points to this practice in the English King Edward:

> A most miraculous work in this good King,
> Which often since my here-remain in England
> I have seen him do. How he solicits heaven
> Himself best knows, but strangely visited people,
> All swoll'n and ulcerous, pitiful to the eye,
> The mere despair of surgery, he cures.
>
> (4.3.148–53)

Shakespeare's strategy of warning against tyranny in a king arguing absolutism, and, perhaps, warning against belief in witchcraft at the expense of belief in the King's Touch, may be basing the play in the idea of equivocation, of "lies like truth" (5.7.42) where, paltering in a double sense, it is not, finally, ascertainable just what Shakespeare himself means to convey. Clearly, the possibilities of censorship in a king who, rather than playing a good host, turns regicide is near the surface throughout the play, and that may explain why the play is so short – perhaps a part of the text was excised – and why a play which must have struck a chord under the nation's first Scottish king's reign was not actually printed until the First Folio of 1623, near the end of James's reign and long after Shakespeare's death.

Censorship, however, was only one of the material conditions under which Shakespeare first conceived and later wrote his plays. Nearly all of the conditions we have discussed are readily apparent in *As You Like It* – or the play for all seasons – that may have opened the new Globe Theater in 1599. There a curtain at the back or perhaps a discovery space could secrete Duke Senior's banquet, ready to be seen of a sudden in 2.5 and 2.7, the exiled court gathering on the *locus* after the wrestling scene, over which Oliver presided, was held in mid-stage and Rosalind and Celia, as spectators to Orlando's success, chatted about it downstage, on the *platea*, where the groundlings could hear their informal remarks. Hymen might close the play after appearing high on the balcony, descending to the stage to welcome the wedding processional, long after Orlando had used stage pillars to pin up his poems to Rosalind. The early disappearance of Le Beau allows him to reappear as Hymen, just as Old Adam probably doubled as Old Corin, the script giving ample time for changes of costume. Playgoers could associate themselves with an exiled duke and a restored one, the courage of Orlando, the farce of Touchstone and Audrey, the exaggerated lovesickness of Silvius, and the conventional Petrarchan coolness of Phoebe to his overtures. For those playgoers who wished for a better existence, there was always the playworld of Arden; for those who wanted social advancement, there was always the personation of Audrey and her attraction to Touchstone; for those women who wanted more authority, there was always Rosalind in the guise of Ganymede, wooing and winning her lover herself. But however topsy-turvy things might seem in this romantic comedy, Rosalind and Celia return to their women's parts; Sir Oliver Martext does not wed Touchstone to Audrey after all; and the exiled duke is welcomed back to court and his dukedom is restored. The ordered society of Elizabethan England has been reordered again, and no harm done. This is not the customary way of looking at *As You Like It*, with its moments of sheer lyricism; it is not the way we often remember the powerful lines of Lear on the heath, either, or King Harry before Agincourt, or Desdemona facing the Venetian court. That Shakespeare could produce such great poetry encouraged by, within, even despite the material conditions we now know he faced, however, makes that assured achievement all the more magnificent.

Notes

Preface

1 Alfred Harbage, *As They Liked It* (New York: Macmillan, 1947), p. 3.
2 Andrew Gurr, *The Shakespearean Stage, 1574–1642* (Cambridge: Cambridge University Press, 1992), p. 122.
3 Gurr, *Shakespearean Stage*, p. 10 (text modernized).
4 E. K. Chambers, *The Elizabethan Stage*, 4 vols (Oxford: Clarendon Press, 1923), IV, 307.

Chapter 1 Stages

1 Thomas Platter, *Travels in England, 1599*, trans. Clare Williams (1937), pp. 166–7, rep. *Elizabethan–Jacobean Drama: A New Mermaids Background Book*, ed. G. Blakemore Evans (London: A. & C. Black, 1987), pp. 56–7.
2 Glynne Wickham, Herbert Berry, and William Ingram, eds, *English Professional Theatre, 1530–1660* (Cambridge: Cambridge University Press, 2000), p. 535.
3 Wickham, Berry, and Ingram, *English Professional Theatre*, p. 598.
4 John Orrell, *The Quest for Shakespeare's Globe* (Cambridge: Cambridge University Press, 1983).
5 Andrew Gurr, "A First Doorway into the Globe," *Shakespeare Quarterly* 41:1 (Spring 1990), 97–9.
6 Bernard Beckerman, *Shakespeare at the Globe 1599–1609* (New York: Macmillan, 1962), p. 164.
7 M. C. Bradbrook, *Elizabethan Stage Conditions: A Study of their Place in the Interpretation of Shakespeare's Plays* (Cambridge: Cambridge University Press, 1968), pp. 32–3.

8 Robert Weimann, *Author's Pen and Actor's Voice* (Cambridge: Cambridge University Press, 2000), p. 192.

9 John C. Meagher, *Shakespeare's Shakespeare: How the Plays Were Made* (New York: Continuum, 1997), p. 73. Other examples are taken from pp. 195, 74–5, 78, 76, 77, 80, 81.

10 T. S. Dorsch, "Introduction," in William Shakespeare, *The Comedy of Errors* (Cambridge: Cambridge University Press, 1988), p. 24.

11 J. L. Styan, *Perspectives on Shakespeare in Performance* (New York: Peter Lang, 2000), pp. 84–5.

12 Beckerman, *Shakespeare at the Globe*, pp. 181–2.

13 Andrew Gurr and Mariko Ichikawa, *Staging in Shakespeare's Theatres* (Oxford: Oxford University Press, 2000), p. 83. Subsequent quotations are from pp. 75, 95.

14 Alan C. Dessen, *Recovering Shakespeare's Theatrical Vocabulary* (Cambridge: Cambridge University Press, 1995), pp. 65–6. The other examples are on pp. 67–8, 78, 83–4.

15 Bruce R. Smith, *The Acoustic World of Early Modern England* (Chicago: University of Chicago Press, 1999), p. 209.

16 Nearly all of these examples of song and dance are taken from Styan, *Perspectives*, pp. 130–41.

Chapter 2 Players

1 E. K. Chambers, *The Elizabethan Stage* (Oxford: Clarendon Press, 1923), IV, 352.

2 S. P. Cerasano, "The Chamberlain's–King's Men," in *A Companion to Shakespeare*, ed. David Scott Kastan (Oxford: Blackwell, 1999), p. 331.

3 John Southworth, *Fools and Jesters at the English Court* (Phoenix Mill: Sutton, 1998), p. 135. Many of my earlier illustrations of Kempe and Armin are drawn from Southworth, pp. 130–5.

4 Cerasano, "Chamberlain's – King's Men," pp. 337–8.

5 Gerald Eades Bentley, *The Profession of Player in Shakespeare's Time 1590–1642* (Princeton: Princeton University Press, 1984), pp. 147–8.

6 Bentley, *Player*, p. 152.

7 Tiffany Stern, *Rehearsal from Shakespeare to Sheridan* (Oxford: Oxford University Press, 2000).

8 Transcribed by James Greenstreet in *New Shakespeare Transactions*, 1887–92, part 3, p. 276, and quoted by Bentley in *Player*, pp. 120–1.

9 Roslyn Lander Knutson, "Shakespeare's Repertory," in *Companion to Shakespeare*, ed. Kastan, p. 347.

10 Knutson, "Shakespeare's Repertory," p. 347.

11 Glynne Wickham, Herbert Berry, and William Ingram, eds, *English Professional Theatre, 1530–1660* (Cambridge: Cambridge University Press, 2000), p. 123.

12 This long account of the repertory of Shakespeare's company is derived directly from Knutson, "Shakespeare's Repertory," pp. 346–60, 475.

13 J. A. B. Somerset, " 'How Chances it they Travel?': Provincial Touring, Playing Places, and the King's Men," *Shakespeare Survey* 47 (1994): 50.

14 Sally-Beth MacLean, "Players on Tour: New Evidence from Records of Early English Drama," in *Elizabethan Theatre X*, ed. C. E. McGee (Port Credit, Ontario: P. D. Meany, 1988), pp. 71–2; Andrew Gurr, *The Shakespearian Playing Companies* (Oxford: Oxford University Press, 1996), p. 45.

15 These routes are taken from Peter Greenfield, "Touring," in *A New History of Early English Drama*, eds John D. Cox and David Scott Kastan (New York: Columbia University Press, 1997), pp. 261–2.

16 Gurr, *Shakespeanda Playing Companies*, p. 46.

17 William Ingram, "The Cost of Touring," *Medieval and Renaissance Drama in England* 6 (1993): 59.

18 The documents and commentary are from Gurr, *Shakespearian Playing Companies*, p. 39.

19 As reprinted in Wickham, Berry, and Ingram, *English Professional Theatre*, pp. 251, 141–2, 252.

20 Quoted by Bentley, *Player*, p. 192.

21 Quoted in Wickham, Berry, and Ingram, *English Professional Theatre*, p. 252.

22 Peter Davison, "Commerce and Patronage: The Lord Chamberlain's Men's Tour of 1597," in *Shakespeare Performed: Essays in Honor of R. A. Foakes*, ed. Grace Ioppolo (Newark: University of Delaware Press, 2000), p. 63.

23 Gurr, *Shakespearian Playing Companies*, p. 72.

24 Thomas Heywood, *An Apology for Actors* (1612), sig. C4.

25 Cerasano, "Chamberlain's–King's Man," p. 342.

26 I. G., *A Refutation of the Apology for Actors* (1615), sig. E3v.

27 Examples are taken from Bernard Beckerman, *Shakespeare at the Globe 1599–1609* (New York: Macmillan, 1962), pp. 115–16.

28 John Bulwer quoted in Bertram L. Joseph, *Elizabethan Acting* (Oxford: Oxford University Press, 1964), p. 16.

29 Joseph, *Elizabethan Acting*, pp. 100–1.

30 This list is taken from J. L. Styan, *Shakespeare's Stagecraft* (Cambridge: Cambridge University Press, 1971), p. 78.

31 Stern, *Rehearsal*, pp. 100–1.

32 Stern, *Rehearsal*, p. 107.

33 Stern, *Rehearsal*, p. 109.

34 Both examples are taken from Stern, *Rehearsal*, p. 103.

35 Alan C. Dessen, *Recovering Shakespeare's Theatrical Vocabulary* (Cambridge: Cambridge University Press, 1995), p. 26.

36 M. C. Bradbrook, *Elizabethan Stage Conditions: A Study of their Place in the Interpretation of Shakespeare's Plays* (Cambridge: Cambridge University Press, 1968), p. 112.
37 These patterns are suggested by Nicole Matos and Christine Mahoney in English 891D, "Material Shakespeare," a graduate seminar at the University of Massachusetts, Amherst, in fall 2000.
38 Carol Chillington Rutter, ed., *Documents of the Rose Playhouse* (rev. edn) (Manchester and New York: Manchester University Press, 1999), p. 111.
39 Reprinted in Wickham, Berry, and Ingram, *English Professional Theatre*, p. 497.

Chapter 3 Playgoers

1 John Webster, *The Complete Works*, ed. F. L. Lucas (London: Chatto and Windus, 1927), I, 107. J. Leeds Barroll has suggested that the harsh winter of 1607–8 may be what caused the King's Men to move into Blackfriars. See Barroll, *Politics, Plague, and Shakespeare's Theater* (Ithaca: Cornell University Press, 1991), pp. 159–60.
2 *Annals of English Drama, 975–1700*, 3rd edn, ed. Alfred Harbage, rev. S. Schoenbaum and Sylvia Wagenheim (London and New York: Routledge, 1989), cited by Andrew Gurr, *The Shakespearian Playing Companies* (Oxford: Oxford University Press, 1996), p. 27.
3 Gurr, *Shakespearian Playing Companies*, p. 27.
4 Gurr, *Shakespearian Playing Companies*, p. 27.
5 Carol Chillington Rutter, ed., *Documents of the Rose Playhouse* (rev. edn) (Manchester and New York: Manchester University Press, 1999), p. 57.
6 Rutter, *Documents*, p. 58.
7 Alfred Harbage, *Shakespeare's Audience* (New York: Columbia University Press, 1941, 1961), appendix B, pp. 174–5.
8 These figures are drawn from Bernard Beckerman, *Shakespeare at the Globe 1599–1609* (New York: Macmillan, 1962), p. 22.
9 Ann Jennalie Cook, "Audiences: Investigation, Interpretation, Invention," in *A New History of Early English Drama*, eds John D. Cox and David Scott Kastan (New York: Columbia University Press, 1997), p. 318.
10 Quoted by Leo Salinger, "Jacobean Playwrights and 'Judicious Spectators,'" *British Academy Shakespeare Lectures 1980–1989* (published for the British Academy by Cambridge University Press, 1993), p. 235; Harbage, *Shakespeare's Audience*, p. 13.
11 Charles Whitney, "'Usually in the Working a Daies': Playgoing Journeymen, Apprentices, and Servants in Guild Reports," *Shakespeare Quarterly* 52: 4 (Winter 1999), 451.
12 Quoted by Harbage, *Shakespeare's Audience*, p. 77.

13 Gayton, quoted by Andrew Gurr, *The Shakespearean Stage, 1574–1642* (Cambridge: Cambridge University Press, 1992), p. 225.

14 Quoted by Whitney, "'Usually in the Working,'" p. 442.

15 Quoted in original illiterate spelling by Whitney, "'Usually in the Working,'" p. 446.

16 Quoted by Salinger, "Jacobean Playwrights," p. 235.

17 Ilana Krausman Ben-Amos, *Adolescence and Youth in Early Modern England* (New Haven: Yale University Press, 1984); Paul Griffiths, *Youth and Authority in Early Modern England* (Oxford: Oxford University Press, 1996).

18 Steve Rappaport, *Worlds within Worlds: Structures of Life in Sixteenth-Century London* (Cambridge: Cambridge University Press, 1989), p. 240.

19 Transcribed by Whitney, "'Usually in the Working,'" p. 455.

20 Whitney, "'Usually in the Working,'" p. 435.

21 Quoted by Gurr, *Shakespearean Stage*, pp. 153–4.

22 Quoted by Gurr, *Playgoing in Shakespeare's London* (Cambridge: Cambridge University Press, 1987), p. 71.

23 Rutter, *Documents*, pp. 230–1.

24 Salinger, "Jacobean Playwrights," p. 236.

25 Harbage, *Shakespeare's Audience*, p. 60.

26 Harbage, *Shakespeare's Audience*, pp. 16–17.

27 Gurr does not cite Digges.

28 Quoted by Salinger, "Jacobean Playwrights," p. 249.

29 Gurr, *Playgoing*, p. 85. The following discussion of hearing and seeing is derived from pp. 88–93.

30 Gurr, *Playgoing*, p. 89.

31 Gurr, *Playgoing*, p. 90.

32 This and the reaction to *Othello* that follows are from Gurr, *Shakespearean Stage*, p. 152.

33 Citations from Manningham and Forman are from Gurr, *Playgoing*, pp. 107–8.

34 Quoted by Gurr, *Playgoing*, p. 112.

35 Quoted by Harbage, *Shakespeare's Audience*, p. 50.

Chapter 4   Equipment

1 Ann Rosalind Jones and Peter Stallybrass, *Renaissance Clothing and the Materials of Memory* (Cambridge: Cambridge University Press, 2000), p. 180.

2 Quoted by Alexander Leggatt, *Jacobean Public Theatre* (London: Routledge, 1992), p. 54.

3 Jones and Stallybrass, *Renaissance Clothing*, p. 178.

4   In correspondence with the author.

5   These facts are derived from Jones and Stallybrass, *Renaissance Clothing*, pp. 179–80.

6   Jones and Stallybrass, *Renaissance Clothing*, p. 178.

7   Andrew Gurr quoted by Jones and Stallybrass, *Renaissance Clothing*, p. 178.

8   Jean MacIntyre, *Costumes and Scripts in the Elizabethan Theatres* (Edmonton: University of Alberta Press, 1992), pp. 56–7.

9   Andrew Gurr and Mariko Ichikawa, *Staging in Shakespeare's Theatres* (Oxford: Oxford University Press, 2000), pp. 53–4.

10 Alan C. Dessen, *Recovering Shakespeare's Theatrical Vocabulary* (Cambridge: Cambridge University Press, 1995), p. 151.

11 Dessen, *Recovering Shakespeare's Theatrical Vocabulary*, pp. 28–9.

12 MacIntyre, *Costumes and Scripts*, pp. 274–5.

13 E. K. Chambers, *The Elizabethan Stage* (4 vols) (Oxford: Clarendon Press, 1923), IV, 205.

14 MacIntyre, *Costumes and Scripts*, pp. 87–8.

15 These examples are also in Bruce R. Smith, *Shakespeare and Masculinity* (Oxford: Oxford University Press, 2000), pp. 76, 4.

16 MacIntyre, *Costumes and Scripts*, pp. 176–7.

17 MacIntyre, *Costumes and Scripts*, pp. 278, 195–6.

18 MacIntyre, *Costumes and Scripts*, p. 157. Her earlier observations on shared costumes are on pp. 188, 198; the following on kings is on p. 156.

19 MacIntyre, *Costumes and Scripts*, p. 284. She suggests the examples from *Comedy of Errors* in part (p. 145); from *Shrew* (p. 145); from *Richard II* (pp. 153, 154); from *Merchant of Venice* (p. 160); from *Hamlet* (p. 29); from *Lear* (p. 283); and, subsequently here, from *Coriolanus* (p. 300) and *Winter's Tale* (p. 305).

20 MacIntyre, *Costumes and Scripts*, pp. 142, 149–50, 313.

21 Lawrence Danson, *Shakespeare's Dramatic Genres* (Oxford: Oxford University Press, 2000), pp. 30–1.

22 These remarks draw on Jean MacIntyre and Garratt P. J. Epp, "'Cloathes Worth All the Rest': Costumes and Properties," in *A New History of Early English Drama*, eds John D. Cox and David Scott Kastan (New York: Columbia University Press, 1997), pp. 279–82; the quotation from Frances Teague is on p. 280.

23 Leggatt, *Jacobean Public Theatre*, pp. 50–1; Gurr and Ichikawa, *Staging*, p. 60.

24 Some of these examples are also in Bernard Beckerman, *Shakespeare at the Globe, 1599–1609* (New York: Macmillan, 1962), pp. 76–7.

25 The information on weapons and this application are drawn from Gurr and Ichikawa, *Staging*, pp. 67–8.

26 Dessen, *Recovering Shakespeare's Theatrical Vocabulary*, pp. 22–3.

Chapter 5   Reactions

1   E. K. Chambers, *The Elizabethan Stage* (4 vols) (Oxford: Clarendon Press, 1923), IV, 271.
2   Chambers, *Elizabethan Stage*, IV, 273–4.
3   Chambers, *Elizabethan Stage*, IV, 322–3.
4   Richard Dutton, *Mastering the Revels: The Regulation and Censorship of English Renaissance Drama* (Iowa City: University of Iowa Press, 1991), p. 107.
5   Glynn Wickham, Herbert Berry, and William Ingram, eds, *English Professional Theatre, 1530–1660* (Cambridge: Cambridge University Press, 2000), p. 102.
6   Chambers, *Elizabethan Stage*, IV, 223–4.
7   Wickham, Berry, and Ingram, *English Professional Theatre*, p. 167.
8   Wickham, Berry, and Ingram, *English Professional Theatre*, pp. 168–9.
9   Chambers, *Elizabethan Stage*, IV, 247.
10 Chambers, *Elizabethan Stage*, IV, 249.
11 Chambers, *Elizabethan Stage*, IV, 204.
12 Chambers, *Elizabethan Stage*, IV, 239.
13 Wickham, Berry, and Ingram, *English Professional Theatre*, pp. 175–7; Chambers, *Elizabethan Stage*, IV, 253.
14 Chambers, *Elizabethan Stage*, IV, 210.
15 These phrases and most of the examples that follow are also in Michael O'Connell, *The Idolatrous Eye: Iconoclasm and Theatre in Early-Modern England* (Oxford: Oxford University Press, 2000), pp. 126–30.
16 David Scott Kastan, *Shakespeare After Theory* (London: Routledge, 1999), pp. 154–5.
17 Chambers, *Elizabethan Stage*, IV, 263.
18 Quoted by Kastan, *Shakespeare After Theory* p. 117.
19 Kastan, *Shakespeare After Theory* p. 114.
20 Gerald Eades Bentley, *The Profession of Dramatist in Shakespeare's Time 1590–1642* (Princeton: Princeton University Press, 1971), p. 147.
21 Chambers, *Elizabethan Stage*, IV, 285–7.
22 Bentley, *Profession*, p. 152.
23 Richard Dutton, "Censorship," in *A New History of Early English Drama*, eds John D. Cox and David Scott Kastan (New York: Columbia University Press, 1997), p. 296.
24 Dutton "Censorship," p. 297.
25 Chambers, *Elizabethan Stage*, IV, 306–7.
26 Dutton, *Mastering the Revels*, p. 80.
27 Bentley, *Profession*, p. 167.
28 Dutton, *Mastering the Revels*, p. 81.
29 Dutton, *Mastering the Revels*, pp. 81–3.

30 From *Statutes of the Realm 1103–1713* in Bentley, *Profession*, p. 182; cf. Chambers, *Elizabethan Stage*, IV, 338–9.
31 Bentley, *Profession*, p. 183.
32 Chambers, *Elizabethan Stage*, IV, 332.
33 Quoted by Bentley, *Profession*, p. 189.
34 Clare, "Censorship and Negotiation," in *Literature and Censorship in Renaissance England*, ed. Andrew Hadfield (Basingstoke and New York: Palgrave, 2001), p. 20.
35 Knutson, *Playing Companies and Commerce in Shakespeare's Time* (Cambridge: Cambridge University Press, 2001), p. 20.

Bibliography

Astington, John H. "Descent Machinery in the Playhouse." *Medieval and Renaissance Drama in England* 2 (1985): 119–33.

———, ed. *The Development of Shakespeare's Theater*. New York: AMS Press, 1992.

Barish, Jonas. *The Antitheatrical Prejudice*. Berkeley: University of California Press, 1981.

Barroll, J. Leeds. *Politics, Plague, and Shakespeare's Theater*. Ithaca: Cornell University Press, 1991.

Beckerman, Bernard. *Shakespeare at the Globe, 1599–1609*. New York: Macmillan, 1962.

Ben-Amos, Ilana Krausman. *Adolescence and Youth in Early Modern England*. New Haven: Yale University Press, 1984.

Bentley, Gerald Eades. *The Profession of Dramatist in Shakespeare's Time 1590–1642*. Princeton: Princeton University Press, 1971.

———.*The Profession of Player in Shakespeare's Time 1590–1642*. Princeton: Princeton University Press, 1984.

Berry, Herbert. *Shakespeare's Playhouses*. New York: AMS Press, 1987.

Bevington, David. *Action Is Eloquence: Shakespeare's Language of Gesture*. Cambridge, MA: Harvard University Press, 1984.

———. *From "Mankind" to Marlowe*. Cambridge, MA: Harvard University Press, 1962.

Bradbrook, M. C. *Elizabethan Stage Conditions: A Study of their Place in the Interpretation of Shakespeare's Plays*. Cambridge: Cambridge University Press, 1968.

———. *The Rise of the Common Player*. London: Chatto and Windus, 1962.

Bradley, David. *From Text to Performance in the Elizabethan Theatre*. Cambridge: Cambridge University Press, 1992.

Bibliography

Callaghan, Dympna. *Shakespeare without Women: Representing Gender and Race on the Renaissance Stage*. London: Routledge, 2000.

Cerasano, S. P. "The Chamberlain's–King's Men." In David Scott Kastan, ed., *A Companion to Shakespeare*. Oxford: Blackwell, 1999.

Chambers, E. K. *The Elizabethan Stage*. 4 vols. Oxford: Clarendon Press, 1923.

Clare, Janet. "Censorship and Negotiation." In Andrew Hadfield, ed., *Literature and Censorship in Renaissance England*. Basingstoke and New York: Palgrave, 2001.

Cook, Ann Jennalie. "Audiences: Investigation, Interpretation, Invention." In John D. Cox and David Scott Kastan, eds, *A New History of Early English Drama*. New York: Columbia University Press, 1997.

——. *The Privileged Playgoers of Shakespeare's London 1576–1642*. Princeton: Princeton University Press, 1983.

Cox, John D. and David Scott Kastan, eds. *A New History of Early English Drama*. New York: Columbia University Press, 1997.

Cressy, David. *Literacy and the Social Order*. Cambridge: Cambridge University Press, 1980.

——. *Travesties and Transgressions in Tudor and Stuart England*. Oxford: Oxford University Press, 2000.

Danson, Lawrence. *Shakespeare's Dramatic Genres*. Oxford: Oxford University Press, 2000.

Davis, W. Robertson. *Shakespeare's Boy Actors*. London: Dent, 1939.

Davison, Peter. "Commerce and Patronage: The Lord Chamberlain's Men's Tour of 1597." In Grace Ioppolo, ed., *Shakespeare Performed: Essays in Honor of R. A. Foakes*. Newark: University of Delaware Press, 2000.

Dawson, Anthony B. and Paul Yachnin. *The Culture of Playgoing in Shakespeare's England: A Collaborative Debate*. Cambridge: Cambridge University Press, 2001.

Dessen, Alan C. *Recovering Shakespeare's Theatrical Vocabulary*. Cambridge: Cambridge University Press, 1995.

—— and Leslie Thomson. *A Dictionary of Stage Directions in English Drama, 1580–1642*. Cambridge: Cambridge University Press, 1999.

Dillon, Janette. *Theatre, Court and City 1595–1610*. Cambridge: Cambridge University Press, 2000.

Dorsch, T. S. "Introduction." In William Shakespeare, *The Comedy of Errors*. Cambridge: Cambridge University Press.

Dutton, Richard. "Censorship." In John D. Cox and David Scott Kastan, eds, *A New History of Early English Drama*. New York: Columbia University Press, 1997.

——. "Licensing and Censorship." In David Scott Kastan, ed., *A Companion to Shakespeare*. Oxford: Blackwell, 1999.

——. *Mastering the Revels: The Regulation and Censorship of English Renaissance Drama*. Iowa City: University of Iowa Press, 1991.

Egan, Gabriel. "Reconstructions of the Globe." *Shakespeare Survey* 52 (1999): 1–16.

Evans, G. Blakemore, ed. *Elizabethan–Jacobean Drama: A New Mermaids Background Book*. London: A. & C. Black, 1989.

Foakes, Reginald A. *Illustrations of the English Stage, 1580–1642*. London: Scolar Press, 1985.

Forbes, Thomas Rogers. *Chronicle from Aldate: Life and Death in Shakespeare's London*. New Haven: Yale University Press, 1971.

Graves, R. B. *Lighting the Shakespearean Stage, 1567–1642*. Carbondale: Southern Illinois University Press, 1999.

Greenfield, Peter. "Touring." In John D. Cox and David Scott Kastan, eds, *A New History of Early English Drama*. New York: Columbia University Press, 1997.

Greg, Walter W., ed. *Dramatic Documents from the Elizabethan Playhouse*. 2 vols. Oxford: Clarendon, 1931.

Griffiths, Paul. *Youth and Authority in Early Modern England*. Oxford: Oxford University Press, 1996.

Gurr, Andrew. "A First Doorway into the Globe." *Shakespeare Quarterly* 41:1 (Spring 1990): 97–9.

——. "Maximal and Minimal Texts." *Shakespeare Survey* 52 (1999): 68–87.

——. *Playgoing in Shakespeare's London*. Cambridge: Cambridge University Press, 1987.

——. *The Shakespearian Playing Companies*. Oxford: Oxford University Press, 1996.

——. *The Shakespearean Stage, 1574–1642*. Cambridge: Cambridge University Press, 1992.

—— and Mariko Ichikawa. *Staging in Shakespeare's Theatres*. Oxford: Oxford University Press, 2000.

Hadfield, Andrew, ed. *Literature and Censorship in Renaissance England*. Basingstoke and New York: Palgrave, 2001.

Harbage, Alfred. *As They Liked It*. New York: Macmillan, 1947.

——. *Shakespeare and the Rival Traditions*. New York: Macmillan, 1952.

——. *Shakespeare's Audience*. New York: Columbia University Press, 1941, 1961.

——. *Annals of English Drama 975–1700*. 3rd edn. rev. S. Schoenbaum and Sylvia Wagenheim. London and New York: Routledge, 1989.

Henslowe, Philip. *Diary*. In facsimile, eds R. A. Foakes and R. T. Rickert. Cambridge: Cambridge University Press, 1961.

Hodges, C. Walter. *Enter the Whole Army*. Cambridge: Cambridge University Press, 1999.

——. *The Globe Restored*. London: Ernest Benn, 1953.

Holmes, Martin. *Shakespeare and his Players*. London: John Murray, 1972.

Honigmann, E. A. J. and Susan Brock, *Playhouse Wills 1558–1642*. Manchester: Manchester University Press, 1993.

Ingram, William. *The Business of Playing*. Ithaca: Cornell University Press, 1992.

Bibliography

——. "The Cost of Touring." *Medieval and Renaissance Drama in England* 6 (1993).

Jones, Ann Rosalind and Peter Stallybrass. *Renaissance Clothing and the Materials of Memory*. Cambridge: Cambridge University Press, 2000.

Joseph, B. L. *Elizabethan Acting*. Oxford: Oxford University Press, 1964.

Kastan, David Scott. *A Companion to Shakespeare*. Oxford: Blackwell, 1999.

——. *Shakespeare After Theory*. London: Routledge, 1999.

King, T. J. *Casting Shakespeare's Plays: London Actors and their Roles, 1590–1642*. Cambridge: Cambridge University Press, 1992.

——. *Shakespeare and Staging 1599–1642*. Cambridge, MA: Harvard University Press, 1971.

Knutson, Roslyn Lander. *Playing Companies and Commerce in Shakespeare's Time*. Cambridge: Cambridge University Press, 2001.

——. *The Repertory of Shakespeare's Company 1594–1613*. Fayetteville: University of Arkansas Press, 1991.

——. "Shakespeare's Repertory." In David Scott Kastan, ed., *A Companion to Shakespeare*. Oxford: Blackwell, 1999.

Lawrence, William J. *Pre-Restoration Stage Studies*. Cambridge, MA: Harvard University Press, 1927.

Leggatt, Alexander. *Jacobean Public Theatre*. London: Routledge, 1992.

Lenthicum, M. C. *Costume in the Drama of Shakespeare and his Contemporaries*. Oxford: Clarendon, 1936.

Levine, Laura. *Men in Women's Clothing*. Cambridge: Cambridge University Press, 1994.

Lincroft, H. and R. Lincroft *The Theatre*. New York: Roy Publishers, 1958, 1961.

MacIntyre, Jean. *Costumes and Scripts in the Elizabethan Theatres*. Edmonton: University of Alberta Press, 1992.

—— and Garrett P. J. Epp. "'Cloathes Worth All the Rest': Costumes and Properties." In John D. Cox and David Scott Kastan, eds, *A New History of Early English Drama*. New York: Columbia University Press, 1997.

MacLean, Sally-Beth. "Players on Tour: New Evidence from Records of Early English Drama." In C. E. McGee, ed., *The Elizabethan Theatre X*. Port Credit, Ontario: P. D. Meany, 1988.

Masten, Jeffrey and Wendy Wall, eds. *Renaissance Drama* 28 (1997).

McMillin, Scott and Sally-Beth MacLean. *The Queen's Men and their Plays*. Cambridge: Cambridge University Press, 1998.

McMurty, Jo. *Understanding Shakespeare's England*. Hamden: Archon, 1989.

Meagher, John C. *Shakespeare's Shakespeare: How the Plays Were Made*. New York: Continuum, 1997.

Mullaney, Steven. *The Place of the Stage*. Chicago: University of Chicago Press, 1988.

O'Connell, Michael. *The Idolatrous Eye: Iconoclasm and Theater in Early-Modern England*. Oxford: Oxford University Press, 2000.

Bibliography

Orrell, John. *The Quest for Shakespeare's Globe.* Cambridge: Cambridge University Press, 1983.

Pritchard, R. E. *Shakespeare's England.* Stroud: Sutton, 1999.

Rappaport, Steve. *Worlds within Worlds: Structures of Life in Sixteenth-Century London.* Cambridge: Cambridge University Press, 1989.

Richmond, Hugh Macrae. *Shakespeare and the Renaissance Stage to 1616 and Shakespearean Stage History 1616 to 1998: An Annotated Bibliography.* Asheville, NC: Pegasus, 1999.

Rutter, Carol Chillington. "Designs on Shakespeare: Sleeves, Gowns, and Helen's Placket." In Grace Ioppolo, ed., *Shakespeare Performed: Essays in Honor of R. A. Foakes.* Newark: University of Delaware Press, 2000.

——, ed. *Documents of the Rose Playhouse.* (rev. edn) Manchester and New York: Manchester University Press, 1999.

Salinger, Leo. "Jacobean Playwrights and 'Judicious Spectators.'" *British Academy Shakespeare Lectures 1980–1989.* Published for the British Academy by Cambridge University Press, 1993.

Shakespeare, William, *The Norton Shakespeare.* Eds Stephen Coreenblatt, Walter Cohen, Jean E. Howard and Katharine Eisaman Maus. New York and London: W. W. Norton, 1997.

Shurgot, Michael W. *Stages of Play: Shakespeare's Theatrical Energies in Elizabethan Performance.* Newark: University of Delaware Press, 1998.

Slater, Ann Pasternak. *Shakespeare the Director.* Brighton: Harvester, 1982.

Smith, Bruce R. *The Acoustic World of Early Modern England.* Chicago: University of Chicago Press, 1999.

——. *Shakespeare and Masculinity.* Oxford: Oxford University Press, 2000.

Smith, Irwin. *Shakespeare's Blackfriars Playhouse.* New York: New York University Press, 1964.

Smith, Warren D. *Shakespeare's Playhouse Practice: A Handbook.* Hanover: University Press of New England, 1975.

Somerset, J. A. B. "'How Chances it they Travel?': Provincial Touring, Playing Places, and the King's Men." *Shakespeare Survey* 47 (1994): 45–60.

Southworth, John. *Fools and Jesters at the English Court.* Phoenix Mill: Sutton, 1998.

Stern, Tiffany. *Rehearsal from Shakespeare to Sheridan.* Oxford: Oxford University Press, 2000.

Styan, J. L. *Perspectives on Shakespeare in Performance.* New York: Peter Lang, 2000.

——. *Shakespeare's Stagecraft.* Cambridge: Cambridge University Press, 1971.

Thompson, Marvin and Ruth Thompson, eds. *Shakespeare and the Sense of Performance.* Newark: University of Delaware Press, 1989.

Thomson, Peter. *Shakespeare's Theatre.* London: Routledge and Kegan Paul, 1983, 1992.

Webster, John. *The Complete Works.* Ed. F. L. Lucas. London: Chatto and Windus, 1927.

Weimann, Robert. *Author's Pen and Actor's Voice*. Cambridge: Cambridge University Press, 2000.

Wells, Stanley. *Re-Editing Shakespeare for the Modern Reader*. Oxford: Clarendon Press, 1984.

Welsford, Enid. *The Fool: His Social and Literary History*. London: Faber and Faber, 1966.

White, Martin. *Renaissance Drama in Action*. London: Routledge, 1998.

Whitney, Charles. "'Usually in the Working a Daies': Playgoing Journeymen, Apprentices, and Servants in Guild Reports." *Shakespeare Quarterly* 52:4 (Winter 1999): 433–57.

Wickham, Glynne. *Early English Stages 1300–1600*. 2 vols. Vol. II. London: Routledge and Kegan Paul, 1972.

——, Herbert Berry, and William Ingram, eds. *English Professional Theatre, 1530–1660*. Cambridge: Cambridge University Press, 2000.

Wilson, Jean. *The Archaeology of Shakespeare*. Stroud: Sutton, 1997.

Index

172

174